The New Historicism: Studies in Cultural Poetics
Stephen Greenblatt, General Editor

# Expositions

# Expositions

*Literature and Architecture in Nineteenth-Century France*

Philippe Hamon

Translated by

Katia Sainson-Frank and Lisa Maguire

Introduction by

Richard Sieburth

UNIVERSITY OF CALIFORNIA PRESS
*Berkeley · Los Angeles · Oxford*

b 29347235

Please note that the translation and citation practices
for this publication follow the translators' preferences.

The publisher wishes to acknowledge the generous assistance of the French Ministry of
Culture and Communication in the publication of this book.

University of California Press
Berkeley and Los Angeles, California

University of California Press
Oxford, England

Library of Congress Cataloging-in-Publication Data

Hamon, Philippe.
    [Expositions. English]
    Expositions : literature and architecture in nineteenth-century
France / Philippe Hamon ; translated by Katia Sainson-Frank and Lisa
Maguire ; introduction by Richard Sieburth.
        p.     cm.—(The New historicism ; 20)
    Includes bibliographical references and index.
    ISBN 0-520-07325-8 (cloth).—ISBN 0-520-07326-6 (paper)
    1. French literature—19th century—History and criticism.
    2. Architecture and literature—History—19th century.
    3. Architecture, French.   I. Title.   II. Series.
    PQ283.H3513   1992
    840.9'357—dc20                                          91-35034
                                                                CIP

Printed in the United States of America

1  2  3  4  5  6  7  8  9

The paper used in this publication meets the minimum requirements
of American National Standard for Information Sciences—Permanence
of Paper for Printed Library Materials, ANSI Z39.48-1984 ⊗

# Contents

# Introduction to Translated Edition

*Richard Sieburth*

"Die Dinge aus Glas haben keine Aura"

—*Walter Benjamin*

Over the past twenty years, Philippe Hamon has established himself as one of the leading critics of the nineteenth-century French realist and naturalist novel. A longstanding member of the editorial board of *Poétique* and frequent contributor to its pages, he has worked primarily within the ambit of formalist or structuralist literary theory. His early (and still influential) essays on the semiology of fictional characters and on the poetics of description, published in 1972 at the high-water mark of structuralism, built on the work of Roland Barthes, Gérard Genette, A. J. Greimas, and Tzvetan Todorov in the fields of semiotics and narratology.[1] True to his intellectual origins, Hamon has always brought to his scholarship an engineer's scientific fascination with the intricate designs and mechanisms of textual systems. He approaches literary works with the modesty and meticulousness of a skilled mechanic, providing diagrams and schemata of their inner workings, defining and labeling each moving part with the precise technical term. It is no accident that his major focus as a literary technician and theorist should therefore involve the poetics of description—a practice based on an art

---

[1] "Qu'est-ce qu'une description," *Poétique* 12 (1972) and "Pour un statut sémiologique du personnage," *Littérature* 6 (1972). Hamon's other books include *Introduction à l'analyse du descriptif* (Paris: Hachette, 1981), *Le Personnel du roman: Le Système des personnages dans les Rougon-Macquart d'Emile Zola* (Geneva: Droz, 1983), *Texte et idéologie* (Paris: Presses Universitaires de France, 1984), and *La Description Littéraire: Anthologie de textes théoriques et critiques* (Paris: Macula, 1991). A portion of *Introduction à l'analyse du descriptif* was translated as "The Rhetorical Status of Description" in *Yale French Studies* 61 (1981).

of encyclopedic nomenclature whose lexical virtuosity assembles (or disassembles, as the case may be) the visible world into a verbal machine available to pedagogic or aesthetic inspection and display.

As its title implies, Hamon's most recent book, *Expositions,* turns specifically on the same issues of referential ostension and deictic display previously analyzed in his ground-breaking *Introduction à l'analyse du descriptif* (1981). What sets *Expositions* apart from Hamon's previous work, however, is that he has conceived this study more as an exploratory essay than as a specialized demonstration of literary semiotics or rhetoric—significantly enough, the book was originally published in France in 1989 by the house of José Corti, known for its quirky belletristic list, rather than by a French university press. Gone are most of the high-tech diagrams and charts that marked his earlier publications, and gone too is much of the forbiddingly technical vocabulary in which his previous arguments were couched. (Even so, his translators have had to work miracles to mold his paratactic, appositional prose into English syntax— Hamon's basic heuristic and stylistic device still remains the inventory or list.) *Expositions* marks a swerve away from the formalist stance of structuralist semiology and narratology and a move toward something that looks more like the "new historicism"—an evolution that may or may not be symptomatic of the recent (re)turn in French literary studies toward the more broadly historical and ideological contexts of literature.

Without sacrificing any of his previous theoretical rigor, Hamon has undertaken an erudite stroll, as his subtitle announces, through the rich precincts of "Literature and Architecture in Nineteenth-Century France." Judging from the many allusions scattered through *Expositions,* Walter Benjamin is the major tutelary presence behind Hamon's *flânerie,* specifically the Benjamin of the 1935 exposé "Paris, Capital of the Nineteenth Century" whose chapter on "Grandville or the World Exhibitions" is in turn quarried from the section (Konvolut G) devoted to world's fairs and advertising in the unfinished publication *Arcades Project.* "Konvolut G" falls between the rubrics devoted to "Iron Construction" (transparency and utopia) and "The Collector" (fetishism and melancholia) and deploys documentary material ranging from the first French national exposition of 1798 (just five years after the founding of the Louvre) and the 1851 London Crystal Palace Exhibition to the great Parisian Expositions Universelles of 1855, 1867, 1878, 1889, and 1900. (These five provide the historical backbone for Hamon's study.)[2]

---

[2] Walter Benjamin, "Ausstellungwesen, Reklame, Grandville," in *Gesammelte Schrif-*

Intent on reading nineteenth-century Parisian architecture both as the "index" of the "latent mythology" of high capitalism and as the crucial "pre-history" of a potentially revolutionary and/or utopian twentieth-century modernity, Benjamin allegorizes the Expositions Universelles into a Janus-like "dialectical image" of the ambiguous dream world of consumerism. He underscores the revolutionary innovations in glass and iron architecture occasioned by these temples of industry and commerce and calls attention to the utopian social practices and theories they spawned: the worker's delegations to the London Exhibitions of 1851 and 1862 eventually evolved into Marx's International Workingmens' Association; the 1855 Paris Exposition inspired Pierre Joseph Proudhon's visionary *Projet d'une exposition perpétuelle;* the 1867 Exposition promoted the establishment of the International Bureau of Weights and Measures; and the 1878 Exposition, a showcase for the Third Republic, hosted an International Congress on the Rights of Women, a Congress for the Protection of Literary Property (which laid the groundwork for the formulation of international copyright laws), and a Congress for the Amelioration of the Condition of the Blind (which led to the worldwide adoption of braille).[3]

These utopias of transparency and equality, the very architecture of which "occupies the role of the subconscious" (inasmuch as it projects both an archaic fantasy of the classless prehistory of society and a wish-symbol of the future)[4] are for Benjamin inseparable from their nightmarish opposite—a phantasmagoria of the *Immerwiedergleiche,* a universe of infinite reproducibility and substitutability whose reified (or zoomorphic) dehumanization is captured by the serial lithographs of Grandville. Significantly enough, it is in the section on Expositions Universelles that Karl Marx's celebrated (and very Grandvillian) definition in *Das Kapital* of the occult, topsy-turvy "theological capers" of the commodity fetish first makes its appearance in the *Arcades Project.* ("It

---

*ten,* ed. Rolf Tiedemann (Frankfurt am Main: Suhrkamp, 1982), vol. 5, 232–268. "Paris, Capital of the Nineteenth Century" exists in two translations in *Reflections,* trans. Edward Jephcott (New York: Harcourt Brace, 1978) and in *Charles Baudelaire: A Lyric Poet in the Era of High Capitalism,* trans. Harry Zohn (London: New Left Books, 1973).

   [3] Among the growing body of literature in English devoted to Universal Exhibitions see Burton Benedict, ed., *The Anthropology of World's Fairs* (Berkeley: Scolar Press, 1983), Patricia Mainardi, *Art and Politics of the Second Empire: The Universal Expositions of 1855 and 1867* (New Haven: Yale University Press, 1987), Paul Greenhalgh, *Ephemeral Vistas: The Expositions Universelles, Great Exhibitions and World's Fairs, 1851–1939* (Manchester: Manchester University Press, 1988), and John Findling, ed., *Historical Dictionary of World's Fairs and Expositions, 1851–1988* (New York: Greenwood Press, 1990).

   [4] Benjamin, *Charles Baudelaire,* 158.

not only stands with its feet on the ground, but, in relation to all other commodities, it stands on its head, and evolves out of its wooden brain grotesque ideas, far more wonderful than 'table-turning' ever was.") Benjamin elliptically extrapolates from Marx in "Grandville or the World Exhibitions":

> The world exhibitions glorified the exchange-value of commodities. They created a framework in which their use-value receded into the background. They opened up a phantasmagoria into which people entered in order to be distracted. The entertainment industry made that easier for them by lifting them to the level of the commodity. They yielded to its manipulations while enjoying their alienation from themselves and from others. . . . [The commodity] prostitutes the living body to the inorganic world. In relation to the living it represents the rights of the corpse. Fetishism, which succumbs to the sex-appeal of the inorganic, is its vital nerve.[5]

Although it builds broadly on Benjamin's investigations into "Paris, Capital of the Nineteenth Century," Hamon's *Expositions* is by no means an orthodox application of Frankfurt School theory. He is not really concerned with working out a Marxian hermeneutic of the relation of base to superstructure or with critically applying the notion of commodity fetishism; instead, he prefers to link social and textual practices via the looser concept of "homology," here used in an anaphoric sense that is far more Lévi-Straussian than Goldmannian. Nor does Hamon particularly claim to be following Benjamin's surrealist mode of dialectical historiography, in which any historical image can potentially flip over into its obverse or any moment of the past suddenly erupt as a political instance of the present—as for example the surprising reversal in Benjamin's "The Work of Art in the Age of Mechanical Reproduction" where the heretofore alienating and anti-auratic "exhibition value" (*Ausstellungswert*) of the commodity is unexpectedly revealed as a possible basis for a new revolutionary praxis of art.[6] Although Hamon follows Benjamin in reading the French nineteenth century as an archaeology of (post)modernity (his footnotes abound with references to Baudrillard, Lyotard, Virilio, and Tafuri), he in the end remains noncommittal as to the purport of the master narrative of the decline of the aura that he constructs over the course of his book.

The real interest of Hamon's study lies elsewhere, namely, in its attempt to define an approach whose methodological openness (or

---

[5] Ibid., 165–166.
[6] Walter Benjamin, *Illuminations,* trans. Harry Zohn (New York: Schocken Books, 1969), 224.

"weakness," as the Italian postmodernists might say) might provision-
ally bridge social, cultural, architectural, and literary history on the one
hand and a more formalist analysis of the specific rhetorical and semiotic features of nineteenth-century literary texts on the other. Hamon
describes his study in his introduction as an experimental unfolding of
the various metaphorical implications of the term *exposition*. The semantic reach of the word in French not only includes the rhetorical
practice of setting forth argument or evidence in *expository* fashion but
also refers to the commercial, industrial, or artistic *exhibitions* which in
turn devolve from considerations of architectural *exposure*. In short, by
playing on the various connotations of this single term—with all that it
implies about didactic or aesthetic ostension, presentation, demonstration, and display—Hamon manages to establish homologies between
(1) architectural theory (exposure as the art of positioning or turning a
building in space), (2) cultural history (the architectural, economic, and
social practices associated with the Expositions Universelles), and (3)
rhetoric (exposition as a specific descriptive and/or explanatory moment in any given literary text). The key issue that connects these three
domains, as becomes clear over the course of the study, is the interrela-
tion between the practice of exposition and the ideology of representation in the nineteenth century.

Hamon's first chapter ("Text and Architecture") is the most densely
theoretical portion of the book. In a mere forty pages, he develops Hegel's
notion that architecture stands as the *archè* (origin and law) of all other
arts. In particular, Hamon examines the ways in which literature has
recourse to the vocabulary of architecture ("structure," "deconstruction" or *Abbau*, "edification" etc.) in order to generate its theoretical
discourses about itself. As he ranges from Vitruvius to Robert Venturi,
Hamon effectively sketches out a tradition of *ut architectura poesis* that
sees in architecture the privileged model or metalanguage for literature,
particularly at those moments (the Renaissance, the nineteenth century,
postmodernism) when the very concept of mimesis enters into crisis.

In addition to exploring the various ways in which literature speaks
of itself as a species of architecture, Hamon also investigates how literature (primarily the nineteenth-century realist and naturalist novel) includes architectural objects or spaces within itself in order to demonstrate that its mimesis in fact originates from the archè of the "real." For
the realist novel, Hamon argues, the architectural object serves as a
privileged "shifter" between text and world, that is, it functions as a
metaphorical "operator" that allows the (nonsemiotic or visual) do-

main of the "real" to be translated into the (semiotic or textual) domain of literary representation. This is possible, he contends, because architecture is, at its root (or in its very archè) already a kind of model grammar—a projection into space of the topoi of rhetoric and the sequences of narrative. By comparing itself to architecture or by relying on architectural constructs for its most persuasive *effets de réel,* the nineteenth-century novel thus bases its claims to mimesis on two complementary semiotic procedures—the narrativization of space and the spatial segmentation of time—that are (always) already at work in architecture. The mimetic effects obtained by the realist novel's description of architectural objects or spaces therefore do not involve the representation of "real" referents, but rather the representation of objects or spaces that are themselves already representations. The mimetic strategies of realism (and here Hamon's thesis rejoins his earlier work on description) can thus be reduced to a species of semiosis—signs rewriting other signs.

It is illuminating to read Denis Hollier's recently translated *Against Architecture* in tandem with Hamon's theoretical exposition. An extended commentary on the work of Georges Bataille (notably his 1929 *Documents* article on "Architecture"), Hollier's study engages in a fiercely antinomian critique of the symbolic authority of architecture (and of structuralist theory in general). Brilliantly dismantling Hegel's arguments in the *Aesthetics* on architecture as the archè of the arts and building on Michel Foucault's insight that architectural devices (reducible in the end to prisons) above all function to produce subjects (or subjection), Hollier proposes a utopian poststructuralist architecture that "rather than performing the subject, would perform spacing: a space from before the subject, from before meaning; the asubjective, asemantic space of an unedifying architecture."[7] The vehemence of Bataille's (and Hollier's) animus against the very term *architecture* has to do with its surreptitious metaphoricity:

> When architecture is discussed it is never simply a question of architecture; the metaphors cropping up . . . are almost inseparable from the proper meaning of the term. . . . Architecture, before any other qualifications, is identical to the space of representation; it always represents something other than itself from the moment that it becomes distinguished from mere building.[8]

---

[7] Denis Hollier, *Against Architecture: The Writings of Georges Bataille,* trans. Betsy Wing (Cambridge, Mass.: MIT Press, 1989), xi.
[8] Ibid., 32.

Hamon of course makes very much the same points about architecture as the archistructure or system of systems, but he seems to inhabit his prison house of *ut architectura poesis* with a lucidity and equanimity that is poles apart from Bataille's iconoclastic wrath. Benjamin wrote of the Paris arcades that they had no "outsides" and the same might be said of Hamon's theoretical construct: its very systematicity and meta-phoricity would seem to exclude any exteriority or alterity that might threaten it.[9] His metalanguage serenely mimes the very phenomenon it describes.

After his expository theoretical introduction, Hamon proceeds to concrete illustrations of his argument in the second portion of his book, "Texts and their Monuments," which is divided into five subchapters. The first of these explores two of the more recurrent forms of architec-tural monumentality in nineteenth-century French literature—the ruin and the glass house, the former a metaphor for the present's experience of the past (recollection and restoration), and the latter a metaphor for the present's imagination of the future (as in the optimistic transparency of progress so visible in Joseph Paxton's Crystal Palace).[10] Establishing a series of homologies between the exhibition of relics and commodities, between archaeological and commercial display, and between museums and department stores, Hamon here extends a number of Benjamin's most crucial insights into the relation of architecture and ideology in the nineteenth century. Hamon's illustrations of the nineteenth century's fascination with various modes of transparency (the panopticon, green-house, conservatory, diorama, etc.) lead him directly back to the formal features of literary texts: this chapter concludes with a suggestive analy-sis of how windows, panes, and screens function within the nineteenth-century novel's expositions (or descriptions) of a world whose very visibility is a measure of its legibility, a world in which the act of reading (or writing) is inevitably associated with the act of seeing something or someone exposed through the transparent medium of realist prose.

Hamon further explores the expository ambitions of nineteenth-

---

[9] This is perhaps most apparent in Hamon's omission of any discussion of the role of the Expositions Universelles in representations of the colonial Other. See Sylvian Leprun, *Le Théâtre des colonies: Scénographie, acteurs et discours de l'imaginaire dans les exposi-tions, 1855–1937* (Paris: L'Harmattan, 1986); Timothy Mitchell, *Colonising Egypt* (Cam-bridge: Cambridge University Press, 1988); Zeynep Çelik and Leila Kinney, "Ethnogra-phy and Exhibitionism at the Expositions Universelles," *Assemblage* 13 (1990); and Zeynep Çelik, *Displaying the Orient* (Berkeley, Los Angeles, Oxford: University of Cali-fornia Press, 1991).

[10] George Kohlmaier and Barna von Sartory, *Houses of Glass: A Nineteenth-Century Building Type*, trans. John C. Harvey (Cambridge, Mass.: MIT Press, 1986).

century literature in the next chapter, "The Book as Exposition." In addition to surveying various guidebooks to expositions and exhibits, he provides an excellent overview of a variety of popular encyclopedic texts whose very titles (*physiologie, panorama, tableau, revue, galerie, magasin*) indicate their claims to function as exhibitions, authoritatively displaying the totality of contemporary urban reality by appropriating it as a visible, consumable inventory of distinctive features. Hamon analyzes the semiotics of lists and the tropological role of detail in these texts, while underscoring the recurrent figure of hypotyposis (a vivid, picturesque description addressed to the reader's eye).[11] In an ingenious move, he in turn shows how the expository portions of many nineteenth-century novels (i.e. the settings of scene or theme at the very outset or archè of the work) tend frequently to involve the description (or exposition) of architectural spaces or objects—a technique which effectively manages to blend the twin functions of the realist house of fiction: mimesis (the transparent display of the real) and mathesis (the coherent ordering or classification of knowledge).

Hamon's following chapter, "Plaster, Plate, and Platitude," presents the negative face of this nineteenth-century plenum of exhibition. The surfeit of detail, the proliferation of things on display, Hamon argues, can easily generate a kind of overexposure or semiotic hypertrophy in which the plethora of signs in circulation leads not to heightened legibility but rather to radical blankness. As the title of this part suggests, Hamon here sketches out how the (French) nineteenth century experiences a disconcerting disappearance of depth, confronted as it is by an urban world increasingly perceived as sheer surface or platitude—a general loss of volume or aura that is symbolized by the reduction of architecture to facades or plastered surfaces which (as with such other sheathing devices as zinc, industrial brick or glass, whitewash, and macadam pavement) tend to reduce bodied depth to superficial skin. Hamon correlates this phantasmagoria of the surface with the later nineteenth-century novel's exposure of a world given over to facsimile, kitsch, and cliché, an exposure no longer grounded in the optimistic belief in the legibility and transparency of the "real" but instead resigned to the ironic quotation of opaque, empty signs and simulacra—

[11] Hamon's analysis of the rhetorical figure of hypotyposis is nicely complemented by Jonathan Crary's investigations into the history of visuality in *Techniques of the Observer: On Vision and Modernity in the Nineteenth Century* (Cambridge, Mass.: MIT Press, 1990).

an anticipation, as Hamon points out, of the disenchanted poetics of postmodernism.

The subsequent chapter, "Characters Exposed," grows out of Hamon's earlier work on the semiotics of fictional characters. Touching on onomastics, point of view, monologue, dialogue, and typology, he traces the same decline of the aura as it effects character portrayal over the course of the nineteenth-century novel, a loss of volume which coincides (say, in Emile Zola's work) with the increasingly exhibitionistic ostension of female nudity or fetishized items of clothing. Although in his discussion of Edouard Manet's *Olympia* and Zola's *Nana* Hamon touches briefly on the relationship between exposition and prostitution (from *pro-statuere,* to set or place forth in public), readers interested in a more sustained feminist (and Benjaminian) analysis of commodification and sexuality in nineteenth-century France should consult Charles Bernheimer's recent *Figures of Ill Repute* (where one learns that the Expositions Universelles provided a bonanza for prostitution, with syphilis reaching an all-time high in the wake of the 1878 fair).[12]

Hamon's closing chapter on "Lyric and Exposition" reads like something of an appended afterthought, for here he leaves the domain of the realist and naturalist novel to focus on nineteenth-century French poetry and, more specifically, on the spatial and architectural metaphors that organize the discourse of the lyric "I." (The very term "stanza," he reminds us, comes from "room.") Hamon focuses on the ways in which many lyric poems of the nineteenth century tend to establish the self in (or as) a locus that is simultaneously closed and open, centripetal and centrifugal, firmly sited in space yet radically dispersed. He also speculates as to how rhetorical features of the lyric (such as deictics) work together with what he calls "technemes" (i.e. architectural objects such as doors, windows, walls, corridors) in order to effect the dialectical "shifting" (*embrayage*) of closure and openness within the poem.[13] Hamon here reveals himself to be an extremely sensitive and original reader of poetry; behind the structuralist and semiotician, one nearly hears a Bachelardian poetician of space.

[12] Charles Bernheimer, *Figures of Ill Repute: Representing Prostitution in Nineteenth-Century France* (Cambridge: Harvard University Press, 1989), 92, 234. On the broader relationship between women and consumerism in nineteenth-century literature, see Rachel Bowlby, *Just Looking: Consumer Culture in Dreiser, Gissing, and Zola* (New York: Methuen, 1985).

[13] Hamon's article "Clausules" in *Poétique* 24 (1975) remains one of the most far-reaching discussions of the entire issue of poetic closure.

# Expositions

*Literature and Architecture in*
*Nineteenth-Century France*

EXPOSITION: *Action d'exposer, de mettre en vue, d'offrir aux regards du public: L'EXPOSITION des marchandises dans les étalages . . . L'EXPOSITION universelle de 1867.*
*—Action d'abandonner un enfant dans un lieu public . . .*
*—Orientation, situation par rapport aux points cardinaux: L'EXPOSITION au midi est indispensable pour une serre chaude. . . .*
*—Littérat. Partie d'une oeuvre littéraire dans laquelle on fait connaître le sujet, on expose les diverses circonstances dont on veut débarrasser tout d'abord la marche de l'action ou des idées.*
*—Liturg. Cérémonie qui consiste à laisser quelques temps en vue des fidèles un objet qu'on veut offrir à leur vénération: EXPOSITION de reliques.*

[EXPOSITION: To expose, to display, exhibit to the public gaze: EXPOSITION *of merchandise in displays . . . The universal* EXPOSITION *of 1867.*
—Abandonment of an infant in a public place . . .
—Position with respect to the points of a compass: *Southern* EXPOSURE *is obligatory for a green house or conservatory.*
—liter. Part of a literary work in which the theme or subject is presented, exposing various matters which once dispensed with allows for the development of the subsequent action or ideas.
—litur. Ceremony openly displaying objects for public veneration: EXPOSITION *of relics.*]

Pierre Larousse, *Grand dictionnaire universel du XIXème siècle*

EXPOSITION: Sujet de délire du XIXème siècle.

[EXPOSITION: Object of delirium in the nineteenth century.]

Gustave Flaubert, *Dictionnaire des idées reçues*

# Introduction

The nineteenth century has often been defined as the century of history. It was a time when Alexandre Lenoir and Eugène Viollet-le-Duc set out to establish history via national landmarks, when Alexandre Dumas fils cast history into novels, and Charles-Augustin de Sainte-Beuve and Gustave Lanson founded a history of literature; above all it was a time that saw history as a discipline to be created. To speak of history is to speak of monuments; each enables the other, each is implicated in the crises of the other. If the notion of *place* is only a function of memory,[1] if even the most insignificant of buildings is always a monument, a concrete incitement to reactivate or produce some sort of history (in the form of anecdotes, legends, or "foundation" narratives), or to produce some sort of fiction, then memory is only a function of architectural spaces, places that haunt the collective unconscious. Lexicographers remind us that to call someone an architect is an insult still current in certain neighborhoods in Brussels that underwent savage urban "renewal" in the nineteenth century. These memories in turn come to haunt that other collective unconscious, which is language. Conserving traces of specific places in its epithets and turns of phrases, language thus acts as the natural conservator of national heritage. For example, in French, one finds expressions like: *fréquenter les lorettes* (to keep company with *lorettes*); *boire du vin de barrière* (to drink *barrière* wine); *se porter comme le Pont-Neuf* (to feel as strong as the Pont-Neuf); *esprit boulevardier* (to have a

[1] Pierre Nora, ed., *Les Lieux de mémoire*, 4 vols. (Paris: Gallimard, 1984–1986).
*Please note that throughout this translation the numbered footnotes are the author's original notes, and the lettered notes are those of the translators.*

3

*boulevard* sense of humor); *être bon à mettre à Chaillot/aux Petites-Maisons/à Charenton* (to be fit to be committed to Chaillot, Petites-Maisons, or Charenton); and *se mettre en grève* ("to go on strike").[a] Moreover, Mnemosyne, the mother of the arts—as the ancient arts of memory and mnemonic devices of the orators remind us[2]—goes hand in hand with architecture. Rhetoric is based on nothing more than a series of places, or *topoi*. Romanticism would seem to be, among other things, an effort to abandon the ahistorical topoi of rhetorical commonplaces in order to rediscover the historical, symbolic, and psychological weight of real places. The connections between Viollet-le-Duc and Jules Michelet, between Baron Georges Eugène Haussmann and Emile Zola, and among Hector Horeau, Gustave Eiffel, and Jules Verne involves more than the mere fact of their contemporaneity. The relations that link one symbolic field to another, one semiotic sphere to another, or one aesthetic project to another run far deeper. Michelet discovered his vocation as a historian in the architectural museums of Alexandre Lenoir and Alexandre Du Sommerard, and among the tombs of Parisian cemeteries. Similarly, Marcel Proust's reveries about architecture owe a great deal to John Ruskin. In his various essays on the latter, Proust as a matter of course comes to speak of resurrection, of memory, of the books and places of his childhood, of reading as a way of wandering through cities, and of cities as books to wander through. The city—book metaphor was inevitable in the nineteenth century. A book is after all a volume, a spatialized measure of a certain time and order of reading—just as literature is perhaps, at its origins, a lapidary object or an inscription.

For nineteenth-century writers, architecture was not merely the framing or punctuation of a given space or the scenery that served as the backdrop for plot. Architecture was not reducible to aesthetics, economics, or the laws of gravity. Rather, it produced, permitted, and concretized not only a concept of history (be it collective or individual) but also, the staging of everyday life and of those rituals which expose social behavior. These rituals are founded on impalpable legal and ethical dis-

---

[2] Frances Yates, *The Art of Memory* (Chicago: University of Chicago Press, 1966); Jonathan Spence, *The Memory Palace of Matteo Ricci* (New York: Harper and Row, 1971).

[a] *Lorettes* are kept women named for Notre-Dame de Lorette, the neighborhood in which they lived; *vin de barrière* is cheap wine sold at Paris's city limits or *barrières; se porter comme le Pont-Neuf* refers to the oldest bridge over the Seine; a *boulevard* is a form of light, popular comedy that was associated with the theaters on the boulevards; Chaillot, Petites-Maisons, and Charenton all refer to insane asylums in and around Paris; the place de Grève, an area near the banks of the Seine where the Hôtel de Ville now stands, was where out-of-work laborers would go in the hope of being hired.

tinctions expressed through such oppositions as movable/immovable, private/public, sacred/profane, inside/outside, and privacy/exhibition. The act of dwelling involves living within these "distinctions" and inhabiting a system of values. These distinctions make up the preferred material of nineteenth-century literature: on the one hand, manners and morals (*moeurs*), or one's social relationship to others, as embodied in the novel (Honoré de Balzac writes at the beginning of *La Fausse Maîtresse* that "architecture is the expression of a nation's mores."); and on the other hand, the subject or the self's relationship to itself through memory and recollection, as embodied in lyric poetry. In a word, the question of society and the question of the subject.

The phrase which Martin Heidegger would comment upon, "poetically man dwells,"[3] was foreshadowed by the Romantics—and not just in Friedrich Hölderin's work, but in Michelet's and Charles Baudelaire's as well. For Michelet, the two major sciences of the future would involve the organization of living space: "A science of emigration and an art of acclimatization. . . . [Man] will only become free and human once this special art transforms him into a true inhabitant of his planet."[4] The origin of all art and the art of origination (archè) according to Hegel, the "pivotal art" according to the Fourierist Victor Considérant,[5] and "the matrix of all other arts" according to Félicité-Robert Lamennais,[6] architecture would become the obsession of the nineteenth century. And literature, particularly fiction, would of course have ample opportunity to bear witness to this obsession.

Both writing (production) and reading (reception) were involved in this process. Admittedly, any literary text—even the "book about nothing" of which Gustave Flaubert dreamed or the "rhythm of nothingness" that Arthur Rimbaud sought to capture—can talk about whatever it pleases. And readers, once they have closed the book, are similarly free to remember anything of what they have just read. Yet it would probably be easy to confirm that the selective and anthological memory of the average reader retains above all the architectural spaces or objects present in nineteenth-century literature. Here too it would seem that textual mem-

---

[3] Martin Heidegger, "Poetically Man Dwells," in *Poetry, Language, Thought*, trans. Alfred Hofstader (New York: Harper and Row, 1971).

[4] Jules Michelet, "Choix du rivage," in *La Mer* (Paris: Hachette, 1861), pt. 4, chap. 2.

[5] "Architecture is the pivotal art that sums up all other arts, and consequently sums up society itself: architecture writes history" (Victor Considérant, *Considérations sociales sur l'architectonique* [Paris: Librairies du Palais-Royal, 1834]), 6.

[6] Félicité-Robert Lamennais, "Du Beau et de L'Art dans leurs rapports avec le langage écrit," in *Esquisse d'une philosophie* (Paris: Garnier, 1865), 40.

ory or readability were entirely dependent upon inscribed or described places: the Vauquer boarding house in *Le Père Goriot,* Fabrice's prison in *La Chartreuse de Parme,* Proust's steeples in *A la recherche du temps perdu,* Emma Bovary's castle-like wedding cake, the symmetrical phalansteries of the good French and bad German engineers in Verne's *Les Cinq cents millions de la Bégum,* des Esseintes's chamber in Joris-Karl Huysmans's *A rebours,* the sewers of Victor Hugo's *Les Misérables,* Baudelaire's balconies and alcoves, the sealed room of Edgar Allen Poe's *The Murders in the Rue Morgue,* Stéphane Mallarmé's casement windows and waning mirrors. The two literary genres that were, by all accounts, first "invented" in the nineteenth century—the detective story (Poe, Emile Gaboriau) and the prose poem (Aloysius Bertrand, Baudelaire)—both feature intricate and most often urban decors that stand out by their architectural specificity. Any number of important works of the nineteenth century bear the name—be it real or invented, proper or common—or the sign of some particular architectural site: *Le Cottage Landor; Cosmopolis; La Chartreuse de Parme; La Maison du chat qui pelote; La Maison Tellier; Au bonheur des dames; La Maison à vapeur; Tableaux parisiens; Notre-Dame de Paris; La Cathédrale; Les Villes tentaculaires,* and so on. Not to mention the innumerable mysteries (of Paris, London, Marseilles, and New York) whose titles catalogue the range of contemporary megapolises. Such titles are lapidary in the full sense of this term and bear witness throughout the century to the writer's growing sensitivity to the symbolic power of architectural frameworks. It is as if these writers—individuals whom Barthes characterizes as afflicted with the "disease" of "seeing language"—suddenly found themselves afflicted with yet another disease, that of "seeing architecture." It is as if the fabrication of fiction were now constrained to gather sustenance systematically from the factories, houses, cities, monuments, and various other habitats that dotted an increasingly urbanized landscape of the real. It is as if the writer henceforth would always have to provide housing for his characters, to make them inhabitants; no longer would he be able to describe any of his heroes' habits (habit being routine, a way of being manipulated by space and environment) without also mentioning their habitat. Above all, it is as if the artifice of literature (an articulated semiotic ensemble that produces meaning) possessed a structural complicity or deep preestablished homology with that very thing whose existence in reality is *already* artificial: namely the building (an articulated semiotic ensemble that produces space). Which thus confounds all the differences between various literary genres and schools.

Significantly, nineteenth-century mass literature was quick to adopt the name of the building most emblematic of the entire era: the magazine (*magasin*).[b] In the same way, such nineteenth-century terms as *panorama, museum, pantheon, ruin, tomb* (those written by Mallarmé being the best known), *tableau, boulevard, salon, Paris,* and *backstage* refer both to a type of publication, or even a particular literary style or genre, and to specific kinds of constructed spaces.

Writers in the nineteenth century took an active interest in architecture. Prosper Mérimée became an inspector of historical monuments, Victor Hugo traveled around as an antiquary, Gustave Flaubert and Maxime Du Camp photographed monuments in Egypt, and Emile Zola photographed those of the 1900 Exposition Universelle. Over the course of the century, writers took part in the great debates whose focus or pretext was various architectural objects, problems, or concepts: for example, Proust's aforementioned dialogue with Ruskin; the polemics and debates surrounding Hector-Martin Lefuel's new Louvre; the demolition of the Vendôme column during the Paris Commune; the erection of Sacré Coeur; Charles Garnier's Paris Opéra; or the Eiffel Tower. Hugo, in *Notre-Dame de Paris* (1831), launched the slogan that would serve as a leitmotif in a debate lasting more than a century: *Ceci tuera cela*—this (the book) will kill that (architecture). Victor Considérant in his *Considérations sociales sur l'architectonique* (1834) took issue with Hugo's slogan in the name of the phalanstery of the future, whereas Zola, in *Le Ventre de Paris* (1873), reapplied Hugo's phrase to the debate around the death of the architecture of the past in the face of the new architecture of steel and glass, exemplified by Victor Baltard's designs for les Halles.[7]

The imbrication of literature and architecture thus appears widespread in the nineteenth century and seems to play on a variety of levels with a relevance that goes beyond mere historical, metaphorical, or anecdotal coincidence. By its very polyvalence the term *exposition,* as defined in the nineteenth-century *Grand Larousse* dictionary, can serve

[7] Both Hugo's book and this phrase have had quite a legacy. Théophile Gautier, beginning with the preface of *Mademoiselle de Maupin* (1835), would make note of the popularity of historical novels set in the Middle Ages and their fondness for descriptions of architecture. Frank Lloyd Wright would also mention Hugo's book and slogan in his autobiography. Michelet would also develop a comparison between Notre-Dame and the "white and gray walls of the Collège de France." Moreover he accused Hugo of seeing Notre-Dame as disorder when in fact it was a "dialectic in stone."

[b] The French term *magasin,* meaning "store" is etymologically related to the term *magazine,* with its various associations of warehousing, storing, stocking, and compartmentalizing.

both as a guide and as a unifying term to explore these different strata of imbricated meaning.

Hence, it is predictable that literature should privilege certain architectural objects, certain "paper monuments" that bring out the contemporary resonances of the term exposition: (1) the *ruin* (ancient or modern) in which the interior is exposed to the exterior and the eye can penetrate through cracks in the walls; (2) the *arcade* (*passage*) and its variants (the covered market, the gallery, the conservatory, the glass canopy) in which products are displayed and people come to stroll and inside and outside become interchangeable (In his great unfinished project on Paris and Baudelaire, Benjamin portrays the arcade as the edifice emblematic of the entire period.)[8]; (3) the *phalanstery* which enables the utopian theorist, like the architect and the belletrist to become a great plotter of fictions. Like Proudhon, who composed a project for an *exposition perpétuelle*, all utopian theorists emphasized the importance of architecture, the need to invent what Le Corbusier would call new "machines for living," and, in the interest of hygiene, the importance of exposing buildings and passageways to facilitate the circulation of fluids and light; (4) and last but not least, the *big city*—London and most notably Paris, a city that Benjamin would call "the capital of the nineteenth century," the site of annual salons and, every ten years or so, of universal expositions, a city laid out panoptically by an administration that imposed a grid of well-lit boulevards on which society exhibited itself, offering the everyday spectacle of its rituals, fashions, shop windows, and worldly manners. For the stroller who gapes and the dandy who is gawked at—two stock characters of nineteenth-century literature—as well as what Poe called the modern "man of the crowd," Paris not only hosts universal expositions but the city itself along with its inhabitants becomes an object of exposition.

First and foremost, universal expositions are an economic and social fact. "Expositions are all the rage," reads the foreword to a catalogue of the 1875 Salon de Peinture.[9] "Too many expositions," writes Hippolyte Taine's character Thomas Graindorge.[10] In *Au bonheur des dames,*

---

[8] On Benjamin and his *Arcades Project*, see Heinz Wisemann, *Walter Benjamin et Paris* (Paris: Cerf, 1986). For Benjamin the key words for the second half of the century would be: "Arcades; fashion; Paris in ancient style; ennui; the eternal return; Haussmannization; iron construction; means of exposition; advertisement; Grandville; collectors; interiors; the trace; Baudelaire" (Burkhardt Lindner, ed., *Paris au XIXème siècle* [Paris: Presses Universitaires de France, 1984] 155).

[9] A. de la Fizelière, (Paris: Librairie des bibliophiles, 1875), iv.

[10] Hippolyte Taine, *Vie et opinions de Monsieur Frédéric-Thomas Graindorge: Notes sur Paris,* 4th ed. (Paris: Hachette, 1868), 292. Yet the battle cry of painters who in the middle of the century, wanted to break free of the tyranny of the sole official salon was "Freedom of exposition!"

Zola speaks of "the neurosis of the huge department stores." An entry in Flaubert's *Dictionnaire des idées reçues* reads, "Exposition: object of delirium in the nineteenth century." Indeed, expositions run through the second half of the century like a leitmotif, providing its punctuation and its absolute referent (or reference point). This "expositionitis," a linkage of the visible and the legible, is authorized by a deep complicity between architecture ("the art of turning a building properly," according to Philibert de l'Orme) and literature (the art of producing meaning and of exposing ideas by means of tropes and turns of phrase). Literature experienced expositionitis by either of two modes: the euphoric mode, which conveys the consumerist mastery of a world reduced to a well-organized department store, or the dysphoric or melancholic mode, which reflects the loss of meaning and value.

There are thus several different aspects to the exposition: on the one hand a delight in the encyclopedia of novelties and in the universal exposition of knowledge and products, on the other, a more anxious experience of fragmentation and discontinuity; on the one hand the domain of home and privacy, of museums and stores with their aisles, on the other the domain of the promiscuous prowlings of "the man of the crowd." The outcast, the recluse, the native, the vagrant, the bourgeois, the bohemian, the lunatic (of whom it is said, "nobody's home"), and the staid person (*rassis*) (or as Rimbaud would say, the stay-at-home (*l'assis*)—such are the literary types who dominate the novels and poetry of the century, a cast of characters that derives heavily from fundamental architectural distinctions. The fact that Verne's *P'tit Bonhomme* (1893) was both an account of an abandoned, "exposed" child wandering the roads as well as an ode to a department store, and the fact that *La Veillée des* **chaumières** (Evening gathering in the **thatched cottage**) published in its first issue "La Fille du juif **errant**" (The **Wandering** Jew's daughter) by Paul Féval, which could be bought at the same time as the Jules Hetzel edition of Verne's **Voyages** *extraordinaires* (Extraordinary **voyages**) (emphasized terms indicate the oppositions in an overall system), stress the existing tensions between different architectural and topographical imaginings. These tensions, particularly noticeable in literature after 1850, criss-cross the entire century. The whirlwind of Haussmann's public works department (the *voirie-ouragan* of Baudelaire's poem "Le Cygne") threw the city dwellers' frame of experience into upheaval with the industrial proliferation of new, hitherto unthinkable buildings and scenery. (But then, isn't all new architecture unthinkable?) Among Parisians in general and writers in particular, Haussmann's projects certainly exacerbated a sense of violent dispossession capable of provoking painful effects of amnesia, or caused them to indulge in a melancholic remembrance that led to the search for imaginable, inhabitable, enveloping forms of architecture.[11] The orphan Kasper Hauser as well as the splenetic hero haunt the century alongside such great classifiers and organizers of well-ordered places as Zola's Octave Mouret in *Au bonheur des dames* or Verne's professor–engineers.

Exposition, be it an architectural phenomenon, a collective obsession, or a specific descriptive moment occurring in texts, is therefore ambiguous. On the one hand it acts as the architectural and rhetorical locus for a given rationality, on the other, it provides a site for eclecticism (both in the sense of bric-a-brac and organization). The exposition is simultaneously utilitarian and picturesque—a place both for entertainment and for the exhibition of knowledge. Although exemplary and universal, the exposition is at the same time temporary, transitory, and easily dismantled. A "storehouse of education," according to Hetzel's children's books, the exposition is also a kind of "school recess."

Perhaps because literature and architecture are the two most "visible" arts, since they organize both the everyday practices of reading and the everyday necessities of shelter, the crises and tensions that affect them seem strikingly parallel. This parallel appears to take root by 1850. With the emergence of politicians and appointed bureaucrats such as Haussmann, the architects trained at the Ecole des Beaux-Arts deemed themselves increasingly dispossessed of their right and their competence to create the city. They furthermore deemed themselves dispossessed of their ability to create personally designed monuments, houses, and interior furnishings, given the emergence of the knockdown modules used by engineers such as Eiffel. Industrial architecture, with its buildings that could be easily dismantled, restored, or put to a variety of uses, brought about a crisis of style and of meaning which Hugo registered as early as 1830: How do we "read" a building? Which in turn leads to another all-encompassing crisis: How do we read the real?[12] These architectural crises came at a time when writers were also

---

[11] Concerning this point and Baudelaire's poem "Le Cygne," see Ross Chambers, "Mémoire et mélancholie," in *Mélancholie et opposition; les débuts du modernisme* (Paris: José Corti, 1987).

[12] On nineteenth-century architecture, see Claude Mignot, *Architecture of the Nineteenth Century in Europe* (New York: Rizzoli, 1984); Eugène Viollet-le-Duc, *Le Dictionnaire d'architecture: Relèves et observations*, ed. Phillipe Boudon and Phillipe Deshayes (Brussels: Margada, 1979); François Loyer, *Architecture of the Industrial Age, 1789–1914* (New York: Skira/Rizzoli, 1983); Loyer, *Paris in the Nineteenth Century: Architecture and Urbanism* (New York: Abbeville Press, 1988).

confronting difficulties in the practice of their profession. Both writers and architects saw their roles becoming increasingly subordinate or accessory: the architect felt reduced to designing bourgeois vacation houses, or "secondary" homes, while the writer felt obliged to churn out entertainment for concierges, to produce gossip columns (*l'écho de Paris*), to write newspaper articles, or to engage in what Sainte-Beuve termed the "industrial literature" of the serial novel. In reaction to the hypertrophy of what Benjamin called "exhibition value" that tends to supplant all other values (notably aesthetic ones), in the production of artworks, architecture turned to the practice of eclecticism, to the "neo-," and to the picturesque while literature turned to the practice of irony, Flaubert's "higher joke" (*blague supérieure*), intertextual montage, and *écriture artiste*. Whether by parody or pastiche, all these practices reflected an effort to recover style, meaning, and memory.

But once again, this effort is not without its ambiguities. Flaubert may well have thundered against the "exposition-as-object-of-delirium," believing that the stupor of the wide-eyed bourgeois gaping at shoddy merchandise and slogans of industry was truly a *dé-lire*,ᶜ that is, an obstacle both to reading and to the private production of meaning. Nevertheless he writes over and over again in his correspondence, "Let's be exhibitors" (*Soyons exposants*).[13] If there is an economy, an ethics, or a pathology (a delirium) of exposition, what then are its stylistics, its aesthetics? Could exposition not also be a (textual) machine or mechanism that facilitates representation and reading (rather than blocking them); that is, could it not also be a machine that produces hypotyposis?

Any examination of the phenomenon of exposition in the nineteenth century must take into account the role as well as the specific status of certain expository and descriptive practices, whether as an accompaniment, a means, or an ends in a given literary work. The nineteenth century is, afterall, the century of realism in all its variations: Edmond and Jules Goncourts' impressionistic realism; Verne's encyclopedic realism; Zola's naturalistic and ethnographic realism (where the novel is a "storehouse (*magasin*) of human documents"); or Flaubert's ironic real-

---

[13] "Let us attack nothing, let us sing the praises of everything, let us be *exhibitors* and not debaters" (Flaubert to Louise Colet, 13–14 April 1853); "Literature will be above all *expository* which does not mean didactic" (Flaubert to Colet, 12 January 1853). Flaubert elsewhere deplores the fact that "the French mind contents itself so little with what I think of as the essence of poetry, that is, exposition, whether done in a picturesque fashion via tableaux, or morally, via psychological analysis" (Flaubert to Colet, 25–26 June 1853).

ᶜ *Dé-lire* denotes "unreading" as well as "delirium."

ism (where the agricultural fair is nothing but the caricature, or the provincial double, of the capital's great universal expositions.

This era of realism could be historically located in relation to a monument destroyed by a painter (as was the Vendôme column by Gustave Courbet); to the Salon des Refusés of 1863 (where Manet displayed his scandalous nude); or to two epoch-making expositions— in 1855 the wildcat exposition of paintings by and of Courbet, which took place on the sidelines of the official salon; in 1881 the official entry of the same Courbet into that most legitimate domain of exhibition, the Louvre. The nineteenth century is thus the site of the Battle of (and for) Expositions.

The term *exposition* elicits many different associations: it evokes the preeminence of the gaze, with its particular pleasures and displeasures; it also conjures an architectural space whose readable design permits a more or less restricted passage; it implies a rational presentation of collected objects, not to mention a set of highly ritualized social and institutional practices; and finally, *exposition* entails an ostentation of knowledge, with an accompanying linguistic practice that is at once explanatory (an exposition explains) as well as designatory and descriptive (an exposition displays items that are named and labeled). No monument comes without its plaque, its explanatory guide; no decent exposition is complete without its catalogue.[14] As might be expected, the nineteenth century would produce a series of conjunctions between architecture and literature. But the analysis of these conjunctions should involve more than a thematic inventory of the numerous nineteenth-century literary works that describe buildings of their time, or a certain shared vocabulary (as in the aforementioned case of the *magasin*). Rather, these conjunctions should be analyzed from the perspective of a textual poetics that would attempt to describe the system or structure of such interconnections, while above all highlighting the function of certain specific objects, metaphors, or textual schemas. Such a textual poetics would focus specifically on exposition-texts or on characters engaged in posturing, posing, being exposed, and exposing others. These characters include, for example, the actress, the gawker, the parvenu, the traveling salesman, as well as other stock figures who at once constitute a system and practice some form of exposition—be it of themselves, of others, or of objects. Such a textual poetics would furthermore illuminate fiction's *topoi* of exposi-

14 "A decent exposition implies a good catalogue," wrote André Chastel in *La Revue de l'art* (Paris: Flammarion, 1980), 104.

tion and inaugural passages in all their various forms: ruins, both ancient and modern; tableaux that display knowledge; descriptive catalogues; tropelike doorways; naturalistic hypotyposis; guidebooks; and gallery books. The modest dimensions of this present work, a study of the extended metaphor of exposition, permit little more than a sketchy analysis of certain points, especially since I wish to devote the chapter that follows to more general considerations of the connections between textuality and architecture.

# PART I

# Text and Architecture

Monuments . . . of paper.

Joachim du Bellay, *Antiquitez de Rome*

Literature depends on other arts to define itself. Comparison, metaphor, and analogy are therefore necessarily inscribed at the core of the very act of definition—not as mere decorative practices, but as indispensable tools. At the end of Proust's *A la recherche du temps perdu*, the narrator, dreaming of the ideal book and its ideal writer, confronts this very problem, namely, how to talk about the literary work. Analogy appears to provide the only recourse: "One would have to borrow comparisons from the loftiest and the most varied arts,"[a] he writes, as he proceeds to string together a very rich and complex series of such comparisons over the next few pages. A first group of comparisons is set into motion by the multiple meanings of the word *volume*. For each character of his book, the writer "would display [that character's] most opposite facets in order to indicate his volume";[1] he then would have to stage his work

> with meticulous care, perpetually regrouping his forces as if on an offensive, and he would also have to endure his work like a form of fatigue, to accept it like a rule, to build it up like a church, to observe it like a strict diet, to overcome it like an obstacle, to win it like a friendship, to pamper it like a child, to create it like a new world . . . [with parts] that have only been

[1] "To feel his volume as if he were a solid" is a variation in the text (Marcel Proust, *A la recherche du temps perdu* [Paris: Bibliothèque de la Pléiade, 1956], vol. 3, 1,302). A deletion in Proust's famous opening of *A la recherche* found in the printer's uncorrected proofs reveals that the narrator, before falling asleep, was reading "A treatise on monumental archaeology."

[a] Marcel Proust, *Remembrance of Things Past*, trans. C. K. Scott Moncrieff (New York: Random House, 1981), 1,089ff.

sketched out, parts, which because of the very amplitude of the architect's design, will no doubt never be completed. How many cathedrals remain unfinished! One nourishes a book, one reinforces its weak parts, one protects it, but afterward it is the book that grows, that designates our tomb, and defends it against the world's clamor, and for a while, against oblivion.

The narrator then follows this up with a comparison of his literary work to a sort of optical device: "My work is but a sort of magnifying glass . . . that would allow me to furnish [my readers] with the means of reading within themselves." Then, "shifting [his] similes from one moment to the next as [he] began to represent [to himself] more clearly and in a more material shape the task upon which [he] was embarking," the narrator goes on to put forward a comparison between his own literary activity and Françoise's sewing ("I would work by her side almost as she herself worked")[2]:

> by pinning here and there an extra page, I would construct my book I dare not say ambitiously like a cathedral, but quite simply like a dress . . . it was my habit to stick together with paste these "paperies" (*paperolles*), as Françoise called the pages of my writing, and sometimes in this process they tore, but then Françoise would come to my aid by consolidating them just as she stitched patches (*mettre une pièce*) onto the worn parts of her dresses, or, as she used to paste a piece of newspaper where a pane of glass had been broken on the kitchen window while waiting for the glazier, as I was waiting for the printer.

The narrator concludes with one final analogy: "I would make my book in the same way that Françoise made that *boeuf-mode* that Mr. Norpois had found so delicious just because she had enriched its aspic with so many choice cuts of meat."[3] This celebrated passage of Proust is exemplary for a variety of reasons. To speak of a literary work, whether completed or still in progress, inevitably raises the problem of what kind of metalanguage one is going to adopt to talk about it, and what kind of metaphors, analogies, allegories, or similes one is going to have to choose. Beyond its references to "the most varied arts," or to images

[2] A comparison with the metonymic referent (Françoise) chosen for its very contiguity to the narrator's habitat ("like all beings without pretention who live near us" [Proust, *Remembrance*, vol. 3, 1,090]).

[3] A long elaboration on the themes of death and time follows. At this point in the text there is a brief return to the architectural metaphor where the narrator speaks of "the edifice that [he] had to construct" and writes that the idea of his construction "did not leave [him] for an instant." He writes that he did not know "whether [his work] would be a church where little by little a group of faithful would succeed in apprehending truths and discovering harmonies or perhaps the grand design, or whether it would remain, like a druidic monument perched on a rocky isle, something forever unfrequented" (Proust, *Remembrance*, vol. 3, 1,098).

that would initially appear fairly disparate, Proust's text at this point seems to choose figures that follow a logic whose legend is provided by architecture, which functions as a kind of mathematical operator that allows some common denominator to become plainly readable. It is perhaps the ambiguity of the two initial terms in the passage—the most "lofty" arts and "volume"—that compelled the subsequent references to architecture, which is the art of configuring and mastering space. Similarly, it was perhaps just as inevitable that this metadiscourse about novelistic discourse—a means of reducing both the distance and space between a work and its commentary, between a text and its metatext—should not only borrow from the art of architecture, inasmuch as it is an art of constructed, measured, and articulated space, that establishes distance and proximity, but also borrow from similes and metaphors which make it possible to "transfer" meanings around in lexical space. Proust, as is well known, had at the outset planned to entitle each part of his book with a different architectural term: porchway (*porche*), the apse's stained-glass windows (*vitraux de l'abside*). But what is remarkable in this passage is how Proust extends strictly architectural references into allusions to clothing, to reading and writing, and even to ingestion. The architectural metaphors are overt in his references to "a church," "architect's design," a "great cathedral," and even in the expression "regrouping forces" (which can be understood architecturally as well as militarily). He then goes on to link architecture to clothing ("like a dress") which in turn is associated with the act of sewing ("as she stitched patches"), for one can patch a dress (*mettre une pièce*) in the same way one can "patch up" a broken window, and moreover, *pièce* also designates a part of a house—a room. The various connotations of *pièce* lock into themes of paper and of reading and writing—as is borne out by Françoise's term "paperies," by the magnifying glass, by the association between the glazier and the printer, and of course by the "piece of newspaper" that replaces the missing window pane. And all this in turn connects up with the theme of bodily ingestion—the passage speaks of sticking to a book "like a strict diet," of "pampering it like a child," of "nourishing" it, and compares it to Françoise's *bœuf-mode* in aspic (not to mention that the room with a broken window is the "kitchen"). It's as if Proust is emphasizing in this play of metaphors that architecture is more than the mere art of establishing or reducing distance or space, but that inasmuch as it organizes the interplay of exterior and interior, of public and private, architecture thereby also emerges as the art of the body, with all its "fatigues," its desires, its envelopes, its articulations, its dislocations, its "reversibilities" and its relations to other bodies. Consider such phrases as "like a rule" (which introduces the notions of restriction and "order," which is physical, linguistic, and legal as well as architectural) or "like an obstacle," "like a friendship": all desire is perhaps but the establishing or the abolishing of the distance between an object of attraction or repulsion, and hence all desire may be reduced to a sort of *proxemics* that architecture simply makes concrete. To speak, to live, or to eat are to establish a relation toward oneself and toward others. Speaking presupposes the reversibility of the act of enunciation; entering presupposes the possibility of exiting; and, if architecture is the art of housing a body inside something, gastronomy (as in the fairy-tale gingerbread house) involves exactly the reverse, the art of housing something in a body.[4] Another thing that literature tells us is that architecture is nothing but the same, on a different scale, as skin and clothing.[5] All three concretize an ambiguity, for skin, clothing, or walls are all sheaths that establish contact and distance, that both bring things together and hold them apart. What becomes of the notions of interior or exterior when one can simply switch around "paperies," or replace windowpanes with a piece of newspaper, or turn a dress inside out, or go through a doorway in one direction or another? In this passage of Proust's, replacing a window

---

[4] Aspic, like ice cream (another typically Proustian object) and sugar are the primary culinary means for creating edible architecture. See the analyses of Jean-Pierre Richard, *Proust et le monde sensible* (Paris: Seuil, 1974). The comparison with the *boeuf-mode* in aspic, a culinary object that reappears many times in Proust's work (notably on one occasion when it is compared to "blocks of marble from the mountains of Carrara" that Michelangelo selected when constructing Julius II's tomb [Proust, *Remembrance*, vol. 1, 23]) is followed by a long passage on the body and the relationship between exterior and interior:

> For the fundamental fact was that I had a body, and this meant I was perpetually threatened by a double danger, internal and external, though to speak thus was merely a matter of linguistic convenience, the truth being that the internal danger—the risk, for instance of cerebral haemorrhage, is *also* an *external* threat. . . . Indeed it is the possession of a body that is the great danger to the mind. (Proust, *Remembrance*, vol. 3, 1,092; emphasis mine)

[5] The everyday vocabulary of the newspaper in fact draws indiscriminately upon these two vocabularies: *manchette* [meaning cuff or headline—trans.], "column," or *rez de chaussée* [meaning ground floor or the bottom of a newspaper page—trans.]. Hugo writes in *Le Rhin*: "You know that I don't disdain any detail, and I think that everything that touches man reveals something about him. I study clothing the way I study an edifice. The suit of clothes is Man's first garment, the house is his second" (Hugo, *Le Rhin: Lettres à un ami*, ed. Jean Gaudin [Paris: Imprimerie Nationale, 1985]). This can be compared to Charles Fourier, who writes: "What I understand to mean artificial clothing are our fabrics, walls, and rooms; by natural clothing, I mean the atmosphere that, by its very contact with us, becomes a natural part of our clothing" (*Oeuvres Complètes*, vol. 3 [Paris: n.p., 1841], 36).

open to the outside world with a printed piece of paper can be regarded as an apt allegory for the writer's work. The problem of representation is thereby posed by this text: Who represents what? How to go about representation? What does architecture, which here represents the literary work, represent in and of itself? Given that architecture is a nonmimetic art that does not "represent," an art that allows us to inhabit reversibility, an art that triumphs over time and therefore death (which is irreversibility par excellence), an art that manufactures privacy and promiscuity and thus regulates our relationship to ourselves and to others, given all this, one can understand how architecture in this passage could become the model for all literature (inasmuch as it "designates a tomb," "protects it against clamor and against oblivion," and serves as an optical "machine" that allows one to read what lies within oneself and others rather than to read the outside world). Ambiguity and reversibility, desire and oblivion, privacy and exteriority, experiencing one's body and the body of others as presence—all these themes central to *La Recherche* converge in this passage, as they do in all passages of the novel that feature references to architecture. This passage also contains within it, as we shall later see, the essential purport of numerous other literary texts, most notably the poetic text, which seems to harbor a curious obsession with architecture.

We can start from the following observation: the critical or theoretical discourse on literature provides the locus for an extended metaphor that insistently borrows from the descriptive vocabulary of architecture. Architectural terms like "construction," "deconstruction," "closure," "point of view," "rhythm," "style," "framework," "lapidary," "monumental," "edifying," and "threshold," to name but a few, permeate the discourse about literature. No matter what the era, theoretical debates concerning the coherence or the definition of the literary work—whether these involve the relationship of the parts to the whole, of details to the overall mass, or of the outline to its outcome—almost automatically resort to references to architecture, to buildings, or to some sort of manufactured object. Proust is of course in no way original on this point. Hugo, in his 1829 preface to *Les Orientales,* announced his intention to compose a work comparable to the medieval city, or to a "mosque." Zola opened the chapter on Balzac in his *Romanciers naturalistes* with a two-page extended metaphor about the novelist's "construction site." Théophile Gautier, in his poem "Après le feuilleton" in *Emaux et Camées,* described the pages of the newspaper in architectural terms that were already standard usage:

*Mes colonnes sont alignées*
*Au portique du feuilleton;*
*Elles supportent, resignées,*
*Du journal le pesant fronton.*[b]

Mallarmé, in his discussion of Poe, wrote that the poet must "avoid the reality of any remaining scaffolding that surrounds this magic, spontaneous architecture" that is the poem. It is as if architecture, precisely because it involves sight, that "most intellectual of the senses" ("To see is to know," wrote Viollet-le-Duc by way of a conclusion to his *Comment on devient dessinateur*), was judged particularly suited to support speculation, to prop up theory, to concretize the abstract, and to serve as a universal extended metaphor or as a preferred metalanguage producing intelligibility and meaning.[6] The same complicity exists both on the level of texts and genres, where architecture acts as a veritable "genre signal." The autobiographical "I" (the childhood home); the characters of the fantastic novel (the house of Usher, Hoffman's "abandoned house," or Verne's Carpathian mountain castle) or the lyric poem (Baudelaire's "*J'ai longtemps habité sous les vastes portiques*"[c]); the characters in the naturalist novel (marquises always leaving somewhere at five o'clock); the heros of the theater (the court, or the garden); the protagonists of the picaresque novel (the wayside inn)—none of these characters can be imagined without their architectural settings. These settings, which can also involve the sheerly physical layout of the volume itself—the portico frontispieces of the sixteenth century, the "cathedral-style" or the "lighthouse" bindings of the nineteenth century, or the supplementary illustrations accompanying the text, such as the diagrams and sections often found in detective fiction—take on a variety of shapes and functions. These architectural contexts thereby render the traditional novel at once highly redundant and therefore

---

[6] Concerning the privileged ties of architecture both as a universally comparable object for reflection and as a metalanguage with poetics or philosophy, see Daniel Payot, *Le Philosophe et l'architecte* (Paris: Aubier, 1982) as well as a special issue of the *Cahiers de CCE*, "Mesure pour mesure, architecture et philosophie" (Paris: Centre Georges Pompidou, 1987).

[b]
My columns are aligned
At the portico of the serial novel;
Resigned they support
The heavy pediment of this newspaper.

It should be noted that serial novels (*feuilletons*) were traditionally printed at the bottom of the first page of the newspaper—an area called in newspaper jargon, the ground floor (*rez de chaussée.*)

[c] "I have long resided under vast porticos."

readable by underscoring the harmonies and disharmonies that obtain between habitat, inhabitant, habit and clothing (*habit*). Furthermore they supply innumerable novels their opening exposition (such as the Vauquer boardinghouse at the outset of *Le Père Goriot*) as well as their illustrations. Architecture, in short, may well offer literature its beginning (*archè*) and its absolute origin, which is linked to rhetoric and thereby to the discourse of the law court (*praetorium*), with its various disputations as inventories, boundary markings, breaking and enterings, and party walls. As a rule architecture therefore conveniently guarantees a certain "realistic effect" (*effet de réel*) to any given literary work, for it provides fiction with a recognizable frame, anchor, or background that creates its verisimilitude. Therefore it comes as no surprise that architecture—be it a practice, a metaphor, or a point of reference—should come into play at those decisive moments when the very notion of mimesis is either being promoted or discredited by Western thought. To briefly summarize its well-known impact in the domain of painting, we might note that the development of perspective during the Renaissance evolves out of what were initially architectural concerns: Leo-Battista Alberti writes treatises both on painting and on architecture; Filippo Brunelleschi's designs for the baptistry and the piazza of Florence blend ornamentation with architectural features; specialists in trompe l'oeil apply their illusionist techniques both to interior decoration of homes (through marquetry) and of theaters. More so than painting, although architecture produces structures that are palpably real and concrete, for the architect it remains nonetheless essentially a fiction, a mental construct.[7] Unlike literature it claims and assumes this fictional status unashamedly—as is borne out by the various ways in which architecture is transposed onto other art forms. Thus by the end of the Middle Ages painting abandons its undifferentiated gold backgrounds for architectural settings that provide the ground and backdrop for the painting, thus framing and reduplicating the fictional subjects of the allegories and religious scenes represented. (Scenes of the Nativity or the Annunciation are often accompanied by elaborate architectural framing devices.) However, these painted settings remain a kind of dream architecture, as utopian and imaginary as the scene they frame. Such architectural scenery serves to distribute into a variety of different

---

[7] Under the entry "architecture" in his *Dictionnaire d'architecture* (Paris: A. Leclerc, 1832), Quatremère de Quincy writes: "This art, which appears to be more dependent on matter than others, was able to become, through this connection, more ideal. In other words, more likely to exert the intelligent aspect of our souls."

"mansions"[d] the actors of the story that is being staged, or else to demarcate the different sequences in its narrative. Likewise, when architecture begins to invade literature—for example, when the medieval text abandons its rarified spaces (crossing the forbidden threshold, laying siege to a castle, traversing the bridge)—it does so by means of a kind of second-degree fictionality, as in descriptions of dreams (see *The Dream of Polyphilius* by Francesco Colonna (1499), which inaugurates a somewhat nostalgic and virtually romantic reflection on ruins). The medieval text also favors descriptions of furniture and art objects which, as in the case of silver and gold objects, tapestries, frescoes, and paintings hanging on the wall, can at once be assimilated into the architecture or in fact represent architectural forms themselves. It is as if architecture governed by fiction can only reveal itself by these sorts of emphatic reduplications of itself or by this type of critical distancing. The presence of architecture in literature would appear to be doubly confined and circumscribed by the epideictic genres. More specifically, it is linked to the practice of *ekphrasis*—detachable rhetorical set pieces that are summoned up for the purpose of praise (as in François de Malherbe's "*Beaux et grands bâtiments d'éternelle structure / Superbes de matière et d'ouvrages divers*"[e])[8] or for the purpose of blame (as in Nicolas Boileau's satires on the clutter of Paris). Ekphratic descriptions, then, indicate the heavy *ideological* investment that occurs at these moments of the literary text (since it is at these points that it turns to speaking of value, of evaluation) and at the same time, they throw into relief how the text turns back in on itself by self-description. It is by means of architecture that the text begins to speak of what basically defines it as a structure, as a fiction, or as a structured fiction. All

---

[8] For an example of an epideictic text praising architecture, see the curious—and unfinished—work of Jean-Baptiste de Monicart, in which each of the buildings of Versailles are given the floor to address the visitor (*Versailles immortalisé par les merveilles parlantes des bâtiments, jardins, bosquets, parcs, statues, groupes, termes . . . avec une traduction en prose latine . . . les merveilles parlantes traitent dans leurs récits de leurs descriptions, origines, propriétés, attributs, et de leurs histoires soit saintes, véritables, ou fabuleuses*, 2 vols. [Paris: E. Ganeau, 1720]). According to the publisher this book was supposedly written by the author while incarcerated in the Bastille "without the help of any book. [Monicart's] memory alone served as his library." The text is preceded by a map of the palace, which included the "walking tour that the king had organized," in order to best see "everything in the gardens." This book is a perfect example of places of memory (Yates, *Art of Memory*), memories of places, royalty, order, organization, building, and language becoming practically synonymous.

[d] "Mansions" are permanent structures used to represent various settings in the staging of medieval and Renaissance plays, especially in France.

[e] "Tall and beautiful buildings of eternal construction / Superb in their material and their various works."

architecture in literature thus becomes to a greater or less degree, an incorporated metalanguage. Hence, from our present-day perspective, the crises that have periodically unsettled architecture both as a discipline and as a profession can certainly be interpreted as the symptoms of its sense of dispossession. Its loss of confidence in its essential and fundamental ability to produce imaginary stylistic objects (*utopias,* be they literary or philosophical genres, hardly differ from simple architectural *projects,* since they almost invariably entail major flights of architectural fancy) goes together with its failure of confidence in its ability to project a reality by means of written (or rewritten) semiotic mediation.[9] The architect's specific skill would above all appear to lie in the ability to manipulate paper beings rather than bricks and mortar; to manipulate simulacra that take the shape of consignments (i.e., commissions he receives from the client), signs, drawings, blueprints, sections, mock-ups, or axonometric projections. In short, architectural skill lies in creating substitutes and representamens of reality. (The expression "building castles in Spain" could be fiction's motto.)[10] The architect's forte is the ability to interpret and rewrite consignments into signs, to transform the semiotic into the iconic, and to proceed from the blueprint to the mock-up, from the elevation to the section, and vice versa, which is to say, the architect must develop a skill in matters that are metalinguistic or meta- (or trans-)semiotic. Every century therefore tends to link inextricably together the crises that beset the areas of the imaginary, of theory, and of architecture. The latter, since it is afflicted most directly by more "visible" economic constraints, serves to reveal, touch off, or amplify the crises in other areas. This might begin to

[9] Design (*dessein*) and drawing (*dessin*) are, we know, one and the same word. From Giovanni Battista Piranesi to Le Corbusier, by way of Jean-Jacques Lequeu, Bibiens, Etienne-Louis Boullée, Claude-Nicolas Ledoux, Hector Horeau, Karl Friedrich Schinkel, and others, architecture and pictoral or literary fiction never cease claiming a complicity and their shared "inventiveness" (Manfredo Tafuri, *Architecture and Utopia: Design and Capitalist Development* [Cambridge, Mass.: MIT Press, 1976]). Concerning the ambiguous relationship between architectural treatises and utopian literature, see Françoise Choay, *La Règle et le modèle* (Paris: Scuil, 1980). What genre do texts like Poe's "The Domain of Arnheim" and "Landor's Cottage" belong to?

[10] It comes as no surprise that one finds this expression either implicitly or explicitly throughout many texts that tend to be self-referential: for example, all of Act III of Henrik Ibsen's *The Master Builder,* Gérard de Nerval's *Petit château de Bohème,* or Baudelaire's "Rêve parisien," where the "I," "architect of [his] own wonderland," dreams of a "Babel of staircases and arcades" from which "erratic plant-life" is banished. In the ironic poem "Paysage" that opens the "Tableaux parisiens" section of Baudelaire's *Les Fleurs du mal,* the "I" shut up in his garret with the doors and windows closed out of hatred of the street, dreams of "chastely composing my eclogues" and "building my faery palaces in the night." This privileged link unifying the lyric text and architecture will be discussed in part 2, chap. 5.

explain Charles and Claude Perraults' position during the battle of the Ancients and the Moderns in the seventeenth century. ("It is better to be a mason if that is where your genius lies.") It might also account for the crisis that occurred in the middle of the nineteenth century, at a point when industrial, repetitive, reproducible technology begins to intrude on art and architecture, with the module replacing the model, and the ornament replacing style. And perhaps it is no coincidence that the postmodern movement, which cuts across so many Western intellectual fields after 1970, originated in architecture (Charles Jencks, Charles Moore, Robert Venturi). This development would appear to be repeating what occurred in the nineteenth century, and can perhaps be interpreted as a symptom of the desire to return to the sign, to scenery, to communication with the user or reader, to history, to fiction, and to "representation."

If architecture often seems so alluring to literature, perhaps it is because it appears to designate and circumscribe a field of diffuse theoretical and practical problems that are intrinsic to value. It's as if architecture cast back on literature like a reflective mirror those very questions that most deeply haunt it—but in a form that is sometimes symmetrical, sometimes exaggerated, sometimes ironically displaced or inverted, and sometimes reformulated in a more paradoxical, or "showy" guise (as it were, more concretely or somehow more petrified). These questions touch upon the problematic status of fiction, of representation, of the sign, and of meaning. Architecture and literature thus seem to need each other as a foil, a metalanguage, or a metaphor in order to fully conceive of themselves in all their complexity. Both join in a complicity of *artificiality*; both enter into an implicit epistemological collaboration. All great architects were prolific writers.

For literature or for the literary text the architectural object (in the most general sense: city, garden, house, machine, clothing, furniture, building, or monument) is endowed with a particularly rich and complex semantic status. First of all, it can figure as a *hermeneutical object*: to the extent that it involves an *inside* (always more or less hidden) that necessarily differentiates itself from an *outside* (more apparent, exposed and visible), and to the extent that a facade, even in the case of the most transparent Crystal Palace, can never entirely reveal the interior, or for that matter allow its function to be guessed. On the one hand there is the facade, on the other, the crypt: the world appears as a juxtaposition of "chambers," or "boxes" of relative darkness, clarity, or transparency.[11] Therefore among various Asmodeus-type[f] complexes, strategies for gaining knowledge (*savoir*), strategies for obtaining information by the actors in a story, and strategies for gaining access to truth (of Ruskin's seven lamps, the lamp of truth is the most important) will naturally be deployed in texts that feature architecture.

Secondly, the literary text can apprehend any architectural object as if it were a differential, *discriminating object* that analyzes space through interfaces and proximities or through partitions and contiguities. This kind of architectural object either opens or obstructs and distinguishes between what is joined and what is disjunct; it welcomes, rejects, or filters while partitioning, distributing, straightening, classifying, and separating objects and subjects. Therefore, this kind of architectural object easily organizes the strategies of desire and the strategies of intentionality (*vouloir-faire*) of the actors in narrative scenarios. Notably, the erotic text is generally a major consumer of such carefully articulated sites (such as Casanova's "escapades at the wayside inn" or Jules Barbey d'Aurevilly's *Le Rideau cramoisi*). As we have already noted, all desire, be it attraction or repulsion, is nothing more than the institution, the abolition, or the confirmation of a distance, of an estrangement, or of a deferral, in other words, of a space between a self and another self, or between a subject and object. Thus as we will see, the shop window, which separates the consumer from the exposed object of his or her desire, will emerge as one of the emblematic objects of the nineteenth-century text. Similarly, an entire city or a particular neighborhood would become either a ghetto to be preserved or a territory to be conquered—as is Paris for Balzac's Rastignac, or Plassans for Zola's Rougons and Macquarts in *La Conquête de Plassans*. The correlative myth of this function is of course that of the two separated

[11] An account by Paul Féval in his novel *Coeur d'acier*: [after Eugène Sue] "there were certain people who saw Paris as an immense box with a false bottom, and who thought that by lifting up any cobblestone they would find a surprise" (*Les Habits noirs*, vol. 1, Bouquins [Paris: Laffont, 1987], 562). On the subject of this dialectic of above and beneath that haunted the entire nineteenth century, see Philippe Muray, *Le XIXème Siècle à travers les âges* (Paris: Denoël, 1984), and to cite but one text among a thousand from the period: François de Nion's *Les façades, roman d'aventures mondaines* (1899).

[f] Asmodeus, a character originally created by the Spanish novelist Guevara and later imitated by, among others, the eighteenth-century writer, Alain-René Lesage in his novel *Le Diable boiteux*, is a devil with the power to lift the rooftops of buildings enabling him to observe the private lives of those inside. The name was subsequently given to a variety of characters who shared the trait of omniscience. See the anonymous *Asmodée à New York* (1868) and *Le Diable à Paris* with its famous frontispiece and cross-section of a building.

lovers, Pyramis and Thisbe, who communicate through a crack in a common wall.[12]

Finally, in the third place, literature could conceive of every architectural object first and foremost as a *hierarchical object*—a system, or better yet, a *system of constraints*. Such a system defines interlocking components as well as the configuration of the main buildings and outbuildings of a work and its "outworks." Furthermore, it defines the architectural hierarchies of service spaces, of levels and landings, the relative ranking of parts to whole, container to contained—containers that are themselves governed by an even vaster, all-embracing fabric of artificiality (since a given building stands on a given street, a given street runs through a given neighborhood, a given neighborhood lies in a given town). Clearly for literature this kind of architectural object enables the deployment of strategies, of *proficiency* (*pouvoir-faire*) by the plot's characters in relation to one another. At the same time it gives rise to descriptions of the dependence or influence that obtains between the characters and their milieu, between the whole and its parts, and between the container and the contained.

Of course, these three general functions of the structure frequently coexist in each architectural referent (or each "paper house") presented by the literary text. Thus all literary architecture is in fact a highly overdetermined semantic object, especially because fiction, when "processing" this object, hesitates between and often combines two important forms of semiotic organization. Literary architecture realizes itself in the form of *descriptions*. These descriptions could possibly be monopolized by one of the three functions we have just seen as well as by one of the four important rhetorical figures that stand in homologous relation to these three functions. These four rhetorical figures are: *metaphor* and *irony,* which establish relations of analogy or difference between exterior or interior; *metonymy,* the figure of contiguity, and *synecdoche,* the figure of the interlocking parts and wholes and of inclusion.

Given this perspective, *exposition*—both as a privileged (and often inaugural) moment and as a descriptive figure in literary texts—is able to submit itself to one of these four dominant conceptions of the architectural object, which are also the foundation for three conceptions of the world. Thus we find three sorts of realism that coexist as do so many

---

[12] A story taken from Ovid, and one that is, curiously enough, often cited in the course of the nineteenth century through descriptions of paintings and pictures hung on walls in various literary texts including Zola's *Madeleine Férat,* Nerval's *Sylvie,* Guy de Maupassant's *Une Vie,* Merimée's *La Chambre bleue.*

aesthetic and philosophic visions during the nineteenth century. We have, first of all, a hermeneutic realism, this is a "vertical" realism, based on decipherments, on "painting what's on top and what's underneath" (Flaubert), for which "the real is that which is hidden" (Bachelard). It is a realism essentially concerned with bringing to light, dismantling, revealing, and flushing out the real from behind its facades, its masks, or its outward appearances. Secondly, there is a "horizontal" realism that clears the grounds, maps out exhaustive neighborhood routes, furls and unfurls encyclopedic juxtapositions, and furnishes methodical tables and classifications. Thirdly, there is a realism that apprehends the real as an intersection of norms, as a system which is itself the effect of a larger hierarchical system of values, scales, and constraints. It would not be difficult to link the names of the major writers of the nineteenth century to each of these three realisms.

It should be emphasized that literary architecture can easily distribute and embody itself in the shape of those places and objects that punctuate plots and narratives. It can do this precisely because of the modal overdetermination characteristic of the architectural object. It can be endowed with a semantic status that allows it to function as a hermeneutic or cognitive object (hence stories concerning actant–subjects in the quest for *knowledge*), or as a volitional object (the *will* of these same actants to overcome obstacles), or as a polemical object (the power these same actants exercise or submit to). Zola's *Le Ventre de Paris* (1873)—where a hero returning incognito to Haussmann's new, unrecognizable city and vies for power in the hostile territory of les Halles—would be an excellent example of the imbrication of these three modalities so rich in narrative possibilities. This novel establishes a powerful unity of place in which architecture—Baltard's pavilions—is omnipresent not only as decor but also as a veritable collective actant.

A further observation. These relations between architecture and the narrative are no doubt special and particularly interesting to study because they are played out on extremely different levels. Architects are quick to present themselves as "story-men"[13] who on the one hand listen to the narrative instructions of their clients and on the other hand, produce places that are stories as well as stories of places. (See Viollet-

---

[13] "I myself am a story-man as well as a scenery-man, in other words, for me architecture is nothing more than the organization of a story whose syntactical elements are constituted by a scenery that carries it. . . . I have built cities; and these cities are themselves operas, stories told; they are great stories in which one can dwell, an inhabitable story" (E. Aillaud, "L'Espace d'un récit," in *Cahiers de la recherche architecturale*, nos. 6–7 [October 1980]).

le-Duc and Félix Narjoux, as well as the innumerable pedagogic works recounting the "history" of a farm, a castle, a house, and so on, so common in the nineteenth century.) To tell stories is to engage in transformation and orientation. Thus the architect who thinks of space—be it public (a street) or private (the interior space of a house)—must, among other things, resolve the difficult problem of the *reversibility* of possible pathways of those who use these spaces, which therefore raises the question of how to organize sequentially a space which can be used in "any which way."[8] In addition, the architect must confront the *ambiguity* of the elements being manipulated—for example, walls both separate and linked. A great part of an architect's work consists of resolving such problems; unlike Mallarmé, who observed in the preface to *Un Coup de dés* that he hoped to "avoid telling a story," architects, by contrast need to think in terms of narrativity, inasmuch as it provides them with configurative patterns that allow them to resolve ambiguities. Whereas writers start out from the building, the cadastre, the parcel, in other words, from a static system of distinctions (be these real houses, or the fictive abodes of memory) and *then* subsequently imagines the travels and the adventures of the characters, architects conceive their projects conversely. They must first think in terms of traffic, usage, schedules, routines, functions, and purposes *before* they erect their partitions or lay down roads. Narrativity consequently becomes of primordial importance. The narratives of architecture can be determined by such nonhuman agents as the cyclical movements of the wind, the light, and the seasons, all of which architects attempt to include, neutralize, filter, or ward off, thus dealing with the fundamental problem of architectural exposure, which must be solved in relation to these transformations. The narratives of architecture can also be determined by human agents, particularly by their activities, such as work, movement, etiquette, social rituals, and the traffic of individuals to be blocked or facilitated. Architecture could therefore be defined as *the art of modulating expositions*—this can involve the exposition of a body to the various bodies of other social agents—that are more or less admitted into zones that are more or less private or public, sacred or profane, and that are more or less screened through a series of valves, doors, and walls. Or this can involve the exposition of a body to various natural agents such as the sun, wind, and the seasons. Therefore every building, once completed, concretizes a sort of social and natural proxemics while realizing

---

[8] A reference to Rimbaud's *dans tous les sens*, where the word *sens* can mean both *direction* and *meaning*.

a previous code of narrative scenarios. These scenarios have of course, already been scripted by real texts such as civil and legal codes, technical manuals, flowcharts, and etiquette books. Thus for example, if the construct of a church "concretizes" a ritual made up of specific acts, processions, and liturgies, this ritual is itself the incarnation of a sacred scripture (the Gospels) or of a Word. In a symmetrical fashion, however, the church in turn becomes a space where differentiated movements and acts of language such as preaching, confessing, reading, singing, praying, and baptizing are produced and each assigned its own place. Following up on Michelet's description of Notre-Dame as a "dialectic of stone," Erwin Panofsky's famous essay on the Gothic cathedral demonstrates the structural homology between scholastic rhetoric and the organization of medieval architecture. This homology is therefore not purely and simply a metaphor. Incarnating as it does prior narratives, the building also permits the subsequent reactivation of this narrativity and thus assumes its role as a shifter or *redistributor of narrativity*. Given its various thresholds, partitions, doors, floors, and discriminating interfaces, architecture is therefore primarily a twofold concretization of narratives and norms (in the legal sense of the word) rather than being merely the way of organizing pure space. After all, a wall, partition, or threshold always involves more than static material separations. (Think of the "rites of passage" described by Arnold van Gennep.) Rather they manifest obligation (*devoir-faire*) far more than strictly reflecting technical know-how (*savoir-faire*); they incarnate the constraints laid down by social or technological norms (such as those defined by assembly lines or user's manuals) far more than merely reflecting a stylistic order.

The building undoubtedly analyzes space and constructs a system of differences, but in producing distinctions between full and empty, opened and closed, movable and immovable, private and social it manifests and reactivates normative notions of prohibited and permitted, of private and public, of sacred and profane, or of mandatory and optional, and thereby manifests and reactivates not just value but meaning itself. The building does not only define sheer decorative distributional and functional space for arranging subjects or objects—the Smiths here, the Joneses there. Haussmann's "great transept" (*grande croisée*) that is described in Zola's *La Curée,* does not merely divide Paris into eastern and western quarters or into Left and Right banks—the standard topography that structures the entire Parisian novel of manners of the nineteenth century. The cross of *cardo* and *decumanus* does not merely inaugurate a place that we can begin to inhabit, or conceptualize, but also inaugurates a place that augurs, that is oriented into auspicious and inauspicious, positive and negative zones. Similarly a text—a discreet, articulated, hierarchical, semiotic whole—is not merely a measure or a marker of the time spent reading it, nor is it merely a metrical and typographical space; it is also an ethical measure, a system of values and ideology. Likewise, the architectural object is not merely a measurement of space, a mere piece of stone cut into shape, or a mere quantitative surveying of an expanse; it is instead a construction of differences that are qualitative, and hence imperative. The architectural object is not merely a static *theater* to be viewed, from which one views, or where people view one another. It is also a place that rehearses *theories*—those ritualized processions and movements of social life.[14] The cadastre is much more than a mere framework; it acts as a virtual *mise en demeure*[h] for its subjects. On the one hand, it casts the subject into the role of the user–inhabitant of the house, someone whose identity is limited to that of an occupant or traveler, a trespasser or a native, a vagrant or a permanent resident. On the other hand, it casts the subject into the role of spectator (as with the tourist or visitor) whose place is constrained to those strategic vantage points specified by guidebooks that enable the full appreciation of the aesthetic value of the site or building. These notions of *constraints* and *values* at the foundation of all ideological systems constitute the privileged material of the literary text in general and of the novel in particular. Hence the novel, through its references to architectural articulations, would over and over again put this normative material to narrative use. This is done in two ways. On the one hand, the novel presents its characters' various dwellings as part of a qualitatively oriented itinerary, in other words, as a path leading to social ascension or decline. Numerous examples can be found in Zola: the successive dwellings of the real-estate speculator Saccard in *La Curée*; Gervaise's various lodgings in *L'Assommoir*; or the Lourdes–Rome–Paris itinerary that links the *Trois villes* series. These various staggered places are given the status of objects to be conquered, defended, destroyed, and known, and therefore acquire the status of objects worthy of attraction or repulsion. Nevertheless, the novel presents

---

[14] Victor Hugo in describing the commodities market (a building he detested) in *Notre-Dame de Paris*, speaks of its "colonnade encircling the monument and beneath which, on days of formal high religious solemnity, the *theory* of stockbrokers and jobbers can be majestically *expounded*" (*Notre-Dame of Paris*, trans. John Sturrock [New York: Penguin, 1978], part 3, chap. 2; emphasis mine. The building the "*envelope*" allows one to develop or "*expound.*"

[h] *Mise en demeure* is a formal demand or a notice. Here the author playing on the word *demeure* (residence) uses this expression to indicate the positioning or staging of a character within the confines of a particular architectural context.

the building as a sort of collective actant: a structure that *manipulates* the actors of the story. Instances of this abound: to take another example from Zola, we have the description of the department store in *Au Bonheur des dames,* presented as a metonymic labyrinth, destined to "seduce" the consumer, and especially to entrap women: "From counter to counter, the customer would find herself taken in. Here she would buy the fabric, further on the thread, elsewhere the coat, she would bundle up, and then she would be ambushed by the unexpected, would yield to the needs of the unnecessary." Elsewhere, Zola describes Nana's townhouse as a man-trap: "engineered like a theater, it was administrated like clockwork . . . it ran with precision." In such Maupassant stories as "Le Signe," "Sauvée," and "Le Verrou" we have numerous apartments that function as snares where people fall into various mousetraps, are caught in flagrante delicto, or become victims of eviction or catastrophic intrusions.[15] In Louis-Ferdinand Céline's *Voyage au bout de la nuit* New York is described as "a suspended deluge . . . it is nothing better than an awful system of constraints made of bricks, corridors, bolts, booths, a gigantic inexpiable architectural torture."[16] And finally, Hugo's *L'Homme qui rit* features the description of "small rooms" of the Corleone Lodge and the maze that would lead the hero Gwynplaine to the spider-woman Josyane: "All was curtains, portières, tapestry . . . an intricate abode which remained unintelligible to someone who might just happen by . . . the junctions were inextricable. Portraits swung open revealing hidden entrances and exits. It was a place full of stage contrivances. This was necessary; dramas were played out there." The building is order (archè; commandment), represents an order, and gives orders to its users. As Hugo wrote in *La Légende des siècles:*

> *Moi, le temple, je suis législateur d'Ephèse;*
> *Le peuple en me voyant comprend l'ordre et s'apaise.*[i]

[15] See Philippe Hamon, *Introduction à l'analyse,* 244ff.

[16] "The space of cities could thus be said to be a mixture of observations and material coercion of bodies and social relations" (Léon Murard and Patrick Zylbermann, "Le Petit Travailleur infatigable, ou le prolétaire régénéré: Villes-usines, habitat et intimités au XIXème siècle," *Recherches,* no. 25 [November 1976]). On this point, there is thus no difference between Mouret's department store, the city, the exposition, or the museum: "In museums, the body is manipulated. . . . [O]ne operates in a space that has already been granted various levels of comfort and volume. Moreover the body is a technical means of acquiring knowledge of a particular discourse . . . read by way of a directed path. . . . [One must] arrive at the maximum amount of congestion. . . . The problem has to do with allotting in time and space a given number of bodies over a given surface" (M. Lamourdieu and Jean-Charles Lebahar, "La Manipulation des corps par l'espace: Le Cas du musée," in *L'Homme et son corps* [Paris: Centre Nationale de la Recherche Scientifique 1985], 152).

[i] "I, the temple, am the legislator of Ephesus / The people upon seeing me understand the order and become calm."

Architecture—be it real or on paper—inasmuch as it is the emitter of categorical imperatives, prescriptions, manipulations, or persuasions which in turn govern social or amorous rituals, local tactics, or global strategies which therefore regulate the sequence of events, the movements of characters, and the story, may well come within the reach of a general poetics of narrativity.

Just as literary narratology constituted itself by parenthesizing and "deconstructing" the term *time,* one of the tasks of a literary poetics devoted to the architectural references of texts might well involve refusing to use the all-encompassing term or theme of *space* in order to consider literary space as an effect, or as a result of a production of meaning at work on different hierarchical levels or landings. In order to do this we must distinguish the five following levels. And to be truly rigorous, we must discriminate on every level between: (a) a *paradigmatic* dimension that would specify lists of manipulated items, and (b) a *syntagmatic* dimension that would account for their "syntax" and narrativization (*mise en récit*). These five levels are:

(1) **The topological level:**
    (a)   the level of abstract logical poles, of fundamental *templas;*
    (b)   the level of operations and of *rhythms* as modes of deep syntagmatic configuration.

(2) **The topographical level:**
    (a)   the level of collective actants constructed by the text and the architectural themes signified by the work: places, dwellings, inhabitants' habitats;
    (b)   the level of tropisms, movements, rituals, and proxemics characteristic of each of these actants and actors.

(3) **The topical level:**
    (a)   the rhetorical level of figures, of descriptive systems, and of *topoi*;
    (b)   the level of the distributions, expansions, and extensions of these figures and systems.

(4) **The typographic level:**
    (a)   the material level of the page, of the volume;
    (b)   where the calligrammic, the diagrammatic or anagrammatic sequentialities of the signifier are deployed, the interplay between text and illustrations, the syntactical embedding.

(5)  **The typological level:**

(a)  the level of various distances between earlier or contemporary texts, types, or genres, in other words the level of
intertextuality; thus the level of the various distances of
enunciation—irony, seriousness, solidarity, or lack of
solidarity—that the narrator takes vis-à-vis the narration;

(b)  the syntax of the rewriting and the reformulation of these
different texts among themselves.

An analogy seems to arise here, but one that ought to be explored
with caution. Namely, architecture is to space what narrative is to time:
a semiotic means of *configuration* that allows us to think the unthinkable (time and space), which allows us to give shape to the amorphous
and to impose discontinuity, plot, and direction on the randomness of
the real. It is an analogy that fundamentally underlies and draws together the terms of an equation that at first glance appears to be based
on an irreducible thematic difference: TIME + NARRATIVE = SPACE
+ ARCHITECTURE.[17] Here an observation concerning the typological
level seems appropriate: From a strictly textual point of view, space—or
a "spatial effect,"—is often the product of spacing operations involving
transferences, transformations, or quotations. Just as the literary text is
generally a rewriting of other texts, a palimpsest, the writer often perceives the city or the house as the visible stratification, or as a "reuse"
(the equivalent in the terminology of architecture of the quotation) of
other constructions, in other words, as the reabsorption of diachrony
into a more or less homogeneous or disparate synchrony.[18] Rewriting
founds the building, as it founds the text. Rewriting exists *before* the
building, inasmuch as to practice architecture is above all to develop a
capacity for projecting and thus for rewriting either signs into images,

[17] For a methodological (and semiological) approach to space, see the essay by Pierre
Boudon, *Introduction à une sémiotique des lieux* (Montreal: Presses de l'Université de
Montréal-Klincksieck, 1981) as well as the work of Denis Bertrand, *L'Espace et le sens*
(Paris-Amsterdam: Hadès-Benjamins, 1985). For a "poetician" approach see Gaston
Bachelard, *The Poetics of Space,* trans. M. Jolas (Boston: Beacon Press, 1969) and Pierre
Sansot, *Poétique de la ville* (1971). For many the essential text remains the analyses by
Claude Lévi-Strauss in *Structural Anthropology,* trans. Claire Jacobson (New York: Basic
Books, 1968) in which he analyzes the structure of the Bororo village.
[18] Eclecticism (see for example the architect Boileau's 1853 design for a "synthetic
cathedral") and reuse (revolutionary barricades and Parisian suburbs were built from the
recycling of materials from Haussmann's demolitions) can be interpreted, along with the
fashion for universal expositions, as attempts to reclaim the functions of utopias and
*bricolage*. These two notions underlie debates in architecture (Charles Garnier), philosophy (Victor Cousin), and literature and run throughout the nineteenth century. Hugo's
dream city, the model for *Les Orientales,* would have to be a composite.

images into blueprints, or consignments into images. Rewriting also exists *within* the building, inasmuch as the latter almost always involves the juxtaposition of recycled component parts. Rewriting also continues to exist *after* the building inasmuch as the latter is perpetually modified by subsequent restorations and reconversions. (To restore a monument, according to Viollet-le-Duc's *Dictionnaire,* is not only to repair it, but to "represent its system," to "reestablish [the monument] in a state of completion in which it may never have existed at any given moment.") Rewriting also exists *between* buildings, for one of their distinctive features is that they are eminently plastic and transposable, *just like narratives.* Just as one can translate, transport, summarize, or paraphrase a text, one can similarly translate a building into narrative or a narrative into a building. (Consider the extraordinary project of the Danteum de Terragni in Mussolini's Rome.) One can likewise modify the scale of a building—or make mock-ups of it, or transpose a building made of stone into one made of sugar (or vice versa), or transform the Eiffel Tower into a paperweight. A piece of kitsch is often nothing more than something constructed that has been modified in scale or function. Thus unpredictably the text–architecture connection meets the domain of gastronomy. The nineteenth century is after all the great century of architecture and architectonic gastronomy. (See Marie-Antoine Carême's *Le Patissier pittoresque* (1815), or the treatises of Gouffé or Urbain Dubois.) Aside from the *boeuf-mode* in aspic mentioned at the outset of this chapter, examples abound: Proust's architectonic ice creams; Emma Bovary's elaborately constructed wedding cake; or the "bi-colored obelisk of multiflavored ice cream" in Baudelaire's prose poem "Les yeux des pauvres." Architecture, which is the only art into which we can enter, the only art that is designed to house bodies, here reverses its essential status by instead lodging itself in bodies. The fairy-tale gingerbread house therefore appears as a fantasy of *reversibility,* which highlights a fundamental characteristic of the architectural object.[19] Thus the *scale model,* which provides a general poietic means of

---

[19] Concerning the idea of reversibility, see Kevin Lynch, *The Image of the City* (Cambridge, Mass.: MIT Press, 1980), 132ff. There are numerous scenes in this period's literature, notably in Zola's work, in which food is associated with architecture: *Le Ventre de Paris,* in which a character metaphorically "consumes" architecture; or Nana who "gobbles up" the farms and townhouses of her victim–lovers; Lantier in *L'Assommoir* both literally and figuratively "eats up" Virginie's confectionery shop. See also Juniricho Tanizaki, *In Praise of Shadows,* trans. Thomas J. Harper and Edward G. Seindensticker (New Haven: Lecte's Island Books, 1977): "You take its [a traditional Japanese candy] cool, smooth substance into your mouth, and it is as if the very darkness of the room were melting on your tongue" (p. 16). This is not far from the famous Proustian episode of the madeleine, where the cake "contains" church steeples, houses, and a village, and rebuilds "the edifice of memory." Elsewhere Proust speaks of the rooms of Combray which are

shifting (from the semiotic to the real, from the real to the semiotic, or from one semiotic system to another, via rewriting or transposition), serves as a means to combat the disengagement specific to all architectural objects—a trait it also shares with the *written* text—and as a key concept for all reflection on architecture.[20]

This last point should be emphasized. As a real object that is at once artificial and articulated, the building (just as any machine that is geared to the body; for Le Corbusier the house was a "machine for living"), can be put to use by the writer as a privileged shifter, an object in which the structural has become concretized or an object that mediates between the text (a semiotic object) and the real (a nonsemiotic object). Moreover, the building functions as a primary operator of metaphor that allows the real to be rewritten into text or vice versa, in other words, that allows one to be translated into the other. The attention given to theatrical, military, or hydraulic machines in traditional architectural treatises is well known. Thus, to follow the subtle analyses of Michel Serres in his books *Hermès III: La Traduction* and *Feux et signaux de brume: Zola*[21] one finds in literary references to architecture at the turn of the nineteenth century evidence of a movement away from an aesthetic of figurative representation characterized by the dominance of the plane, the focal point, or the visible world conceived as a network, a measure, or a reticulation. In its place emerged an aesthetic dominated by models of energy or entropy. To cite examples from specific literary genres, the nineteenth century saw a passage from the taxonomic and descriptive genres of *magasins* (youth-oriented or otherwise) and *jardins* (such as the collection of poems with this title by Abbé Jacques Delille) to a literature dominated by the model and by the structures that it unconsciously reproduced and translated from the steam engine. Hence there were individual or syncretic, mobile or immobile architectures of the nineteenth century that tried to reconcile these two ways of conceiving of architecture, the former more static, the latter more dynamic. One could cite such examples as Verne's "steam-driven house" and "floating city," or Zola's description of the covered-market as a steam engine in *Le Ventre de Paris*. Or one could cite that

---

"thickly powdered with the motes of an atmosphere granular, pollenous, and edible" (*Remembrance*, vol. 1, 495).

[20] On the concept of scale in architectural theory, or in general semiology, see the works of Philippe Boudon, in particular *Sur l'Espace architectural* (Paris: Dunod, 1969), and Jacques Bertin, *Semiology of Graphics, Diagrams, Networks, and Maps*, trans. William Berg (Madison: University of Wisconsin Press, 1983).

[21] Michel Serres, *Hermès III: La Traduction* (Paris: Editions de Minuit, 1974), *Feux et signaux de brume: Zola* (Paris: Grasset, 1975).

particular form of architecture that would become the emblem of the century—the Gallery of Machines that figured prominently in universal expositions. In these galleries machines were exhibited as functioning displays—a clear attempt to reconcile the stable geometry of the display area (the *cadre-magasin*) with the mobility of the machine itself. These pavilions represent an effort to combine the moving parts of purely energy-*producing* machines—with the fixity and *fixation* of a frame where one exposes the real by stockpiling industrially *reproduced* objects within the frames of shop windows, glass-covered markets, camera lucidas of the crystal palaces, and camera obscuras of photography with its "exposed" plates.[22]

Thus in literature's selection of particular specialized architectural objects, a certain logic is at work. Similarly, one can read the literature of the nineteenth century as containing the outline of a sort of architectural system that groups together six specific preferred objects, or technemes: (1) the *window*: the title of a short story by Maupassant and of numerous poems; (2) the *stained-glass window*: the title of a José-Maria de Heredia poem as well as a Flaubertian and Proustian object; (3) the *door*: the title of another story by Maupassant; (4) the *shop window* or the *sheet of glass*: as in the many conservatories, screens, and shop windows found in the work of Zola; (5) the *wall*: as it functions in the urban decors of Balzac or Baudelaire; and (6) the *mirror*: as found in the poems of Mallarmé. Each of these six objects enter into a relationship of opposition or resemblance to each of the other five objects on the list (or six including the possible relationship of an object to another object of the same type— window to window, mirror to mirror). Certain other objects (the two-way mirror, the trapdoor, the venetian blind, the arcade, the translucent screen, or the balcony), could of course find a place in this system as variations upon these six principal types of objects that create a *mise en demeure* for a literary cast of characters. For example, one could add that

---

[22] This attempt at reconciliation of the planar and the energetic appears clearly in the following description of les Halles in Zola's *Le Ventre de Paris*:

> They grew more solid . . . they crowded higher and higher their geometric shapes . . . so square and uniform in design . . . like some modern machine of immeasurable dimensions, like a steam engine, or a cauldron intended to perform the digestive process for an entire nation, a gigantic metal stomach, bolted, riveted, made of wood, glass and cast iron. . . . It had all the power of a machine's motor at work, with the heat of its boilers . . . and the furious rotation of its wheels."
> ([Paris: Livre de Poche, 1984], 39)

In this novel, Zola takes up Hugo's famous dictum from *Notre-Dame de Paris* ("This [the book] will kill that [the cathedral], the book made of stone") to reuse it in a strictly architectural parallel: "This [modern architecture of glass and iron] will kill that [the cathedral of stone, Saint-Eustache in the novel]."

portable variant of the wall, that mobile folding screen, the *fan,* a paper
object analogous to the book which can be folded or unfolded and behind
which its owner hides. Mallarmé indulged in numerous reveries about
this "insulating" object that, like the book, interposes itself between sight
and the real site.

The relationships of resemblance and difference that found this system
follow two principal semantic axes: *mobility,* which determines more or
less mobile, fixed, or pivoting objects, and *transitivity,* which determines
objects as "valves," that is, objects more or less translucent or opaque
that more or less allow light to pass; objects more or less transparent or
reflecting that more or less permit the gaze; or objects more or less open
or filtering that more or less block movement. Mobility can refer to an
object's transportable characteristics—furniture (*meubles*) as opposed to
an apartment building (*immeuble*). It can also refer to an object's more or
less articulated characteristics, as in the difference between a dormer and
a swinging window. Transitivity can instead be reciprocal: for example, a
window allows gazes to move from the interior to the exterior and vice
versa. Transitivity can also be selective: the stained-glass window lets
through light, but not the gaze; a wall reflects the voice; a mirror, the
gaze. Or transitivity can be univocal: a door might let one through in only
one direction, just as a venetian blind permits a gaze in only one direction
and the stained-glass window is admired only from the inside looking
out. Therefore the mirror, being both an immobile and reflecting object,
differs from the window (a pivoting and opaque object), from the wall
(an opaque and immobile object), and from the stained-glass window (a
translucent but not transparent object)—although when the exterior
light of day is replaced by an interior lamp at night, the spectacle of the
window as seen from the outdoors inverts the viewing of a stained-glass
window. The fact that classical painting, at the very moment when it
began to invent and refine most of its illusionist or scenographic techniques, displayed a predilection for pictures in which a door, a window,
or a mirror interact within an enclosed space (*Arnolfini and his Wife* by
Jan van Eyck, or Diego Velasquez's *Las Meninas* come to mind, although
Brunelleschi also used doors, windows, and mirrors in his ground-

breaking experiments), reveals the perceptible structural link between these various elements. As we will see later on, the lyric text favors precisely such a system when situating its subjects, a system that therefore defines a particular kind of site. Other types of sites of course also exist, and these will both vary and evolve over time according to specific requirements of different literary genres and to technological changes brought to bear on the architectural object itself. There are those who predict that the postmodern era will witness the exemplary fulfillment of Hugo's prediction ("this will kill that"), with architecture destroying itself under the pressure of a wholesale invasion of the digital and in the process inverting the determining features of traditional sites we have just sketched out. According to some, the modern house of the twenty-first century may well consist essentially of two things: an automobile and a computer terminal screen. The car as Paul Virilio describes it—"the door that soars" (*la porte qui emporte*)—is a mobile door in a mobile object that permits one to go elsewhere. The computer terminal screen is a mobile, portable, autonomous window that allows one to receive everything from elsewhere.[23] A general poetics of these sites remains to be constructed.

In thinking about what is most abstract in the real, in other words, its machines and buildings, one is led to reconsider a problem that also haunts the literary text, namely, the problem of representation. Even though the metaphors and allegorical models that are deployed by the metadiscourse of theory and criticism point to architecture as the paradigm of the literary work (always the comparison when it comes to questions of completion, coherence, or the harmony of parts to the whole), these traditional typologies are generally at a loss when they try to place architecture within a conceptual framework that is broadly mimetic. Hence the endless speculations about "Adam's house in Eden,"[24] or about the way in which architecture imitates or might have originally imitated nature. Some theorists, convinced that architecture is an art that does not signify anything, liken it to music; others, like Abbé Batteux in his *Beaux Arts réduits à un même principe* of 1766, see it rather as the art closest to eloquence since, like the latter, its goal is to be at once useful and pleasing. One might observe when rhetoric speaks of architecture, it often does so indirectly and always in normative terms. Furthermore, rhetoric locates its discussions of architecture in two areas of theory that enjoy a curious symmetry: First, architecture tends to play a crucial role whenever rhetoric addresses the notion of the *sublime*, that grandest of

---

[23] Paul Virilio, *L'Espace critique* (Paris: Christian Bourgois 1984), passim.
[24] See J. Ryckwert, *La Maison d'Adam au paradis* (Paris: Seuil, 1976).

styles or genres, which surpasses or possesses the individual. According
to Edmund Burke, architecture could never match the sublimity of nature
and its spectacles; yet virtually every treatise on the sublime makes mention of such renowned examples of architectural grandeur as St. Peter's in
Rome, which is in turn related to speculations concerning the all-
embracing, enveloping, and dizzying sublimity of such rounded forms as
cupolas, spheres, domes, and vaults. Second, architecture tends to come
up whenever rhetoric discusses the practice of *description,* which, in contrast to the sublime, is "disreputable" because it allows "useless detail" to
thrive and lacks any internal, local necessity, thus threatening to under-
mine the necessity of the work as a whole. When rhetoric speaks of those
descriptions and lists which would be best banished from all writing, it
almost always cites the negative example of descriptions of buildings.
Ironically then, descriptions of buildings become the prime examples of
what must not be done if one wants one's work to be as coherent as . . . a
building. Boileau's *Art poétique* provides a well-known instance of this:

> S'il [le mauvais écrivain] recontre un palais, il m'en dépeint la face;
> Il me promène après de terrasse en terrasse;
> Ici s'offre un perron; là règne un corridor;
> Là ce balcon s'enferme en un balustre d'or.
> Il compte des plafonds les ronds et les ovales.
> "Ce ne sont que feston, ce ne sont qu'astragales";
> Je saute vingt feuillets pour en trouver la fin,
> Et je me sauve à peine au travers du jardin.
> Fuyez de ces auteurs l'abondance stérile,
> Et ne vous chargez pas d'un détail inutile.[j]

The issue of what is *describable* or *indescribable* that is raised here with
reference to architecture provides an opportunity to discuss broader
problems of coherence, representation, readability, and of thresholds, or
limen, as well as problems involving the relation of the whole to its parts

---

[j]
> Sometimes an Author, fond of his own Thought,
> Pursues his object 'til its over-wrought;
> If he describes a House he shews the Face,
> And after walks you 'round from place to place;
> Here is Vista, there the Doors unfold,
> Balcone's here are ballustered with Gold.
> Then counts the Rounds and Ovals in the Halls,
> "The Festoons, the Friezes and the Astragales."
> Tir'd with his tedious Pomp, away I run,
> And skipp'd over twenty Pages to be gone.
> Of such Descriptions the vain Folly flee,
> And shun their barren superfluity.
> All that is needless carefully avoid.
> (Sir William Soames trans. [London: n.p., 1710])

or the work to its readers. Thus for example, readers are said to be possessed by the sublime in the same way that inhabitants are possessed by their habitats; or readers are said to be dispossessed by descriptions which bore them and which they skip. In any case, architecture— whether it plays the role of paradigm or foil—gives pause to even the most subtle of typologies.

Rhetoricians and architectural theorists found an expedient for elegantly solving this irritating question of architectural representation. Since nature is harmony, symmetry, law, rhythm, and order, (archè after all means both beginning and commandment), the building if it is harmonious—or to use Fourierist vocabulary, "harmonian"—will therefore reproduce the harmony of the cosmos.[25] Hence the importance accorded in all architectural treatises to the problem of exposure. (As we have seen, Philibert de l'Orme defined architecture as the "art of turning a building properly.") Exposure is a means of regulating the ways in which the static is geared to the cyclical—as in Michelet's ultimate dream of a revolving or half-moon-shaped house. Reconciling as they do the microcosm and the macrocosm, architects on the one hand deal with the body, its humors, its hygiene, its salubrity (and for this they must be well versed in medicine) while on the other hand they contend with the sun's course, the seasons, and the winds. The architectural imaginary of every era always sees Vitruvius, the founder of architecture, as leaning on Hip-

---

[25] Significantly, the encyclopedist and theoretician of architecture Quatremère de Quincy also published a lengthy theoretical work entitled *Imitation: Essai sur la nature, le but, et les moyens de l'imitation dans les beaux-arts* (Paris: n.p., 1823). It is as if the questions of architecture (which represents nothing), and literature (which exhausts itself in representing) were in some way correlative. A large part of the *Encyclopédie*'s entry "architecture," written by Quatremère, was devoted to exploring and criticizing the status of imitation in architecture: "It is not about . . . giving architecture models to imitate in the strictest sense. We will see that everything that concerns its imitation rests upon analogy, induction, and free association." And Quatremère notes in the entry "architecture" in his own *Dictionnaire d'architecture* (Paris: A. Leclerc, 1832): "[Architecture] imitates nature by the rules it itself prescribed." Its history, according to Quatremère, would be that of a sort of purge or gradual liberation from the most direct and immediate *mimesis*: either by (a) direct imitation of visible nature (pillars imitate tree trunks; a fictional copy of Adam's original hut); (b) imitation of the human body and its secret proportions (the module replacing the model; this theory is already elaborated by Vitruvius in *De Architectura Libri decem* (bk. 3, chap. 1); or (c) imitation of hidden laws of nature (order, rhythms, measures, laws of physics). The classical discourse on architecture asserted that the connections between habitat, inhabitant, and the cosmos were made according to the theory of temperaments (the building, by its exposure must maintain the good health of those who use it and must not upset the balance of their temperaments) as well as to the theory that the structures and laws of the universe can be made geometric. Concerning the passage from an architecture of measure to a modern and industrial architecture, see Alberto Perez-Gomez, *Architecture and the Crisis of Modern Science* (Cambridge, Mass.: MIT Press, 1983).

pocrates, the founder of medicine. A theory of *temperaments* underlies both architecture (and its theory of exposures) and literature (and its theory of character) well through the nineteenth century, with its naturalist literary characters subjected to their milieu. Thus measure and exposure became almost synonymous.

Hence the paradigmatic importance in these same treatises of the example of the *garden* and of references to *music*. The garden, on the one hand, is purely planar, the bare design of a "house" laid flat without a facade; it is pure vegetal geometry with no volume and completely "exposed." Music, on the other hand, involves "measure."[26] The completed building thus represents this quintessence of the real known as measure, and thereby embodies a sort of pure analogy; an ideal unison of nature and culture. At the same time, however, the building would represent just as concretely, the fiction of the various blueprints, plans, measures, and drawings which preceded and warranted it. In architecture, it is fiction (the blueprint) that precedes the real (the constructed building) and it is an invisible reality (the harmonies, rhythms, measures, and laws of nature) that links together two visible realities—the building on the one hand, nature on the other. Finally, since all architecture is social and human, it must necessarily be "representation"[k] in the theatrical sense of the word. Architecture thus functions as an ostensive (or ostentatious) way of displaying the signs of private social vanity or of flaunting official power. It can also be a way of marking off or putting under surveillance a territory that one has claimed—Paul Valéry called official monuments and buildings the "geodesic signals of order." Architecture can also be a way of affirming the will to appearance (as in a facade) that is more or less

---

[26] According to Vitruvius—whose *De Architectura* plays the same role in architecture that Aristotle's *Poetics* plays in literary theory—the architect must be completely versed in musical science: (1) to know how to bend catapults properly; (2) to know how to position the bronze vases designed to carry the actor's voices through the theater "so that the voices of the performers hit the spectators' ears with the greatest strength, distinction, and gentleness" (Claude Perrault, *Les dix livres d'architecture de Vitruve: Corrigés et traduits nouvellement en français avec notes et figures* [Brussels: Margada, 1979]). In lengthy notes, both Vitruvius and Perrault return to music and the voice in regard to theater (book 5, chaps. 3, 4). We will see further on the privileged ties that the lyric text seems to establish between the voice and architecture. Curiously enough, many of Rimbaud's poems in *Illuminations* systematically combine references to music, architecture, and theater. To cite two examples: "The lighting comes back to the house beam. From the two far sides of the room, commonplace settings, harmonic elevations merge." ("Veillées") and "all the possibilities of harmony and architecture will rise up around your seat" ("Jeunesse IV"). On the notion of measure see of course Heidegger in the previously cited chapter "Poetically Man Dwells." Heidegger thinks of all things like buildings as a union of fundamental relations and measures.

[k] In French, *representation* not only has all the connotations of the English representation, but it can also mean a performance.

embodied by a decor that demonstrates the various roles and scripts that its occupant can manage to act out.[27] To represent styles of architecture and monuments in texts is therefore to represent referents that are certainly part of the real but that are also concretized representations in the various meanings of this term—representations of preliminary plans and consignments, representations of the harmony of nature, representations of the power of the inhabitant and, as we have seen, representations of a social theater that governs its user's *theories*. For this reason, it was the *theater,* for both the architect and the classical theorist, that tended to become at once the building par excellence and the literary locus par excellence, since it is a place dedicated to language and song. In the theater acoustics, design, and performance are almost synonymous; it is the voice of the actor that regulates the degrees, or the tiers, of the hall (Vitruvius).[28] Innumerable novels of the nineteenth century included something akin to a mandatory "theater phase" in the itinerary of their characters. Moreover, writers often tended to identify the various sites of their fiction as *sites where language was on show,* or as a series of small theaters, differentiated both by custom and by language. The *bedroom* became the site for confiding secrets or for domestic squabbles, where husbands and wives made "scenes"; the *library,* the place for reading, where the walls were made of books (which according to Gérard Genette in *Figures II* is the "clearest and truest symbol of literature's spatiality"); the *kitchen* or the pantry was the place where orders were given and gossip about the master dished out; the *threshold* and *vestibule* were the places for announcing guests or for ritualized salutations; the *balcony* provided the place for public harangues; the *study,* or the poet's *mansard,* the place for writing; the *courtroom,* the place for performative language; the *workshop* or the *street,* the place where advertisements are written or cried out; the *salon*—this room was obviously crucial to Stendhal's novels—the place where the voice was "staged" and where gossipers and chatterers carried on multiple conversations. In a novel the sites of the city and the rooms of the house are but specialized *parlors (parloirs)*

[27] On the subject of the different meanings of the term *representation* (How does one represent architecture? What does architecture represent?) the collective work *L'Architecture en representation* (Paris: Ministère de la Culture, Direction du Patrimoine, 1985). Photographs of deserted Paris taken by Eugène Atget, a failed actor himself, were correctly described as a "theater of crime" by Benjamin.

[28] Mallarmé, in his *La Dernière Mode* of 20 September 1874, speaks of the relationship between the tenor and his audience: "One of their voices, goes up to the balcony, the boxes, the ceiling, and the chandeliers to find the lavish gold for which it was made, the voices of tenors."

that rehearse and distribute lists of the major functions and social usages of language.

It should come as no surprise that architecture and literature are fascinated by one another, and that architecture often provides referents for the literary text. Apart from preliminary consignments that give rise to a building, the completed architectural object is infused by the various texts that are written before, in, around, and about it. A place is never truly a place until it has become a named locality (*lieu-dit*). Any constructed surface has the authority to become a bearing structure. Language, whether written, painted, or calligraphic, often can be found already inscribed in the architectural object. These inscriptions in return propose stylistic models to literature which are sometimes trivial or impressively prestigious: hieroglyphics, graffiti, votive inscriptions, dedications, signatures, decorative symbols, narrative bas-reliefs, posted political proclamations, advertisements, mottos, and coats-of-arms whose heraldry more or less "speaks for itself."[29] Certain communication mechanisms, such as the enigmatic Chappe telegraph of the first part of the nineteenth century, plant themselves on architectural semiotic creations and become miniatures of the structures—Rimbaud writes, in his poem "Les Ponts," of "bridges . . . supporting signal-lights." Thus figurative elements such as sculptures, narrative frescoes, images on billboards, or commercial advertisements collaborate with nonfigurative elements such as arbitrary inscribed signs. This creates semantic spaces that are more or less polyglot, monophonic, or polyphonic and—depending on whether these signs compensate for the silence of the

---

[29] Paul Claudel, writing on 17 August 1913 to Victor Segalen, the author of *Stèles*, speaks of a "lapidary" art. Abbé Batteux writes in his *Principes de la littérature* in a chapter entitled "De l'inscription":

> Inscriptions are put on temples, altars, at the bottoms of statues, in short, on everything that can attract a curious eye and merit the attention of posterity. . . . The Moderns created in the tradition of certain ancient inscriptions a sort of lapidary style that seems to be midway between poetry and prose. They are thoughts, turns of phrase, clauses of a sentence which gradually increase, intersect, and are symmetrical. ([Paris: n.p., 1774], vol. 3, 416)

Batteux also devotes a chapter to the inscriptions of medals and another to emblems ("A thought expressed by an allegorical image and words. The image is called the body [*le corps*], the emblem and the motto are its soul [*âme*]" [429].) Let us remember the title and mission of the *Académie des inscriptions et belles lettres*. We know that François Rabelais parodied the use of references to the lapidary: Gargantua is in a sense framed by chapter 2, entitled "Antidotal Jokes, Found in an Ancient Tomb," and the "enigmatic poem which turned up set into the foundations of the Abbey at Thélémites on a great bronze plaque," mentioned in chapter 57 and set out in chapter 58. (François Rabelais, *Gargantua and Pantagruel*, trans. Burton Raffel (New York: W.W. Norton, 1990), 11, 125.

stone—more or less talkative or mute. Perhaps because architecture
does not signify anything other than its own sheer presence and because
one must at all costs "reinject" meaning into it, literature often turns it
into the preferred semaphoric bearer of a compensatory proliferation of
scripts.[30] Writers, particularly if they subscribe to the project of realism,
will find this to be the way of pursuing their project "to the letter," of
"copying by means of language a reality which is itself not made up of
language"—in other words, by returning to architecture in order to
copy by means of signs a real that is *already* inscribed with signs. In fact,
the literary text, especially in the nineteenth century, seems fascinated
with the semaphoric properties of certain architectural objects. For example, Nerval's gardens of the Valois inspired by the novels of Jean-
Jacques Rousseau are strewn with follies on whose walls are engraved
philosophical maxims and formulae borrowed from Rousseau as well as
other eighteenth-century philosophers. Elsewhere we find walls of stone
plastered with labels and advertisement in Zola's *Au bonheur des
dames*; the traveling caravan–theater (a place for mobile speech) or the
Green Box whose walls are covered with inscriptions in Hugo's
*L'Homme qui rit*; Homais's dispensary in *Madame Bovary*; Captain
Nemo's Nautilus in *Vingt mille lieues sous les mers,* filled with maps,
books, and musical scores; and of course the innumerable Balzacian
dwellings covered with more or less legible "hieroglyphics." For the
literary text to describe a monument is to describe such an object situated in the real, which is therefore already predisposed to becoming a
sort of book. But to describe such an object is also a way of rewriting
and reactivating the diffuse nebula of latent or absent discourses that
surround the building, such as anecdotes, myths, historical narratives,
legends, etiological accounts of "foundation," or stories involving the
origin of place names. The foundations or atmosphere of a building are
first and foremost narrative, textual, and literary, a building merely
being a kind of "frozen speech" (Rabelais), or merely the sum total of

[30] *Notre-Dame de Paris* begins with describing graffiti in an obscure corner of the
church; "It is upon this word (*Anankè*) that this book was made" concludes the preface of
February 1831. François-René de Chateaubriand, who was unable to visit the pyramids in
Egypt at his leisure, asked one of his friends to engrave his name there. "I asked Monsieur
Caffe to write my name on these great tombs, according to custom at the first opportunity.
One must fulfill all the small obligations of a pious traveler. Doesn't one read on the ruins of
Memnon's statue, the names of the Romans who had heard him sing at dawn?" (*Voyages en
Orient*). The references here to the myth of Memnon is significant; this is a myth of
resurrection, to which we will return, that is directly homologous on the one hand to the
practice of religion (the pious pilgrimage, the obligation, or the prayer spoken in front of the
relic or commemorative tomb) and on the other hand to the lyric stance (voice and death).
Finally it is homologous to the very activity of reading, which resurrects a lost meaning.

the discourses (usually official) which are pronounced within it (in its parlors) or about it. Therefore buildings serve as a pretext for the writer to reactualize a textuality and become the occasion for recalling or inventing a body of knowledge, anecdotes, or memories. The travel account, that great consumer of architectural descriptions (romantic travels in the Orient, naturalist strolls down the boulevard, "travels around my room," or pedagogic tours of France), is nothing more than a journey through various discourses or voyages through the already-anchored versions of public or personal history. Buildings thereby always lay themselves open to activities involving the production of meaning or respond to the urge to write, paraphrase, gloss, or read. One reads the monument at its behest and its suggestion: in dedicating his prose poems to Arsène Houssaye, Baudelaire declares that his attempt to write was born from "frequenting enormous cities" and "their countless intersections." The Goncourts, in their preface to *Germinie Lacerteux* (1865) likewise affirm "this book comes from the streets," and in effect the succession of microspectacles or microevents that the street offers the gawker may well have given rise to the succession of "snapshots" which are so dear to the impressionist style of the two brothers. Henry James's prefaces to his various novels, written between 1906 and 1910, constitute an extraordinary anthology of the instigating, or "germinating" functions of architecture. Architecture suggests the initial idea of the literary work, the "germ of its subject," or its governing themes (as in the case of *The Princess Casamassima,* with its hero who "sprang up out of the London pavement" and was confronted by the spectacle of the big city). But in addition, architecture accompanies both the composition of the work (the writer's windows, workplaces, or hotel rooms and the noise of the city surrounding the writing desk—see the evocation of the "intrigue of Paris" that surrounded James's Parisian hotel room during the 1889 Exposition and the concurrent composition of *The Tragic Muse*) as well as the author's subsequent rereading of the work. Marguerite Duras in 1985 said that for her the creative process always began with her visiting or remembering a specific architectural structure that she was familiar with, and whose layout and "discrete articulations" suggested to her the initial outlines of the narrative movements of her characters. The Baudelairian "intersection" relates somehow to the crossed lines (*croisée*) of religious *templum,* which mark the place of oracular prediction and is analogous to the cross (*croisée*) of innumerable window casements that open and authorize so many wordy descriptions in the naturalist novel. Inasmuch as it functions as an incitement that inaugurates and generates the literary work, architecture can extend its influence to the most minute details of form and style. Thus, to cite only a few comparable examples: in both Zola's *Pot-Bouille* (1882) and Georges Perec's *La Vie mode d'emploi* (1978) simultaneous action occurs on different floors and in different apartments of the same building. Given their respective themes (old Vabre's file for Zola, and the puzzle for Perec), the fragmented distribution of plot, and their shared tendency toward "montage" and toward the dissolution of a *hero,* both novels appear to derive from this initial architectural choice.

Of course, the major problem, which is linked to the question of representation, remains the meaning of the architectural object. Even though the latter constitutes, like articulated language, a discrete system (producing discontinuities and differences), even though it establishes communication between the subsidiary spaces that it incorporates while being itself incorporated into a more encompassing space, and even though it is defined by its articulations or directions (*sens*), it is far from certain that the architectural object produces meaning (*sens*) directly, that is, without the mediation of another system such as language which, as we have seen, has been massively reinjected into the building. And more specifically, it is far from certain that the architectural object has a syntax. This particular issue lays at the core of the first attempts by Umberto Eco and Sir John Summerson to construct an architectural semiotics, and it has forever haunted the history of architecture—see for example the classic debates of ancient architects over the meaning or character of the different orders, as well as the various attempts at "eloquent" architecture at the end of the eighteenth century. Many writers and philosophers have pointed to the silence of edifices, which contrasts sharply with the talkativeness of literature.[31] One need only

---

[31] There is a national language of monuments. . . . This language gave birth to sculpture and painting . . . which are closely linked to the building . . . [and] signs . . . ; the very beauty of these signs will always be that they only announce themselves. . . . All these beautiful figures, and especially those related to a building, express silence: this is the reason why silence strongly establishes itself in these buildings full of signs; this type of language suppresses the other language. (Alain, *Système des beaux-arts* [Paris: Gallimard, 1931], 183)

Baudelaire's poem "Rêve parisien," which we have already cited, finished, "Everything for the eye and nothing for the ear, a silence of eternity." Hugo writes in his introduction to Lacroix's *Paris-Guide* in 1867: In the middle of these enigmas, we think we hear behind us [inside Paris's monuments] the Sphinx's "quiet bursts of laughter" (xiii). Hegel's analyses of architecture in his *Aesthetics* are entwined with metaphors of riddles, sphinxes, and silence. Hegel sees architecture at once as an essence (before any symbolism) and a moment (originating a sort of childhood of art).

recall the endless debates of art historians over what the famous "urbinate" paintings with their meticulously composed architectural perspectives, exactly *represented*. Similarly, some of the most obscure texts of literature (such as Rimbaud's *Illuminations*, certain poems of Mallarmé or Pierre Reverdy, or Poe's "Lanor's Cottage" and "The Domain of Arnheim") also present themselves as architectural descriptions. Perhaps it is only the notion of narrativity discussed above that might permit us to readdress the question of what architecture signifies.

Let us recall a few of the givens of the problem: the meaning of an utterance (*énoncé*) is tied to how it stands in relation to the two parameters that serve as the basis of all meaning—first, its relationship to a real context (a moment, a locus), and second, its relationship to the act of a speaking subject (the presence of a voice). The fact of speaking (*énonciation*) brings the context into being; speaking thus inaugurates a real *site* by means of deictics (here, there, to the right or left, in front, or behind) while at the same time establishing *chronology* (yesterday, today, tomorrow). Architecture would therefore seem to have more to do with absence than with presence, and thus have more to do with writing. Just as writing is triply removed from the real *qua* sign, *qua* written sign representing oral signs, and *qua* activity that institutes an unbalanced, deferred form of communication, and just as writing lives on longer than the spoken word (*scripta manent*—*manere* is also the etymological root of *manor*), so architectural structures seem to be equally removed from the real and barely subject to passing time. This state of "abstraction" (in Wilhelm Worringer's terms) in comparison to the real, obviously makes it possible to master the real. The glory of monuments, writes Ruskin, "resides in their tranquil contrast to the transitory nature of all things."[32] Yet for the written literary text, as for the building/monument (since all buildings are monuments), this comes at a cost. Any edifice, even one that has been designated a monument, is by nature forgetful (innumerable religious edifices have been converted to other uses; the most notorious example in the nineteenth century being the Pantheon in Paris). The era to which the edifice refers back becomes unrecognizable, its interior and exterior spaces become dilapidated and in order for it to be restored to its original condition, in order for it to reacquire meaning through its location in a specific time and place, the building needs the

---

[32] John Ruskin, *The Seven Lamps*. Alain echoes Ruskin: "Monuments are the first written words, since writing is nothing more than a lasting sign" (*Système*, 183). Or Hugo: "Architecture is the great book of humanity . . . dictated by an era" (*Notre-Dame de Paris*, bk. 5, chap. 2).

language of the historian, the discourse of the guidebook, or explanatory plaques. Similarly, the literary text, situated as it is at the crossroads of absence, seems to be always attempting to recover the concrete presence of the speaking voice by imposing a *style* upon its linguistic material. This strategy of style is a nostalgic effort to compensate for the triple loss of those three categories on which all meaning and all identity are founded: time, space, and voice. The effort at recovering these three is therefore essentially a lyric one; and there is a notable presence of architecture in the texts belonging to this genre, which is the genre of self-exposure, described by Valéry as the "development of an exclamation," and which Baudelaire, in *Mon coeur mis à nu,* identified as a hesitation between the "vaporization" and the "centralization" of the self. We shall return to this in the final chapter of this work.

It was not the aim of these last remarks to develop a systematic parallel between text and architecture, nor to found some sort of all-encompassing *ut architectura poesis.* The idea was merely to provide a general introduction to the more focused and detailed analyses that are to follow while underlining some of the problems, situations, and operations that appear to writers themselves as potentially homologous. Since the literary text elects certain architectural objects (furniture, buildings, cities, gardens, monuments, houses, or machines) as preferred referents, and since it allows itself to be in turn questioned by the very silence and nonrepresentativeness of the architectural object, these various problems, situations, and operations allow literature indirectly to think about itself as text, as work, as communication, and as representation of a subject "I" and a world. Hence we should again recall the insistent presence of references to architecture in general, or in particular at those historical moments involving a crisis—of meaning, style, or of the subject. Nor should we forget literature's particular alertness to the architectural changes of its time. Both the lyric genre, which meticulously and obsessively elaborates the ecological sites and niches of the subject as well as its localizations and disloca(liza)tions, and the realist genre, which seeks to expose exhaustively the discreet articulations of a world conceived as a storehouse of documents—seen from this perspective, certainly take on a primary importance as objects of study, and nowhere more so than in the nineteenth century.

# PART II

# Texts and Their Monuments

# CHAPTER I

# Ruins and Glass Houses

"As you know, I have a habit of questioning buildings at close quarters," wrote Victor Hugo in *Le Rhin* before describing his encounter with a particularly enigmatic funerary inscription.[1] For the Romantic antiquary, the world was a succession of more or less meaningful edifices and each one provided a hermeneutic adventure. Such structures enabled face-to-face encounters with other cultures whose architectural objects had to be identified, qualified, described, and resuscitated; thus, two sorts of plenitudes were brought face to face. Antiquaries were not just great surveyors of cities, monuments and archeological sites; they were above all connoisseurs of engraved inscriptions—ambulatory enthusiasts of signs. They delighted in inscriptions on such noble materials as marble, bronze, or freestone carved in such noble typographies as hieroglyphics or Roman characters, in such noble languages as Latin or Greek, and found on such noble architectural supports as plinths, tombstones, steles, pediments, or altars. The travel account, which is a discourse about touring, is first and foremost a tour through discourse. Voyagers, who had previously journeyed about the various bookshelves in their libraries, considered each stop on their tour an opportunity for decoding inscriptions—a philological confrontation with engraved stones. Inscriptions, even when incomplete or written in an unknown language, seemed to exist solely to provoke and justify translation, a self-indulgent rewriting of the Baedecker or Joanne guidebook, a recollection of general cul-

[1] Victor Hugo, *Le Rhin* (Strasbourg: Bueb and Reumaux, 1980), 197ff.

ture, or a more or less melancholic personal elegy. Moreover they inspired rhetorical exercises which drew parallels between past and present times, reactivated anecdotes or momentous historical events, or caused the traveler to meditate on the differences and similarities of civilizations and their demise. Without a doubt, Hugo's *Le Rhin* remains one of the finest examples of this fascination with the lapidary. In this work the *ceci* (the book and the written word) merges with and confronts the *cela* (the monument) as the lapidary style of the concise phrase (which in Hugo rarely remained concise) inscribed in the traveler's (pseudo)notebook acts as both a mirror and a rival to the constructed building's lapidary prose.[2] In the encounter of word and monument, travel through the real blends into the reading of a certain reality that conceals or disguises itself or does not readily answer the questions it is asked. After all, the real is meaning and meaning is always hidden. Despite this, meaning is always nonetheless presumed to exist in this lapidary inscription. For the antiquary, the building was both document and monument, as well as an excuse for generating a textual commentary. The more obscure the hieroglyph, the more chance it had of being loaded with history. Consequently, its decipherment would be a testament to the abilities and culture of its decoder.

The novelist exhibited a similar obsession with deciphering the real. A prime example can be found in the description of the doors of Saumur in the first pages of Balzac's *Eugénie Grandet* (the beginning of novels always being the site of exposition and of semantic void). These doors are doubly enigmatic since they are at once hiding interiors which the reader has yet to see and are located at the beginning of an as-yet-undiscovered plot.

> [These doors are] studded with huge nails, on which our ancestors recorded the passions of the age in hieroglyphs, once understood in every household, the meaning of which no one will now ever again unravel. In these symbols, a Protestant declared his faith, or a Leaguer cursed Henry IV, or some civic

[2] Victor Hugo writes in *Le Rhin*: "I am going to enter the ruin. I am there. I am writing on a little green velvet console that I have taken from the old wall" (157). Hence the production of a lapidary discourse, the brief, paratactic note taken on site in a "telegraphic" style, that reproduces the discourse of the ruined, fragmented stone, as the narrator of *Le Rhin* writes to his correspondent: "I can do no better than to transcribe here what I wrote in my notebook at every step. Presenting things seen in any which way, but meticulously, written down as they happened and therefore true to life" (156). All nineteenth-century attempts to produce a form of writing that was both modern and mimetic of the modern world would be haunted by the fragment: *écriture artistique*, impressionist style, the "slice of life," intermediary style, narratives "broken into little pieces," Rimbaldian illuminations, or Coppée's *dizains réalistes*.

dignitary traced the insignia of his office, celebrating the long-forgotten glory of his temporary high estate as alderman . . . the history of France lies written in these houses.[a]

The same term, *hieroglyph,* recurs in the opening scene of *La Maison du chat qui pelote.* For the traveler, the reader, or for the novelist who deciphers the real, the building, a layer similar to other semaphoric envelopes like skin and clothing, acts as an interface where the urges or impulses of the inner as well as the outer world are inscribed in sunken or raised characters. We have already cited Hugo's remark "I study clothing the way I study an edifice. The suit of clothes is Man's first garment, the house is his second."[3] Moreover, in *L'Homme qui rit,* Hugo specifies: "A man's physiognomy is shaped by his conscience and his life, which etch a multitude of mysterious furrows. "Such a theory posits a readable world dedicated to synecdoche (inclusion) and metonymy (contiguity). In this world, where character is a psychological as well as a typographical term, life imprints its stigmata on the skin. Thus consciousness rises to the surface by way of symptoms, and social standing shows through one's clothing and habitat. A readable world could be conceived as a series of systematically interlocking envelopes which interpret each other, or as pages to be read in which hermeneutics, anthropology, sociology, and physiognomy can be practiced at leisure. Redundancies, harmonies, and disharmonies can be deployed between these envelopes, thereby lending them to reports and commentary. Therefore, the traveler's pleasures (Francis Ponge, playing on the erotic sense of this expression, writes of the "pleasures of the door") upon arriving before an edifice, are accordingly numerous. In front of concrete objects the traveler experiences the pleasure of reading, recognizing, and verifying knowledge previously acquired, not to mention the pleasure of that cultural qualifying exam which, when confronted with the sphinx-like monument, affords him the pleasure of evaluating not only his historical but also his semiotic prowess.[4] The monument in particular and the architectural object in general is often a complex

---

[3] Hugo, *Le Rhin,* 317. If the mosque fascinates Hugo (see his preface to *Les Orientales*) it is undoubtedly because this building is covered with inscriptions, with "verses from the Quran on every door."

[4] Of course, a thorough study of hermeneutic postures in the Romantic travel account demands that one make the distinction between the compulsive exposition of knowledge of someone like Hugo, for example, and the offhand way Stendhal deals with the discourse of the cicerones. Stendhal sides with an underexposure of the real rather than its overexposure.

[a] Honoré de Balzac, *Eugénie Grandet,* trans. Marion Ayton Crawford (London: Penguin Books, 1955), 34.

multisemiotic system, where figurative icons such as statues combine with: empty deictics (the statue's pointed index finger), orality (etiological rumblings, a cicerone's accompanying discourse or echoes) and writing (the votive inscription, or the official account in an official history). This brief passage, taken from Chateaubriand's *René*, saturated with *semiosis*, exemplifies such a system:

> One day, as I was walking in a large city, I passed through a secluded and deserted courtyard behind a palace. There, I noticed a statue pointing to a spot made famous by a certain sacrifice.* I was struck by the stillness of the surroundings; only the wind moaned weakly around the tragic marble. Workmen were lying about indifferently at the foot of the statue, or whistled as they hewed out stones. I asked them what the monument meant; some knew little indeed, while the others were totally oblivious of the catastrophe it commemorated. Nothing could indicate so vividly the true measure of human events and the vanity of our existence. What has become of those figures whose fame was so widespread? Time has taken a step and the face of the earth has been made over.[5]

> *At London, behind Whitehall the statue of Charles II [note of Chateaubriand].[6]

Apparently, the big-city stroller/reader takes pleasure in warding off vacuums of meaning. The passage that begins with a series of indefinite articles to describe this "secluded and deserted" courtyard and the "stillness of [its] surroundings," fills the void by imitating a historical text with an explanatory note at the bottom of the page.[7] The narrator's pleasure in rambling on verbally in a place where "only the wind moaned" is also apparent. In an aristocratic fashion these reflections create a cultural difference between the narrator and the natives. They are mere stonecutters not to be confused with artists or sculptors who produce icons;[8] they are "indifferent workmen," men of nature devoted to nonlanguage since their "whistles" seem more closely related to nature's moaning wind than

[5] François-René de Chateaubriand, *Atala-René*, trans. Irving Putter (Berkeley, Los Angeles, London: University of California Press, 1980), 90–91.

[6] Ibid.

[7] This text, monument—so often evoked in Chateaubriand's work—and footnote have their own history. The footnote is in fact *false*. Charles's pointed index finger is not indicating the place of his father's execution; it is actually the place where James II met his end. Hence the question asked in this text, which has not only to do with restoration but also filiation (and any reflection on heritage (*patrimoine*) naturally speaks of fathers): Why did Chateaubriand *deliberately* afix this false footnote to a passage where he is attempting to prove his ability to interpret a place? Concerning this point, see Maurice Regard's footnote to the Bibliothèque de la Pléiade edition of Chateaubriand's *Oeuvres romanesques et voyages*, vol. 1 (Paris: Gallimard, 1969), 1,203.

[8] See Victor Hugo on modern architecture in *Notre-Dame de Paris*: "It no longer explains anything . . . It calls for laborers, instead of artists" (Part 5, chap. 2).

to human speech. This traveler delights in drawing parallels while also considering the notion of scale (the "measure of human events.") Moreover, he can take pleasure in constructing his own monument–text, a sort of "tomb" or "exemplum" with a consecrated lapidary phrase as its clausula ("time has taken a step . . ."), traced from inscriptions on tombs and sun dials, that acts as a final *epiphoneme*. Thus the stroller maps out a rhetorical itinerary evident in the *periphrasis* of the beginning, which is analogous to the circular course of the tourist; after all to do a tour of a country is to go around it in much the same way one walks around a statue. Finally, this text bespeaks the pleasure of restoration: Chateaubriand, proponent of the restoration of the monarchy in France now exiled to England, restores the forgotten meaning of the monument, a meaning which coincides with a story out of English history and which deals with the restoration of its monarchy after Oliver Cromwell. In passing let us note that if *restoration* as a political concept and debate runs throughout the entire revolutionized nineteenth century, in the architectural arena the problem of restoration of edifices constitutes in a parallel way a subject of a particularly lively debate from Viollet-le-Duc through Ruskin and Alois Riegl. While Viollet-le-Duc is for restoration, Ruskin and Riegl (with some slight differences) are completely opposed to it.[9] According to Ruskin, beautiful architecture is one that is, from its inception, planned and built as "historical"; it must in a sense program its own demise, and "render architecture of the day historical."[10] Ruskin's penultimate lamp, as we know, is the Lamp of Memory; the building has no real significance or value if it cannot stimulate the exercise of memory. Ruskin disliked the architecture of iron and glass that was beginning to invade the real because it was easily dismantled, repetitive, polyvalent and perpetually renewable, thereby losing any historical or geographical anchor and immune to the effects or the patina of time. He writes: "In architecture, there is much in that very treatment which is skillful or otherwise in proportion to its just regard to the probable effects of time."[11] According to Riegl, restoration often has disastrous consequences. Restoration, which deprives us of the somewhat melancholy pleasures of participating in nature's cyclical movements, is not necessary: "Any building, no matter how insignificant, takes on an 'added' historical and memorial 'value,'

[9] Concerning Viollet-le-Duc, see Philippe Boudon, Hubert Damish, and Philippe Deshays, *Analyse du Dictionnaire raisonné de l'architecture française du XIXème siècle par Viollet-Le-Duc, architecte* (Paris: A.R.E.A., 1978).
[10] John Ruskin, *The Seven Lamps,* 165.
[11] Ibid., 173.

by the mere fact that one day it will be deemed ancient—and this, regardless of its function and its original purpose."[12] This debate on restoration therefore centers on the possibilities of exercising both the imagination and memory—themes we will encounter again further on.

One architectural object of particular concern to the nineteenth-century literary text is of course the *ruin,* whose role extends well beyond Romantic travel writing. In an inverted way, the ruin, which was not an invention of the nineteenth century, seems to underline the very essence of architecture. The ruin involves the *decomposition* of the real, whereas architecture is the art of spatial *composition.* Of course, there are ruins and there are ruins. On the one hand there is the ancient ruin of the distant past, which is laden with history. On the other hand there is the modern ruin whose literary status is far more ambiguous and far more difficult to interpret—ruins such as those created by Paris riots, the ruins of shanty towns, or the construction sites created by real-estate speculation, actual ruins of the past, or the fake ruins of the Marquis de Girardin's Ermenonville.[13] Decomposing and recomposing indeed constitute the fundamental operations of any act of comprehension of the text of the world, or rather, the world as a textual palimpsest to be deciphered. The ruin is a kind of hyperbole of the building, and this despite the fact that it constitutes a sort of reduction. Like any other fragmented object, the ruin calls for acts of semantic completion on the part of the narrator, the reader, or any literary character assigned to visit or interpret it. The hermeneutics of the ruin resembles the paleontology of Georges Cuvier that so appealed to Balzac in which the whole is reconstituted from fragments and totality is induced from absence.[14]

---

[12] Alois Riegl, *Le culte moderne des monuments: sa nature, son origine,* trans. Jacques Boulet (Paris: Villemin, 1984), passim.

[13] Certainly, the nineteenth century is not the only century implicated. From Joachim du Bellay's *Antiquitez de Rome* (1558) through Constantin François Volney's *Ruines* (1791) to Jacques Réda's *Ruines de Paris* (Paris: Gallimard, 1977), the very ambiguity of the ruin fascinates painters such as Hubert Robert, sculptors such as Martin and Poirier, and writers of any era. Let us not forget that, according to the *Encyclopédie,* the term *ruin* can only be used to designate "palaces, sumptuous tombs, or public monuments" (from the article "Ruin"). Becoming a tourist attraction or even the purely kitsch kiosk in industrial centuries, the ruin would lose its noble status as the aesthetic object if it took on the role of the purely decorative object. In chapter five of Daudet's *Les Rois en exile,* we see two parvenus, the merchant Tom Lévis and the couturier Spricht try to outdo each other through architectural feats performed on their respective homes: Spricht builds an artificial ruin in his backyard that is like a didactic diorama from a universal exposition, complete with Bengal lights reproducing the Paris Hôtel de Ville set afire during the Commune.

[14] Balzac, in the 1842 forward to his *Comédie humaine,* cited "Charles Bonnet's interlocking matching parts" as another model.

The ruin, like the bone of the paleontologist or the relic of the faithful, provokes, incites, and demands an effort of close and meticulous interpretation. More so than the "normal" building, it appears to be a litotic quotation of the past that instigates reading and writing. Of course, this quest for meaning may be difficult. The ruin can resist the restoration or institution of meaning, but there is no doubt as to the existence of this meaning; that resistance can itself offer further gratification for the traveler–hermeneut is borne out in many of Hugo's writings. Thus, in *Le Rhin,* traveling from Lorch to Bingen and encountering a "dark ruin," Hugo writes:

> What is this chateau? I could not say, I did not know where I was. . . . I came and went in the rubble, rummaging, ferreting, questioning; I overturned broken stones, in the hope of finding some kind of inscription that would signal some fact. . . . This ruin, so perfectly mute, intrigued me yet also grieved me. I never grant a ruin, not even a tomb, the right to remain silent to this extent.[15]

As is the case of all great travelers and consumers of architecture, this quote shows the near athletic, physical investment that goes into reading and writing the ruin: climbing, descending, blazing a trail, scaling, hiking, scratching out, and excavating. The traveler is not only rewarded by the spectacle of the ruin but is also recompensated by the panoramic view of the surroundings from its vantage point, like the famous *Gipfelblick* of the German traveler perched on the summits.

Thus, travelers' "readings" put their entire body and senses into play: they hear the wind and echoes; they see the ruin as a spectacle and an observatory; they smell the musty scent of interiors and the odor of vegetation that grows in and around the ruin; they feel the roughness, smoothness, coldness, or dampness of its surfaces and surrounding air; they even take great interest in tasting the local cuisine. It is as if this abandoned building, although housing no living bodies, only the recumbent statues of those laid to rest, exacerbates and multiplies the corporal functions of its visitors. In certain cases, when travelers confront a lapidary or an entire building that resists legibility, it will be their own poem, whether composed on site or after the fact, that will serve to fill the void. At least this is what Hugo leads the reader to believe.

Above all, it is the semantic complexity of the ruin that makes it so fascinating. The ruin embodies not only a particular *conjuncture*, recall-

---

[15] Hugo, *Le Rhin*, 197, 199. Concerning this passage, see C. Reichler, "Hugo, déchiffreur des pierres," in *Rivista di letterature moderne e comparate*, 39, fasc. 2 (Pisa: Pacini, 1986).

ing an earlier time, furnishing a story with reference points, or resuscitating the commentary or the discourse on an event, but as a concrete object it also unveils and exhibits its *structure*. The cracked or crumbling wall that allows the gaze to penetrate into the interior of the building as well as expose its privacy, is a cut-away or, in other words, an autopsy of the building. In this way, the Romantic alpine meadow prefigures the pavilions and crystal palaces of the universal exposition that would exhibit, like so many modern ruins, the numerous sections, mock-ups, encyclopedic charts, and cut-aways of displayed objects, machines, and buildings. Just as the ruin unveils its interior design, it also reveals the preparatory blueprints and projects that presided over its architectural genesis: its *after* reveals its *before*. The ruin exhibits its initial mental representation, and therefore recovers the absolute origins (archè) of the building that corresponds to its ideal representation. In the words of Claude Perrault, the ruin suggests to the eye a "sciography" or an "ichnography"—a kind of concrete, natural axonometry of the building.

In fact, according to Perrault's notes in his translation of Vitruvius, *sciography* provides a view of "the building . . . as if cut from top to bottom," while *ichnography* is "the representation or the design of the vestiges of a building . . . *ichnos* in Greek meaning vestige, or the imprint left by something when placed on the ground." . . . The manner of graphic representation of the building via *axonometry* thus combines the blueprint, the section, and the elevation of the building, yet its use was widespread in architects' works and blueprints only near the end of the nineteenth century. Therefore, the Romantic ruin somehow anticipated modern architecture (in its exposed frameworks and ribs) as well as its manner of representation: an ideal, all-encompassing, and voluminous representation of a kind of hologram, or a kind of glass house, where the facade loses its status as the primary component of the building. Yet in playing the role of its negative, or shadow image, the ruin prefigured the great transparent architectural styles belonging to the exposition halls of the mid-nineteenth century, intended for the didactic circulation of the gaze.

The lyric poet, like the traveling antiquary or the philosopher, could thus recognize in the ruin some favorite themes—the soul turning in on itself, the transparency of meaning, the dialectics of the visible and invisible and of the before and the after, as well as the meaning of history. The poet thus extracted from it a double hermeneutical benefit: access to structure and access to conjuncture. The ruin is therefore an object that elicits, in the words of Constantin-François de Volney, the finest of "lofty, solemn, and profound" thoughts. In a curious and almost mimetic way, it elicits some particularly architected forms of reflection and writing, notably in the use of the parallel: "it was that way then, it is this way now"; or else: "one day in the future, today's civilization A could become like civilization B, whose ruins I am now familiar with." This last parallel constitutes the literary genre of the anticipatory ruin a futurology of the type exemplified by Hugo's 1837 poem "A l'arc de triomphe."[16] The parallel is the simplest form of evaluation; evaluating is after all comparing something to a model, a standard, or a norm. The ruin's semantic ambivalence and its embodiment of contradictory categories (such as temporality) occasion poetic reflection; just as the ruin creates parallels in the viewer's mind by telescoping past, present, and future, on a more formal level, so the parallel is a distinctive trait of all poetic expression. Furthermore, the ruin instigates ethical reflection,[17] while giving rise to such pedagogic or encyclopedic techniques as the overview, the synthesis, or the exposition. As a monumental way station along an initiatory journey, the ruin easily lends itself to the pedagogic discursive form of the presentation or *exposé*. In chapter 4 of Volney's *Ruins*, entitled "Expositions," the narrator conjures the ghost of the ruins to offer a bird's-eye view of the vast geographic and historic panorama of the world. (It is the same pedagogically descriptive bird's-eye view that Hugo uses to describe Paris from the belltowers of the cathedral in *Notre-Dame de Paris*), a

[16] See Philippe Junod, "Ruines anticipées, ou l'histoire au futur antérieur," in *L'Homme face à son histoire* (Lausanne: Université de Lausanne-Payot, 1984). For a more recent "ruin in the future tense," see the description of Saint-Sulpice in Jacques Réda's *Le Chateau aux courants d'air* (Paris: Gallimard, 1986), 85–86.

[17] Denis Diderot was the great promoter of a pictoral "poetics of ruins" (the expression appears often in his article on the Salon of 1767 in reference to Hubert Robert). About one of Robert's paintings, Diderot wrote: I walk between two eternities. . . . What is my own ephemeral existence in *comparison* . . . to these masses suspended over my head, shaking? (emphasis mine) Similarly: "The memory of time past, the comparison with the present state, all of this raises my heart to the loftiest of thoughts" wrote Volney in chapter one of *Les Ruines*. In his well-known chapter "Paris à vol-d'oiseau" in *Notre-Dame de Paris*, Hugo elaborates a parallel between ancient and modern Paris and concludes by saying: "Compare!" In his introduction to Lacroix's *Paris-Guide* he also writes: "Contrasts and parallels are everywhere." Structurally, this parallelism defines the lyric text as a textual type. From his perspective, J. Cohen in *Le Haut-langage* seeks to explore and extend the notion of poeticity in which the ruin is made into an ambiguous poetic element of the real which he compares to glass and mirrors: "The ruin is an oxymoron made of stone. It is present-past, a mix of now and then" ([Paris: Flammarion, 1979], 267). Concerning ambiguity, aside from the abovementioned technemes, see the book that has become a classic, a postmodern Bible: Robert Venturi, *Complexity and Contradiction in Architecture* (New York: Museum of Modern Art, 1966).

vast geographic and historic panorama of the world: "I will expose to your gaze this truth that you call for, . . . I will reveal to you the wisdom of the tombs." Just as the photographic black box "reveals"[b] the real, the ruin, as it opens up and "ex-plicates itself," develops its envelopes and elicits further "development" by the explicatory and descriptive text.

Ruins, whether real or imaginary, prospective or retrospective, fabricated or pre-existing, are, like all buildings, only in a more exaggerated fashion, semantic objects that are overdetermined, paradoxical, and ambiguous. Whether because it often occupies a strategic position on some bit of uneven ground, or because it sticks out from surrounding buildings or vegetation, the ruin somehow leaps forth from its context (whether by virtue of its anachronism, its incompleteness, its artificiality, or its dilapidation). Constituting an intrusion that is at once historic and detached from any history, the ruin seems to demand to be reattached, but to whom, to what, or to which events? Providing both an "unobstructed view" and "an ocular trap,"[18] the ruin lures the eye as it lies there exposed while thwarting all attempts to give it meaning. Representing the presence of an absence, embodying something virtually depleted of meaning, the ruin functions as a sort of negative punctuation of space, as an "objective riddle."[19] Perceived in emphatic relief, exposed in a natural or artificial framework, or as a moment in a museographic journey, the ruin is thus homologous on the one hand to an item displayed in a store window, and on the other, to a relic that is similarly put on view to attract and hold the attention of the pilgrim. (Both of these objects—the relic and the shopworn item—will be frequently associated in the imaginary of the century.) A kind of camera obscura of memory, the ruin is responsible for giving meaning to the "as is" of history, for the ruin provokes the pure effect of memory (according to Flaubert's *Dictionnaire des idées reçues,* the ruin "induces reverie") and can therefore send the visitor back to the image of his impending death. To borrow Roland Barthes's expression applied to photography (the art of "exposure" and of "development"), the ruin constitutes a poignant "punctum" that refers back to a private

---

[18] Jean-Pierre Richard, *Paysage de Chateaubriand* (Paris: Seuil, 1967), 68. Regarding the literary theme of the ruin, see Roland Mortier, *La Poètique des ruines en France, ses origines, ses variations de la Renaissance à Victor Hugo* (Geneve: Droz, 1974).

[19] This is Hegel's formulation regarding Egyptian architecture in his *Aesthetics: Lectures on Fine Art*, trans. T. M. Knox (Oxford: Clarendon Press, 1975).

[b] In French, *révèler* (to reveal) and *développer* (to develop) can both be used in speaking of photographic development.

history.[20] The black box of the ruin can thus become an anxiety-producing apparatus. For those who visit or gaze upon the ruin, it can easily become the mirror reflection of their own pure artificiality (as in the case of the fake ruins (or follies) in Ermenonville, where the narrator of Gérard de Nerval's *Sylvie* pursues the memory of three "fake" women). The ruin can also bring about a threefold erasure. First, it erases the architectural object itself. Incarnating universal entropy, it verges into nothingness, gradually dissolving into the earth, becoming overgrown by plants, and thus becoming invisible. Second, it erases meaning: an empty place, a theater of the void, unreceptive to the memory of the visitor or reader (as in the empty tomb of Rousseau in the center of Ermenonville), the ruin becomes an illegible *rune*. Third, it erases the subject: fascinated by this void, the contemplative subject becomes absorbed, loses himself, even loses his voice as it reverberates through the echoes and then fades off, as he himself does, into the ruin.[21]

But readers of a ruin cannot tolerate the (semantic) void and therefore always tend to fill it. In order to neutralize any "insignificant" site, they develop a reading activity that saturates its subject with meaning. They do so by endowing these sites with indexical and allegorical functions that derive from a given history and serve to impart some sort of coherence be it mythical, historical, or anecdotal. Of course, the activities of the ruin's visitors can go beyond merely reading and writing; they will readily pilfer a piece of the building they visit. Thus, by taking a "souvenir" back with them, travelers not only contribute to the erosion brought by time but also to the cohesive structure of his own personal history. The piece of stone brought home by the traveler becomes part of an autobiographical recapitulation or reassessment, which in turn enables the development of a personalized narrative serving a cohesive and configurative function. Travel accounts are filled with such lapidary pillaging. Take for example this passage from Chateaubriand:

> As I climbed down from the citadel I took a piece of marble from the Parthenon; I had already collected a fragment from Agamemnon's tomb-

[20] Roland Barthes, *Camera Lucida: Reflections on Photography*, trans. Richard Howard (New York: Hill and Wang, 1981). In his book *Le Philosophe et l'architecte* (Paris: Aubier-Montaigne, 1982), Daniel Payot asks the question, "Is the idea of architecture essentially the idea of death?" Larousse reminds us in his dictionary of the funerary meaning of the word *exposition*: "In Paris, the dead are exhibited in the doorways of houses." One can thus reread the passage in Proust of the death of Bergotte, in which the character of the writer, visiting an art exhibition, dies fascinated by the "insignificant" detail in a Vermeer painting—"a little patch of yellow wall."

[21] See Richard, *Paysage*, 67ff.

stone; and since that time, when visiting a monument I have always taken
something from it . . . when I see these trinkets, I immediately recall my
journeys and adventures; I say to myself: "I was there, and such a thing
occurred."[22]

In this banal touristic act of defacement (the tourist is also someone who
writes on and destroys walls) we glimpse an interesting case of parasitic
reappropriation or abduction. This commandeering of mementos (interestingly, in the name Agamemnon we find the name of Memnon, the
eponym for living stone) is in a sense homologous to the fundamental
operations of reading or writing. The traveler who ransacks a tomb or
monument dedicated to the memory of another and appropriates a
piece of it to bring home and display in the sitting room is in fact
engaged in constituting a *collection*. We should note that collecting is
the other source of delirium of the nineteenth century which Walter
Benjamin so rightly compares to Flaubert's delirium of the exposition.
The travelers construct their own personal relics, their own tombs or
private museums; by erasing someone else's history, they insure their
own memory as well as the cohesiveness of their autobiography. They
bring home these mementos (or mental images) and descriptions in
much the same way that Chateaubriand did. The latter writes in the
preface to the first edition of his *Itinéraire de Paris à Jerusalem* that he
voyaged "in search of images" for his epic *Les Martyrs*. The traveler
may also bring back material that will serve as explanatory legends for
other objects placed on exhibit. For example, when reprefacing his
*Itinéraire*—which he calls his "logbook of ruins"—Chateaubriand
boasts that "excerpts from the book served as the accompanying text
for the Panorama exhibits" on view in Paris. Whether the traveler
brings back rocks, objects, or texts, these mementos in some way fore-
shadow the collection that would miniaturize and bring into the bourgeois interior the great monuments of the world. The act of collecting is
both effectively and etymologically related to the act of *reading*; just as
it is related to that act of spiritual composure (*recueillement*) that as we
will later see, is an essentially *lyric* posture. Collecting is also related to
the act of *citing*, which involves removing a fragment from someone
else's authorized discourse in order to integrate it into one's own autho-
rial discourse. The reverie prompted by the monument inextricably
blends reading (sighting traces), writing (printing traces), traveling (visiting traces), and collecting (juxtaposing traces). The act of citation al-

[22] Chateaubriand, *Itinéraire de Paris à Jerusalem* (Paris: Garnier–Flammarion, 1968),
147.

ways involves situating oneself within a certain history or bringing about an institutional or resurrectional transformation of the self (and of others) through the other. One of the terms most often used by Proust in his preface to Ruskin's *Amiens Bible* is precisely the word *resurrection*; Ruskin is explicitly compared to the Christ figure found on tympana—the traditional iconographic sites for depictions of Last Judgments and Resurrections. Proust raises Ruskin from the dead while Ruskin's commentary itself revives a minuscule detail of this great book of stone, a small sculpted figure from one of the cathedral's portals which, as chance would have it, is referred to as "the portal of the bookseller." In Proust's text literary criticism, the history of architecture, reading, the writing of history, and architecture itself all become metaphors for each other.[23]

In the case of certain modern ruins[24]—buildings in the course of being constructed or demolished—heterogenous, unusual, or incongruous qualities that attract the eye are the very categories called upon to give them meaning. As the narrator of Baudelaire's "Le Cygne" walks across the construction site at the new carousel—a term which can be interpreted anachronistically by way of the technical terminology of photography—he writes:

> A l'heure où sous les cieux
> Froids et clairs le Travail s'eveille, où la voirie
> Pousse un sombre ouragan dans l'air silencieux.[c]

---

[23] See Proust's *On Reading Ruskin* (New Haven, Conn.: Yale University Press, 1987). It is significant that Proust, while in dialogue with Ruskin, would choose to speak of both the "book of stone" (Ruskin's *Our Fathers Have Told Us* [1904]) and reading (Proust's preface to *Sesame and Lilies* of 1906), and that his text on Ruskin is almost entirely devoted to an exegeses of minute detail of the sculpture of the Amiens cathedral. Proust also devotes the entire beginning of his preface to *Sesame and Lilies* to evoking the reading places of his childhood, and the end to extending the comparison between reading and the visit to a city or a monument.

[24] The theme of the modern ruin appears frequently in the literary works and newspaper articles of the nineteenth century. See, for example, the chapter in Lacroix's *Paris-Guide* by E. About entitled "Dans les ruines"; the poem "Démolitions," by Flaubert's friend Louis Bouilhet, in *Festons et Astragales* of 1895; and "Un Chapitre des ruines de Paris-moderne" in Victor Fournel's *Paris nouveau et Paris futur* (Paris: LeCoffre, 1865), 21, 26. In an "irony of history," the ruins resulting from Haussmanns's public works would be reinforced by the ruins created by the Paris Commune. Hence, this ironic grievance from Huysmans: "To embellish this dreadful Paris that we owe to modern builders, shouldn't we—if all the proper precautions were taken to ensure people's safety—plant here and there a few ruins, burn down the Bourse, the Madeleine, or the Ministry of War, or the Church of Saint-Xavier . . . so pathetic when it is raw, the architecture of the century would become imposing, even superb, when cooked" (*L'Art moderne / certains* Union Générale Editions, 1975), 399.

[c] "At the hour when beneath the chill, clear sky, Toil stirs from sleep, When the department of Public Works fills the silent air with its dark whirlwind" (*The Complete Verse of Baudelaire*, vol. 1, trans. Francis Scarfe [London: Anvil Press, 1986], translation modified).

This is a world with no historical depth that is nonetheless thinkable, and therefore easily mastered through allegory:

> Palais neufs, échafaudages, blocs,
> Vieux faubourgs tout pour moi devient allégorie.[25,d]

In *Colonel Chabert*, Balzac's description of his hero's lodgings is a sort of allegory of this displaced phantom come back from beyond.

> Although recently built, this house seemed on the brink of falling into ruins. None of the materials had been put to their original intended use. They all came from the demolished buildings torn down daily in Paris. Derville could read on shutters made out of planks from a sign the words: "Novelty shop." The windows were all mismatched, and grotesquely placed.[e]

In *Les Misérables,* Hugo describes the modern ruins of the barricades, these "frightening masterpieces of civil war" as a similar allegory of randomness:

> What was this barricade made of? Of the material of three six-storey houses torn down for the purpose. . . . It had the woeful aspect of the works of hatred: Ruin . . . Look! A door! A grating! A shed! A furnace! And cracked pots! Bring all! Throw everything on it! . . . It was a haphazard composite of pavement, rubble, timber, iron bars, rags, smashed window panes, stripped chairs, cabbage stalks, . . . and malediction, . . . the mingling of debris, . . . overturned carts, . . . an omnibus . . . as if the architects of this savagery had wanted to add mischief to the terror.[f]

Of course, this jumble of items is not without meaning; it signifies the *peuple* who take other people's objects, tinker with them, and by juxta-posing and reusing these old objects invent ways of introducing disorder into the well-marshaled world of the old order. This revolutionary dia-lectic of old and new would alternately be treated seriously, as in the Hugolian dread, or ironically, as in the case of the remains of the novelty store in the second-hand debris of Chabert's house. Thus, the traveler (or voyeur) who visits these "modern" ruins is someone who

---

[25] Concerning this text as a complex allegory of exile, see Ross Chambers, *Mélancholie et opposition* (Paris: José Corti, 1987), and Richard D. Burton, "The Context of Baude-laire's Le Cygne," Durham Modern Languages Series (Durham, N.C.: University of Dur-ham, 1980).

[d] "The new palaces and scaffoldings, blocks of stone, old suburbs, everything for me is turned to allegory," Baudelaire, *Complete Verse*, translation modified.

[e] Honoré de Balzac, *The Celibate and Other Stories*, trans. Clara Bell (Philadelphia: Gebbie, 1900), 264–265, translation modified.

[f] Victor Hugo, *Les Misérables*, trans. Charles Wilbour (New York: Modern Library, 1931), 984–985.

wanders through the space of social classes and traverses historical time.[26]

After 1850 the Romantic tourist, whose activities consisted of traveling, visiting, watching, marveling, wondering, defining, naming, and commenting, would be replaced by comparable daily ventures of the boulevard *flâneur* and the exhibition-goer. Visiting an exhibition (be it a universal exposition mounted in Paris every ten years, or the annual Salon de Peinture) entailed surveying a space organized by architecture, where the visible was staged as a spectacle and was rendered legible because of its very architectural organization. The exposition offered exemplary objects, scale models, blueprints and cut-aways of machines, as well as examples of art and industry, all accompanied by descriptions. All these items on display were rendered transparent by the very transparency of the great glass housings of the exposition palaces. Similarly, on the boulevard, items bearing names and labels were exposed behind shop windows accompanied by a laudatory epideictic discourse—the advertisement. The street, which offered the flâneur an inexhaustible juxtaposition of changing fashions and trifling events, turned into a permanent stage whose ongoing commentary was furnished by the journalistic buzz of miscellaneous news items, society pages, and gossip sheets. Furthermore those impalpable things—the new and the modern—that had been until then reserved for an elite or a clique were now exposed for all to see. Thus the street managed to replace the pedagogical role of the school, not to mention the inspirational role of the Romantic muses and the genii of the ruins. Emile Souvestre describes the wanderings of his hero in his edifying *Philosophe sous les toits* (1850) in just this way:

> I crossed from one pavement to another, I retraced my steps, I stopped in front of shops and posters! How many things there are to learn on the streets of Paris! What a museum! . . . The world is there to be sampled. . . . Look at those people whose knowledge is gained from shop windows and merchants' displays! . . . This variety of exhibitions makes Paris the world's

---

[26] See in chapter 7 of Zola's *La Curée*, a novel about speculation and the demolition of Paris during the Second Empire, the scene of the visit to the construction site of what was to become the boulevard Prince-Eugène by Saccard and the developers who are his accomplices. They find still erect in the wreckage and exposed to the gaze of passers-by the gutted room where one of the businessmen had lived in his student days and the eighteenth-century follies where the nobility came to hide their orgies. It is also the only moment in the novel when the speculators encounter other social classes (the workers on the construction site).

fairground. . . . It is a constant spur to the imagination, a first rung of the ladder always set up before us in a vision.[g]

Just as Italy was an obligatory stop and (common)place for every Romantic tourist, painter, or student of architecture, the exposition and the boulevard become obligatory passages for writers of the second half of the century because they allowed the transformation of real places into a series of topoi, literary themes, metaphors, or subjects for newspaper articles. The links between literature and journalism on the one hand and the world of expositions on the other are numerous throughout the century. Jules Hetzel, writing under his pseudonym P. J. Stahl, set some minor scenes of his *Morale familière* at an exposition; Théophile Gautier wrote a newspaper account of the 1855 Exposition in London; the Exposition of 1855 incited Proudhon to write his *Projet de société de l'exposition perpétuelle,* which he published in 1871 with his *Théorie de la propriété*; Hans Christian Andersen used the 1867 Paris Exposition as the backdrop for his tale "The Dryad"; in 1871 Walt Whitman composed "Song of the Exposition"; Mallarmé reported on the 1872 Exposition in London for *L'Illustration*; Zola devoted an entire novel, *L'Oeuvre,* to the problem of artists gaining access to the annual Official Salon; as a correspondent for St. Petersburg's *Le Messager de L'Europe,* Zola also wrote about the 1878 Paris Exposition and later photographed the 1900 Exposition in Paris; Huysmans, in his article on the Salon of 1889, spoke at length on the iron architecture of his times; Henri de Régnier reported in *La Vogue* on the 1889 Paris Exposition that would inspire France's first cartoon strip by Christophe as seen in the pages of *Le Petit Français illustré,* which presented the unforgettable Fenouillard family as they visited the exposition; the Douanier Rousseau wrote a light comedy in three acts entitled "Visite à l'Exposition de 1889"; even musicians like Modest Mussorgsky, in his piano work "Pictures at an Exhibition," drew inspiration from the exposition. The various accounts by these writer–journalists provided the forum for aesthetic debates concerning the existence of a nineteenth-century style, or the possibility of industrial or decorative arts. Clearly, for the belletrist, the voyage to the Orient or to Greece had been replaced by travel to the Three Babylons of the modern age—Paris, Lon-

---

[g] Emile Souvestre, *The "Attic" Philosopher* (New York: Current Literature, 1910), 35–37.

don, and New York[27]—or to the innumerable national, international, specialized, or universal, expositions held in most of the major cities of the West. These places were fascinating not only because of their *contents* (crammed as they were with new objects and arts from the world over) but also because of their *containers* (showcasing the latest architecture in its most rational or delirious guises): "One must look to our modern exposition palaces," wrote the architect Paul Planat, "in order to see original work that is truly new and without example in the past."[28] For the first time, the new took on a pride of place—a place that lent itself to exposition; at the same time an exposure of place collaborated to promote novelty itself as a visible universal value.

The physical or athletic investment of the visitor to the salon or the exposition, or that of the flâneur of boulevards or arcades, certainly seems, at first glance, less than that of the Romantic tourist–antiquary who bumped along in coaches, scaled belvederes, and slept under the stars. Although they traveled from the provinces at great expense, Mr. Fenouillard's family's visit to the Exposition of 1889 could not be compared to the journeys of Nerval, Chateaubriand, or Lamartine along the roads of the Near East. Like the *Grand Larousse* and *L'Illustration*, the exposition called itself universal because it brought the entire universe within the grasp of its visitor. The Exposition of 1900 would even carry visitors on a moving sidewalk through its marvels or install them comfortably in front of enormous, moving *panoramas*. By reproducing novelties at an ever accelerating pace, industry and fashion furnished them with spectacles in a far more continuous fashion than did history or national landmarks. The store and the magazine replaced history and the historian just as the catalogue of the exhibit replaced the personal recollections of its visitor. As we will see later on, this development contains elements of a universal crisis of connection to the real.

Certainly the plenitude of the store is more quantitative and quantifiable than the historical and symbolic fullness of the monument visited

[27] *Three Babylons* is the title of a trilogy sketched out in 1864 by Chevalier and Labourdieu. In the trilogy of novels, *Trois Villes*, by Zola (*Lourdes, Rome, Paris*), Lourdes and Rome only serve as dialectical moments in the evolution that would lead to Paris.
[28] Quoted by Mignot, *L'Architecture au XIXème siècle*, 12. On universal expositions see Adolphe Démy, *Essai historique sur les expositions universelles de Paris* (Paris: A. Picard, 1907); John Allwood, *The Great Exhibitions* (London: Studio Vista, 1977); Pascal Ory, *Les Expositions universelles de Paris* (Paris: Ramsay, 1982). On the catalogue, see *Le Livre des expositions universelles, 1851–1989* (Paris: Union Centrale des Arts Decoratifs, 1983); Patricia Mainardi, *Art and Politics of the Second Empire: The Universal Expositions of 1855 and 1867* (New Haven, Conn.: Yale University Press, 1987).

by the Romantic traveler, a fullness achieved by narratives, cultural
memories, or allegories. The store is a result of the rational organization
of customer traffic and space to ends that are at once utilitarian and
pedagogical given that its organization is often encyclopedic, didactic,
even seductive. Accommodating quantity rather than quality, the bourgeois store can be seen—as Baudelaire saw it in his review of the Museum of the Bonne-Nouvelle Bazar and the Salon—as realizing the
democratic dream of making the world accessible to the multitude by
replacing the traditional aristocratic itinerary that obtained between the
antiquary and his ruin. In his *Salon de 1846*, Baudelaire writes:
"Bourgeois—be you king, legislator, or merchant—you have established Collections, Museums and Galeries. Some of these, which sixteen
years ago were only open to greedy buyers, have now enlarged their
doors to accommodate the multitude." The store and the exposition
belong more to the world of balance sheets, inventories or summaries
than to that of lyrical effusion; their policy can be summed up as one
which hopes to: "pile up in a small space the productions of all climates,
the monuments of all centuries, . . . one might say, to shut in the universe."[29] The dream of the late eighteenth-century landscape architects
such as the Marquis de Girardin, or landscape writers such as Delille
who shared the taxonomical spirit of so many of the encyclopedists,
herbalists, and entomologists of the Enlightenment, foreshadowed the
expositionitis of the more industrial century to come. The universal
expositions, wrote Huysmans in his review of the Salon of 1881, "en-
velop entire worlds in their immense aerian vessels." The landscape
architect of Poe's "The Domain of Arnheim" also hoped to concentrate
in one location "the most direct and energetic effects of Nature at
physical loveliness," in order to make "its adaptation to the eyes which
were to behold it on earth." And Sir Joseph Paxton, the architect of the
celebrated Crystal Palace of the 1855 London Exposition, was originally a gardener whose specialty was designing hothouses.

Of course, there are expositions and there are expositions. Throughout the nineteenth century, each served a variety of economic, aesthetic
and political purposes which can be detailed by the historian. Certainly,
all these expositions were, for various reasons, "vital"[30] and diverse:

[29] *Claquemurer, pour ainsi dire, tout l'univers; la mise en exposition* (Paris: Centre
Georges Pompidou, 1986). The sentence in the title of this work is borrowed from the
Marquis de Girardin, *De la composition des jardins* (n.p. 1777).
[30] "Showing is the vital issue," wrote Zola of Manet and his 1867 exhibition (also the
year of one of the universal expositions and Lacroix's *Paris-Guide*, prefaced by the exiled
Hugo.

The phalansterian, rational, imperial exposition of Frédéric Le Play in 1867 had nothing to do with the very republican one that followed in 1889, nor with the Parisian Disneyland of 1900. Yet all these expositions had something in common; unlike the Romantic journey that was dominated by melancholic retrospection and meditation on lost civilizations, these expositions marveled at the new in all its guises.[31] Because staging the marvels also demanded certain skills, all these expositions involved the organization of pedestrian traffic, the mastery of lighting, and the display of certain juxtaposed objects (or of certain people and social classes in the case of the boulevard) that would grant them a certain value. In other words, expositions offered a world whose conception was as coherent as a balance sheet, or as a series of aisles, departments, or compartments, a world where objects could be mastered by their labels, and individuals controlled by rituals and manners. One of the most frequent scenes in the Parisian novel of manners is the obligatory stroll in the Bois de Boulogne, to take in the ever-changing display of fashion.[32] A panoptic and democratic obsession with transparency, display, openness, lighting, and free-flowing traffic (i.e., everyone can see everyone else) was thus established. Its disquieting double and logical reverse would be the prison architecture described by Foucault (i.e., one person can see those who can in turn see nothing).[33] Paxton's Crystal Palace exercised a fascination long after the 1855 Exposition for it provided an absolute model that would offer to aesthetic reflection in general and to literature in particular their most frequently recurring extended metaphors as well as the buildings most commonly described

[31] The word "wonder" (merveille) is a key word for a study of nineteenth-century titles, a word that recalls the famous list of "the seven architectural wonders of the world." See La Bibliothèque des merveilles (Merveilles de l'architecture, Merveilles de la photographie, Merveilles du monde invisible, among others) published by Hachette as well as the innumerable thick, copiously illustrated volumes entitled Merveilles de l'exposition, that flourished in bookstores after each Universal Exposition. The key word for the epideictic genre, it is also linked to the rhetorical figure of preterition, in which the exposition allegedly discourages presentation: the almanac of the periodical Illustration from 1856, which summarizes the Universal Exposition of 1855, writes: "To enumerate all the wonders enclosed in the Palace of Industry would be too long a task." Verne's work contains many examples of preterition.

[32] See, for example, in the opening scene of La Curée, the description of the carriages returning from the Bois: "Silent glances were exchanged from window to window. . . . All of Paris was there." The obligatory scene, whose model remains, for Zola as for others, the ambulatory descriptions of Paris in Flaubert's Education sentimentale.

[33] Fourier's phalanstery (see his blueprint in Considérant's Considérations sociales), entirely based upon the right exposures and the right circulation of fluids, people, and objects, has no less than a "Tower of Order" in its center where a telegraph, a lookout, a clock, a carillon, an observatory, and a pigeon coop serve to communicate with the outside world.

within their pages: conservatories, prisms, panopticons, shop windows, arcades, glass canopies, and various glass walls and roofs.[34] Camille Pissaro painted the Crystal Palace in Sydenham in 1871; Zola photographed it during his brief exile in England; Verlaine admired it,[35] and numerous stores, both in Paris and elsewhere, adopted it as their logo. The new iron-and-glass architecture practically became a moral style, for it expressed honesty in exhibiting without so much as dissimulating the framework of the building. A spectacle in and of itself, such architecture at the same time organized the free circulation of gazes and bodies, as in Zola's description of the department store in *Au Bonheur des dames*:

> The courtyards had been glazed and turned into halls, iron staircases rose from the ground floor, iron bridges were thrown from one end to the other on the two storeys. The architect, who happened to be a young man of talent, with modern ideas, had only used stone for the underground floor and the corner pillars. . . . Space had been gained everywhere, air and light entered freely, and the public circulated with the greatest ease, under the bold flights of the far-stretching girders. . . . And all this iron formed, beneath the white light of the windows, an excessively light architecture, a complicated lace-work through which the daylight penetrated, the modern realization of the dream palace, a Babel-like heaping up of the storeys, enlarging the rooms, opening up glimpses onto other floors and into other rooms without end. In fact, iron reigned everywhere, the young architect had had the hon-

[34] The conservatory, freed of the constraints of geography and seasons, encyclopedically domesticates "vegetal irregularity" (Baudelaire). The fashion for conservatories spread throughout the middle of the nineteenth century, often appearing in literary texts. Eugène Sue, in *Les Mystères de Paris* describes at length a winter garden—conservatory where a brilliant reception is held. Balzac, in *La Fausse Maîtresse*, describes a conservatory belonging to the Comtesse Laginska, with "fantastic constructions" like an "immense garden in which the air is laden with perfumes, where one walks in the winter as though it were burning summer. The means of which one may compose an atmosphere as one pleases, the Tropics, China, or Italy are skillfully plundered in its view" (*La Comédie humaine*, vol. 2 [Paris: Bibliothèque de la Pléiade, 1983]), 201–202. The conservatory is always rather like the acclimatization of a utopia in private architecture; the most famous is undoubtedly Saccard's conservatory in *La Curée* (Georg Kolmaier and Barna Von Sartory, *Houses of Glass, A Nineteenth-Century Type*, trans. John Harvey [Cambridge, Mass.: MIT Press, 1986]).

[35] See Paul Verlaine's account in "La Décoration et l'art industriel à l'Exposition de 1889," a brief article that appeared in *L'Artiste* in 1890:

> In the entire history of almost a half-century of international universal expositions there has yet to be one worthy of this redundant title. There are two exceptions that are complete successes: Sydenham's Crystal Palace, which is imposing, light, white, and blue against the pale sky, like a Shakespearian castle enchanted in an apotheosis of fresh greenery and gracious hills; and the *tubalcainesque* Gallery of Machines from our [Universal Exposition of] 1889.

esty and courage not to disguise it under a layer of whitewash that imitated stone or wood.[36,h]

For writers like Zola, this architecture embodied the very notion of what the modern work of art should be. Characterized at once by honesty and clarity, yet possessing a certain fluidity or legibility that permits movement (perhaps of information), this artwork would function as the "fantasmagoria" (in Benjamin's sense of the word) of a society that is itself ideal. Having become purely aesthetic, given over to the euphoric exercise of the gaze—as it looks at and through a world increasingly made up of store displays, telescopes, dioramas, portholes, the doors of train compartments, or simply windows—this ideal society now perceives its surroundings as a series of juxtaposed spectacles or a collection susceptible to comfortable visual inspection.

Huysmans, in his article on the Salon of 1879, described the architecture of the expositions as "enveloping in its wide frame the superb grandeur of machines, or sheltering with its enormous vessels aerial and light as tulle, the prodigious swell of buyers or the ecstatic circus crowds." The narrator of Rimbaud's *Illuminations,* "a temporary and not-too-discontented citizen of a metropolis obviously modern" ("Ville"), strolls along "crystal boulevards . . . City!" ("Métropolitain"), visits palaces with "an artistic framework of steel about 15,000 feet in diameter" ("Villes II"), "visits painting exhibits in rooms twenty times larger than Hampton Court" (Villes II), and makes his way through "chalets of crystal" or "great glass houses" (Après le Déluge).[i] "Will you take me to see the stores in the beautiful arcades?" Rigolette asks Rodolphe in *Les Mystères de Paris* (1842). Numerous characters in Zola's works seem to be thus transformed into human cameras enraptured by the permanent euphoria that comes from living in their city. Renée and Maxime, the incestuous lovers of *La Curée* are good examples:

> They were in love with the new Paris. They often drove through the city by carriage, making detours in order to pass certain boulevards that they loved with personal affection. The tall houses with great sculpted doors, their heavy balconies, where in gold letters names, signs, and names of firms

[36] Zola, *Les Rougon Macquart,* vol. 3, 612, 626. The architect, who, "by a happy coincidence," is "intellegent," should be compared to Flaubert's architect in the *Dictionnaire des idées reçues*: "All of them are imbeciles, they always forget to build stairways in houses."

[h] Emile Zola, *The Ladies' Paradise* (Berkeley, Los Angeles, Oxford: University of California Press, 1992), 207–208, 221.

[i] Arthur Rimbaud, *Illuminations,* trans. Wallace Fowlie (New York: Greenwood Press, 1953).

delighted them. As the brougham sped along they followed with a friendly eye, the grey bands of the wide, unending pavements with their benches, their variegated columns, their spindly trees. This bright gap, which ran to the limit of the horizon, growing narrower and opening onto a pale blue square of empty space, this uninterrupted double row of department stores where the clerks smiled at their customers, this flow of the crowd trampling and buzzing gradually filled them with an absolute contentment with the life of the streets. . . . Each boulevard became a corridor of their townhouse.[j]

In Zola, the conservatory of *La Curée* and the shop windows of *Au Bonheur des dames* correspond to doors and windows left ajar in *Pot-Bouille*, the glass canopies of train stations in *La Bête humaine*, the stained-glass windows of *Le Rêve*, Les Halles in *Le Ventre de Paris*, and Hélène's belvedere in *Une Page d'amour*. Elsewhere, in the Nautilus of Verne's *Vingt milles lieues sous les mers*, Professor Aronnax, Ned Land, and Conseil discover wonder upon wonder in the display cases of Nemo's museum, where shells and marine animals are arranged and labeled. Here an ideal kind of reading of the underwater world can be practiced "in vitro."

> In elegant display cases fastened by copper rivets were classified and labeled the most precious products of the sea that had ever been presented to the gaze of the naturalist. My delight as a professor may well be imagined. . . . It was simply impossible to estimate the value of this collection which, for lack of time I could not possibly describe in its totality.[k]

These display cases are arranged in the middle of a museum of paintings whose exhibition space adjoins a magnificent library while opening onto the underwater world through two crystal portholes. As in any genuine visit to an exposition, a cicerone, here played by Captain Nemo, is on hand to dispense information. "The Captain spread out a sketch that gave the blueprint, the cross section, and the elevation of the Nautilus. And then he began his description in these terms."[l] Here Verne's text anticipates the aquariums, marinoramas, and dioramas of the Paris Universal Exposition of 1900. Furthermore, he delegates to his three spectator-heros, each stationed at a porthole, the three cardinal functions that the epideictic genre traditionally attaches to any descriptive discourse: naming, classifying, and giving thanks: "We kept exclaiming as

[j] Emile Zola, *La Curée*, trans. Alexander Teixeira de Matteo (New York: Boni and Liveright, 1924), 204.
[k] Jules Verne, *Twenty Thousand Leagues Under the Sea*, trans. Walter James Miller (New York: Washington Square Press, 1965), 82ff., translation modified.
[l] Ibid.

our imagination was challenged again and again. Ned identified the fishes by name, Conseil classified them, and I was ecstatic over their vivacious movements and beautiful forms."[m] The ruin, a fetish of the Romantic traveler, offers itself to ideal observation "in vitro," through the lens of the diving suit and crystal-clear water. In *Vingt milles lieues sous les mers,* these ruins are the underwater remains of Atlantis, with its "remnants of a gigantic aquaduct," its "vestiges of docks," its "floating Parthenon-like outlines," its "temples," its "arches," its "acropolis," its "long lines of crumbling walls"—"an entire underwater Pompei brought to life by the Captain before my very eyes!"[37] The Nautilus, like any other of Verne's wheeled, flying, or floating machines, is nothing more than a vehicle for systematically exploring certain environments—in this case, the ocean. They allow characters to take inventory and to compound their gaze. Just like Paulina Barnett in Verne's *Le Pays des fourrures* (1872) who proclaims "one must see everything, or at least attempt to see everything," Aronnax wants "to have seen what no man has ever seen." Captain Nemo is presented as a man with a particularly keen sense of sight:

> One outstanding feature was his eyes, set a little far apart, which—I verified this later—could take in almost a quarter of the horizon at a single glance. This faculty gave him a range of vision far greater than Ned Land's. When he focused upon an object, his eyebrows met, his thick eyelids closed around so as to contract the range of his field of vision, and he looked as if he magnified the object. How he penetrated your very soul! How he pierced through those liquid sheets, so opaque to our eyes, as if he could read the depth of the seas![n]

Thus the dream of transparency goes hand in hand with the dream of transforming the world or the house into a collection, a museum, or a palace at a universal exposition. The hidden laws of this transformed

[37] See Verne, *Vingt Milles lieues sous les mers,* pt. 2, chap. 9. His description of the ruins of Atlantis, with the reference to Pompei and the presence of a nearby active volcano that Verne places underwater, constitutes a nice oxymoron (fire/water, nature/architecture, solid/liquid), a rhetorical figure whose complicity with a certain type of poetics has already been noted. These ruins will reappear above ground, after a widespread cataclysm, in another one of Verne's texts written toward the end of his life: *L'Eternel Adam* reissued in *Hier et demain* (Paris: Livre de Poche, 1967), 255. At the end of *Une Page d'amour,* a novel in which Zola wanted to both demonstrate the descriptive practice of naturalist writing and prove that such writing could master the subtleties of feminine psychology, Zola ends a series of its descriptions of Paris with a panoramic description of the city during winter, a "frozen" city, almost crystalized and petrified; it is readable in the in vitro sense.

[m] Ibid., 98.

[n] Ibid., 102.

world must be plumbed and deciphered quadrant by quadrant until its fullness and order are finally revealed.[38]

One encounters the same cluster of leitmotifs and images involving visual inspection, transparency, collection, and glass houses, in the critical discourse about literature. The novelist Pierre Sandoz in Zola's *L'Oeuvre* (1866) dreams of composing novels that would contain "life in its totality, universal life, that extends from one end of the animal kingdom to the other." In the same novel, Claude Lantier, a painter, exclaims: "Ah! To see everything and to paint everything!" In Zola's critical texts, when speaking of his novels or of novels in general, he alternates between the metaphor of the "glass house," the "crystal clear sentence," or the "screen." In a chapter devoted to Stendhal in *Romanciers naturalistes,* Zola writes of Stendhal's desire for "simple composition and clear language, something like a glass house which allows one to see the ideas within it."[39] Elsewhere, in his address "A la jeunesse" he returns to this extended metaphor which seems to be borrowed from discourse on the work of Paxton and Horeau. Zola proclaims: "I want crystal-clear sentences so clear and simple that the ingenuous eyes of a child could penetrate them, delight in them, and remember them. I want ideas so true and bare, that they themselves appear to be transparent as well as solid, like diamonds in the crystal of the sentence."[40] From this it is a small step to the metaphor of the *screen* which is taken up from Alberti, and which Henry James will also use in

[38] According to Roland Barthes, the Verne of *Vingt mille lieues sous les mers* had

an obsession with plenitude: he never stopped putting a last touch to the world and furnishing it, making it full, with an egg-like fullness. His tendency is exactly that of an eighteenth-century encyclopedist or of a Dutch painter: the world is finite, the world is full of numerable and contiguous objects. The artist can have no other task than to make catalogues, inventories, and to watch out for small, unfilled corners in order to conjure up there in close ranks, the creations and instruments of man. (*Mythologies,* trans. Annette Lavers [New York: Noonday Press, 1972], 65)

[39] To cite Zola again: "Criticism exposes, it does not teach" (*Oeuvres complètes,* vol. 2 [Paris: Cercle du Livre Precieux, 1968], 92). "I do not judge, I expose facts" (vol. 14, 543). Régine Robin showed in her work *Le Réalisme socialiste, une esthétique impossible* (Paris: Payot, 1986) the persistence of the metaphors and themes of the glass house of transparency, and the image and theme of the Crystal Palace in the Soviet Union of the 1920s and 1930s which occurred at the same time that the notion of social realism was evolving. This is notable in the ideal city in the dreams of the character in Nicolai Chernychevskii's novel *Chto delat?* On these metaphors and the philosophical postures for which they are vehicles, see Jacques Catteau, "Du Palais de cristal à l'age d'or ou les avatars de l'utopie," *Dostoevsky Cahiers de L'Herne,* 197, and Marshall Berman, *All That is Solid Melts into Air* (New York: Simon and Schuster, 1982), 235ff.

[40] Zola, *Oeuvres complètes,* vol. 14, 725. The same metaphor of the glass house is found in Louis Reybaud's novel *Ce qu'on peut voir dans une rue* (1858).

his preface to *Portrait of a Lady*. In an oft-cited letter to his childhood
friend Anthony Valabrègue, Zola writes:

> Every work of art is like a window open onto creation. . . . In a work,
> creation is made visible through a man, his temperament, or his personality.
> The image produced on this new type of screen is a reproduction of the
> people and things placed beyond the screen. This reproduction, which can
> never be completely faithful, will in turn change every time a new screen
> interposes itself between our eye and creation. In a like fashion, colored glass
> alters the color of objects seen through it. . . . If the window were totally
> unobstructed, the objects placed beyond it would appear in their reality, but
> the window is not and could never be unobstructed. . . . The artist places
> himself in direct contact with creation, he sees according to his own lights.
> He allows himself to be penetrated by it and he reflects the luminous rays in
> our direction, after having refracted and colored them like a prism in accor-
> dance with his own nature. . . .

Zola pursues this train of thought by drawing up a typology of screens,
which include the "classical" screen and the "Romantic" screen. He
concludes: "The realist screen is a simple window pane—very thin and
clear—which claims to be so perfectly transparent that images cross
through it and are subsequently reproduced in all their reality."[41] Zola's
window is therefore the exact opposite of the colored pane of glass
demanded by the "hysterical" narrator of Baudelaire's prose poem,
"The Bad Glazier":

> What? Have you no colored panes? No pink panes, no red, no blue, no
> magic panes, no panes of paradise? You are shameless! You dare walk
> through poor neighborhoods and you don't even have panes which render
> life beautiful?[o]

Similarly Verlaine, that sly architect of irregular meters, considered that
traditional alexandrines should be reserved only "for limpid speculation, . . . clear statements, . . . and the rational exposition of objects,
invectives, or landscapes."

These period metaphors involving the pane of glass or the window can
also be found in Barbey d'Aurevilly, Mallarmé, and elsewhere in Baudelaire. These metaphors suggest either a way of framing a particular aspect
of the real in order to domesticate it, intensify it, or single it out, or a more
or less translucent window on the real. A scene from Champfleury's *Sen-
sation de Josquin* describes a bunch of bourgeois tourists who stupidly

[41] Zola, *Oeuvres complètes*, vol. 14, 1,309ff.
[o] Charles Baudelaire, *The Paris Prowler*, trans. Edward Kaplan (Athens: University of
Georgia Press, 1989), 15.

insist upon looking at nature through a window's multicolored panes of glass, while their servant, a simple and common woman, gazes at the world directly, "through her own eyes." We know that at one time Flaubert had planned to introduce an identical colored-glass scene in *Madame Bovary*. Furthermore, mention of stained-glass windows in private architecture appeared any time a writer wanted to underscore the foolish and faddish petty bourgeois fancy for kitsch and eye-catching objects in general. Thus, Flaubert includes a "Gothic cloister with stained-glass windows" in his description of the eclectic Alhambra in *Education sentimentale*, while in *Bouvard et Pécuchet* his heros dig up a Gothic stained-glass window, and insert it into the casement of their window, so that "the steeple of Chavignolles could now be seen in the distance, producing a splendid effect." Huysmans, in *Là-bas*, writes that the style of naturalist writers was "like badly colored glass," while in Courteline's *La Paix chez soi* "a lantern of colored glass and fake wrought iron" prompts a domestic squabble between the writer of serial novels and his wife.

The metaphor of the screen at once complements and extends the various metaphors involving the glass house, the display case, or the camera lucida—be it a room or an exhibition hall—all of which serve to expose and organize the real. The metaphor of the screen is related to all of these, in that it derives from the camera obscura associated with photography, for it is on a frosted glass screen that the photographer, his head hidden beneath a piece of black serge, studies the image of the real world which is to be reproduced—an image that he must focus on before introducing the glass plate to be exposed. All the technical vocabulary of photography (plates, exposures, developers, cameras, poses, lighting, transparencies, screens, rays, lenses) would furnish the discourse of literary criticism as well as the discourse of fiction with an array of distinctive objects, themes, structures, and metaphors related both to the optical and the architectural.[42] I will return to this point in the next chapter.

---

[42] Curiously enough, in his definition of the word *exposition* Pierre Larousse does not mention its technical or photographic meaning. An example of the use of this metaphor in discourse is seen in this excerpt from an interview with Daudet by Jules Huret in 1895 where Daudet speaks of his first impression upon arriving in London: "The strongest and most powerful impression I had upon arriving here was one received without analysis in the *camera obscura* of my brain, like a ray of light that has hit a photographic plate and never erases" (Huret, *Interview de littérature et d'art* [Paris: Thot, 1984], 127). It is no coincidence that Zola towards the end of his life became an excellent amateur photographer. See François-Emile Zola and Massin, *Zola Photographe* (Paris: Denöel, 1979) for the description of his studio with the sitters' room, windows, and glass roof exposed with care, his sunny terrace where plates are exposed, his darkroom, and the photographer's tools. See also *A History and Handbook of Photography*, trans. J. Thomson (New York: Scovill Manufacturing, 1877).

The Romantic traveler had a particular affinity for visiting monuments at night. Hugo upon visiting Geneva wrote that: "The moon
camouflages the foolishness of architects." These "shadow zones" or
sfumato (as Stendhal would say) that plunged objects into real or
semantic darkness served to highlight the feats of memory and the
author's cultural prowess at interpreting signs, signals, and inscriptions. But Zola's project of "seeing all and telling all" (or Viollet-le-
Duc's dictum that "seeing is knowing") could no longer accommodate
this kind of obscurity: given the development of the historical and
social sciences toward the end of the nineteenth century, the aim was
now to arrive at a total elucidation of the real. The whole world was
now a crystal palace. Traditional "cabinets de merveilles" (or curiosity
shops—ancestors of modern universal expositions) as well as traditional notions of sublimity were based on the assumption that natural
phenomena were anarchic, nocturnal, amorphous, monstrous, and indescribable. These phenomena—at least in the eyes of the most optimistic supporters of an exposition mentality—came to be perceived as
suceptible to the control of a museum mentality, a logic of techniques,
dictionaries, frames, tableaux, descriptive systems, or rhetorical processes in general. This type of reasoning constructs texts as if they were
exposition architecture while at the same time conceiving architecture
as if it were a spectacle or text through which one moved: as in the
case of boulevards, galleries of machines, stores, panoramas, arcades,
or museums.[43] Eclecticism and exposition—which juxtapose and set
off objects or spectacles, create discontinuities, and organize differentiated moments along the exhibition's various pathways—would replace
the traditional sublime, which involves the (ef)fusion of spectator and
spectacle—the spectator's possession by the spectacle. Even the sea, an
extreme example of nonarchitecture, is mastered either through work
and technology, as in Hugo's *Les Travailleurs de la mer*, Verne's Nautilus, or, by museums and their catalogues. Thus, in Michelet's *La Mer*,
the author demands that museums be established that would "display"
and "fully exhibit" all sea monsters. He also congratulates the nineteenth century ("a great century, a titanic century, the nineteenth cen-

[43] Larousse in its first dictionary's supplement's entry for *exposition* speaks of universal expositions with several separate pavilions and exhibition sites as being "expositions
in several volumes." When speaking of Jean-Martin Charcot's La Salpétrière, it compares
the hospital to an optical machine and a "pathological museum" for classifying a thousand aberrations of normalcy through photographs, plaster casts, its staging of the spectacle, and the exposition of "case studies" (Georges Didi-Huberman, *L'Invention de
l'hystérie: Charcot et l'iconographie photographique et La Salpétrière* [Paris: Macula,
1982]).

tury") for managing to write the book of the indescribable, "the encyclopedia of storms at sea"—the storm being the "sublime" spectacle
par excellence. Monsters would be henceforth tamed by the well-lit
display case; there is no longer any shadow area or any night. After
the play of the sun and moon on Romantic ruins, the harsh, uniform
light of modernity is ushered in. Gas lamps, in anticipation of electric-
ity, furnish the bourgeois salon—like the exhibition hall, the boulevard sidewalk, or the department store—with permanent footlights for
the display of worldly objects and manners. "The gas lamps in delirium, on ruddy walls" (Rimbaud, "L'Orgie parisienne, ou Paris se
repeuple"), gas lamps that "flame and swim" before "vermilion signs"
(Verlaine, "Sonnet boiteux") punctuate all the descriptions of the city
in the literature of the middle of the century.

The display case exhibited the product of industry as though it were a
spectacle. Like the houses described in literary texts, the ideal workplace
existed only on paper and tended to take the shape of a glass house or of
a "rotating" house, always regulating its own exposures. For the ideal
workplace, there was the phalanstery, in which the open gallery always
played an important role, where a network of pipes "circulated comfort."[44] In the case of the house, there was the home of the parvenu, the
typical residence of a character in transition between social classes, or
else there was the vacation home, evoked by various literary works,
where the problem of exposure proved equally crucial, embodying and
defining in all its different aspects this ideal of transparency.

Thus, Victor Fournel constructs a city of 1965 in his ironic and
polemical book of 1865, Paris nouveau et Paris futur. In this model,
exacerbated by Haussman's urban-renewal projects, the dreamt-of Paris
approaches an encyclopedic design both through its concentric traffic
and through the aisles that would also be adapted by the Exposition of
1867. Its panoptic design also recalls the phalansteries of Fourier:

> At its center stood a vast square one league in circumference from which
> there radiated, in every direction, fifty boulevards of equal beauty, like the

[44] Considérant, Considérations sociales, 45. See also Fourier: "The street galleries are
a means for internal communication which alone make the most beautiful palaces and
cities of civilization seem detestable. Whosoever will have seen the street galleries of the
phalanx, will from then on envisage the most beautiful palaces of civilization as places of
exile, as manors for idiots, who, after 3,000 years of architectural study, have yet to learn
how to house themselves in a healthy and comfortable way." Fourier, op. cit., 462–463.
A great debate on the proper exposure of the artist's workplace runs through the nineteenth century. The studio, according to academicians, should have northern exposure, or
for the impressionists, exposure in any direction. The studio is the place of excess, where
the artist exposes his paintings.

corridors of Mazas around its chapel. Each of these boulevards was fifty
meters wide, and was lined with buildings fifty meters high, with fifty windows on each facade. . . . Standing in this square, one could spin around and
take in all of Paris and its gates at a single glance. Its center was occupied by a
monumental, circular barracks, topped by a beacon—an immense and vigi-
lant eye—from which a strong flash of electric light reached over the city
each night. . . . Out-of-town visitors no longer needed guidebooks to find
their way around the city; all they needed to do was walk straight down the
boulevard upon leaving their hotel; in the evening, they would find themselves back where they started, having thoroughly inspected everything in the
first circle. . . . The next day, they would begin again with the next circle. . . .
We had attained the long-sought goal: to remake Paris into a luxury and
curiosity item; instead of a merely utilitarian object, it would become *a city
of exposition.*

In this urban design, the city itself becomes a book:

The fifty boulevards that radiated from the center to the circumference bore
the names of the fifty largest cities in France; their fifty gates corresponded to
the departments of which these towns were the capitals; . . . hence just as the
geography and history helped the visitor find his way around Paris, so a walk
in the city provided a lesson in history and geography. . . . Paris was a large,
synchronical and chronological mnemotechnical table.[45]

Fournel here concentrates, although in an ironic mode, all the themes,
metaphors, and structures of numerous philosophic, technical, or literary texts of the period, that express some reflection upon the ties between the legible and the visible, knowledge and seeing, and memory
and modernity. One can think of the aesthetic of the table or the mnemonic devices found in the pedagogical tours of France published by
Bruno and Hetzel—to which we will later return. In Charles Fourier's
ideal city—a city which he termed, at various points, "guarantist,"
"harmonian," or "of the sixth period"—"each street should lead toward a picturesque sight be it a public or personal monument, a mountain, bridge, or waterfall." For such a city, built for the euphoric practice of the gaze, Fourier invents the term "visuism," claiming that the
eye of the citizen of a harmonic group would evolve so as to possess full
peripheral vision.

Similarly, there was the more serious philosophic reverie which took
the phenomenon of the exposition as its subject and point of departure,
namely, Proudhon's project for a Permanent Exhibition. In response to

---

[45] Fournel, 234ff. The reference to Mazas (a prison) and to the barracks are both types
of collective habitats and terms that Zola will use in *L'Assommoir* for one of Gervaise's
dwellings.

the question of what might be done with the Palace of Industry following the Exposition of 1855, Proudhon provides a hyperbolic and quintes-
sential version of the themes of transparency and of display:

> [The 1855 Exposition] was merely an industrial joust undertaken from the
> sterile, theatrical vantage point of national vanity and commercial arro-
> gance. Once this temporary exposition is over, we must establish a Perma-
> nent Exposition. . . . Today's commerce as a rule establishes absolute secrecy
> in its operations. . . . The organizers of the Exposition will replace such
> excessive secrecy with complete openness. . . . The report of the annual and
> biannual Society must divulge everything and fully submit itself to public
> opinion. Everything must be displayed in plain view of the master, who is
> none other than the public itself.[46]

One might note in passing that this policy of telling all would later be
the program of realist and naturalist writing.

On the individual scale of the Parisian townhouse, the habitat of a
*homo novus,* such as Zola's parvenu Saccard in *La Curée,* offers a
showcase for the same themes and metaphors. Saccard's home is described as having a

> huge glass conservatory embedded in the very flank of the house and con-
> nected to the ground floor through the French windows of the drawing
> room. . . . [It was] a large construction, new and utterly pallid, . . . a small-
> scale version of the new Louvre. . . . Strollers in the park would stop and
> look. . . . Sheets of glass so wide and clear that they were like the windows of
> the new department stores were there to display its vast interior to those
> outside. Petits-bourgeois families gawked at the stunning riches: corners of
> the furniture, bits of upholstery, and patches of ceiling. The sight paralyzed
> them with admiration and envy, right in the middle of the pathways.[47]

Significantly, this "new" man's residence imitates Lefuel's new Louvre,
the object of harsh criticism at the time of its construction. The house
also mimics the novelty shop featured in Zola's *Au Bonheur des dames*
as well as the fresh produce stands of Les Halles in Zola's *Le Ventre de
Paris.* The profusion of fruits and vegetables in the latter novel is paral-

[46] *Théorie de la propriété suivie d'un nouveau plan de l'exposition perpétuelle: Oeuvres
complètes de Pierre Joseph Proudhon* (Paris: Flammarion, 1926), 251–252, 286. We can
compare Proudhon's title to Taine's character, Thomas Graindorge's phrase: "Paris . . . is a
kind of permanent exposition open to all of Europe" (283). The notion of transparency is as
we know, a political concept—in Russian it is *glasnost*—as well as a technically aesthetic or
linguistic concept (Régine Robin, "L'Obsession de la transparence," 191ff.).

[47] *Les Rougon-Macquart,* Bibliothèque de la Pléiade, vol. 1, 482. Louis Veuillot soon
afterwards describes in almost the same terms Lefuel's new Louvre in *Les Odeurs de
Paris:* "It has the look of enriched vulgarity, loaded with trinkets. . . . The Louvre is not
content in displaying ugliness, it also speaks nonsense."

leled by the small-scale gathering and display of every plant in the world in Saccard's conservatory. As evidenced by the wordplay of the inhabitants of the Vauquer boarding house in *Le Père Goriot*—in which the suffix *-rama* was added to any term introduced into the conversation— all of modern reality seemed predestined in the shape of panoramas and dioramas.

In this organization of a legible space that coincides with a visible space, display cases, partitions, or streets at once connect and separate classes of the real. Thus, the various characters from the working or middle class, high society or demimonde, like items on the writer's filecards, shape the exposition-text on all levels. Most notably, Zola's novels feature a careful montage of all the living spaces of his characters, who are governed by a very dense grid of lines of sight that tend to cover the whole of the novel's referent. Each character continually sees and meets everyone else from windows, connecting doors that are either open or ajar, in shadow play from behind screens or curtains, or from belvederes or garrets. Mademoiselle Saget, the spying gossip of *Le Ventre de Paris* who is the novelist's transparent double or stand-in (she knows everything about the characters who in turn know nothing about her) spends her time on the thresholds of stores, at the corners of intersections, or most often, at her upper-story window from where she can observe the living spaces of the other characters. For Mlle. Saget, as for all gossips—and the journalist or newsmonger is but a variant of her— Paris is a glass house:

> Before her . . . lay the square, the three faces of the houses, pierced by their windows into which she sought to penetrate her gaze; she seemed to grow taller and move along each story seeking visual footholds from each window until she reached the *oeil de boeuf* windows of the garret floors; she stared at the curtains, reconstructing a drama out of a simple appearance of a head between two shutters and ended up knowing the stories of the tenents in each of the houses, without having seen anything more than their facades.[p]

Because Zola's works impose a strict unity of place, the cast of characters tends to converge on a highly confined living space. Sometimes this space is vertical, with all the characters living on different floors of the same building (as in *Pot-Bouille*), or inhabiting the same huge barracks (as in *L'Assommoir*). Sometimes the space is horizontal, with the characters living at the four corners of the same intersection, and thus enabling

[p] Emile Zola, *Savage Paris*, trans. David Hughes and Marie-Jacqueline Mason (New York: Citadel Press, 1955), 221. Translation modified.

them to spy on each other (as in the case of *L'Assommoir,* which is set at the crossroads of the exterior boulevards and rue de la Poissonniere, or *Le Ventre de Paris,* at the corner of Pirouette and Rambuteau). The very term *carreau*—which in the case of the mine in *Germinal* applies to the bank where extracted materials are deposited and in the case of Les Halles in *Le Ventre de Paris* refers to the space where fruits and vegetables are displayed and sold—recalls the *carreau* of window panes, casements, or shop windows that stage the spectacle.

In such a world dedicated to general transparency, secrecy—one might venture to say narrative—has no place. Zola, on two occasions wrote mystery novels; the plot of *Le Ventre de Paris* hinged on the question: "Who is Florent?" just as *La Bête humaine* asked: "Who murdered Grandmorin on the train?" Yet Zola was unable to maintain the suspense for the reader who knew from the first page the identities of both Florent and Grandmorin's killer. It is as if Baltard's covered markets on the one hand and the glass architecture of the railway station on the other had exposed both novels to too harsh a light. Edgar Allen Poe, instead, would know how to make the excessive exposure of the hidden thing the province of efficient modern dissimulation. In "The Purloined Letter" for example, the police are baffled until Inspector Dupin's intervention, despite the various searches of premises and interrogations.

The ideal leisure home, the seaside vacation house, observes the same logic of the same metaphor of "seeing it all." This variation on the *locus amoenus* was already established by Pliny the Younger's description of his country house by the sea in his famous letter which, incidentally, was reproduced in 1852 in the very serious-minded *Moniteur des architectes.* The home described in the letter, with its curving portico, galleries, carefully regulated exposures, organized play of light, belvederes, and meticulously positioned windows was a veritable machine for analyzing both time and space. This logical tool for understanding land and sea, leisure and work, air and ground, can be related in its logical functions to the house whose carefully regulated exposures Michelet describes in *La Mer:*

> Oh to be able to build the house of the future. . . . It must not be shaded from the sun, rather it must gather up the sun like a precious object. Let's set aside ridiculous playthings such as imitation chapels and Gothic churches, which make for impractical lodgings. The side of the house which faces land must be perfectly sheltered, and one must be able to forget the commotion of the sea, in order to find peace. To address these . . . needs I would choose the form least susceptible to wind: the semicircle or crescent. The convex part

would allow for a diverse panorama on the sea and would afford a view of the sun moving from window to window while receiving its light at all times. . . . There would also be a crescent-shaped gallery for use during bad weather . . . with flowers, an aviary, and a small, seawater pool in which [the woman of the house] could store those small curiosities that fishermen would give her to take home.[48]

This ideal panoramic house, a model of universal exposition in that its exposures open out onto the universe, acts as a shifter for a series of binary oppositions: sea/land, open/closed, good weather/bad weather, inside/outside, concave/convex, leisure/work (in this passage, the latter is represented by the fisherman). Furthermore it realizes the dream of total acclimatization—which Michelet foresees as the science to be invented by the nineteenth century—not to mention miniaturization illustrated by the aviary and the saltwater pool where marine samples gathered from the neighboring sea would be collected. In his poem "Promontoire," Rimbaud would in a sense rewrite the ideal belvedere, by creating a seaside site composed of a "villa and its outbuildings," "tremendous views of modern coastal defenses," "outside launderies surrounded German poplars," and "circular facades of the 'Royals' or 'Grands' of Scarborough or Brooklyn" with "windows and terraces full of lights."[q]

Of course the body, which inhabits protective envelopes such as skin or clothing, did not escape this logic of transparency and exposition, which is in turn legitimized by the discourse on hygiene and medicine as well as the obsession with comfort, a criterion that signals the satisfactory acclimatization of the inhabitant to his habitat. Hygiene and comfort (both terms appear frequently in Rimbaud's poetry) can both be reduced to nothing more than the regulation and control of exposure to natural agents such as air, sun, wind, and seasons on the one hand and, on the other, to optical instruments of science (microscopes) and their accompanying elucidating theories such as physiology, physiognomy,

[48] Michelet, La Mer, pt. 4, chap. 3. Michelet's panoptic dream of a crescent-shaped house materialized, toward the middle of the century, not only in the fashionable bow-window, which like the arcade brings the interior outside, but also the American architect Fowler's plans for "octagonal houses for all." Note that Michelet's house was expressly designed for a woman on vacation with her children. The man is working in the big city ("someone works back there for them"). We can also note the 6 December 1874 La Dernière Mode with Mallarmé's sensational decoration tip, which was a part-nautilus porthole, part universal exposition "marinorama" and part seaside house. The "aquarium wall," "an extraordinary magic panel . . . that can be placed above a credenza's top shelf" and the sunk "into the depths of either a common wall of adjoining rooms or with an outside garden or courtyard" (Stéphane Mallarmé, Oeuvres complètes [Paris: Bibliothèque de la Pléiade], 821).

[q] Rimbaud, Illuminations, 207.

psychology, and theories of heredity that underlie much of the literary discourse of the nineteenth-century. Once again in *La Mer* Michelet gives a modern heliotropic and hygienic twist to the ancient idea of "exposing a child": "A child must be lightly dressed so as to always be in contact with fresh air. Air and water, nothing more." He also suggests that city dwellers acquire suntans:

> This rich color should not be considered an illness of the epidermis, rather it manifests the skin's healthy and deep saturation of sun and life. I have a wise doctor friend who used to send pale Parisian and Lyonnais clients to bask in the sun. He himself used to expose himself to the sun by lying on a rock for hours on end.

For the person immersed in nature, the tan is the equivalent to the patina left on edifices immersed in history. The importance of patina for Ruskin in particular and for antiquarians in general is well known; if they protest against the excessive restoration of monuments, it is because the patina constitutes the mark of truth.[49]

Exposure to natural agents is carefully specified in Professor Sarrasin's ideal city, France-Ville, in Verne's *Cinq cents millions de la Bégum*. The city is located

> near a mountain range that blocks the winds from the north, south, and east, leaving only the Pacific breeze to cleanse the surrounding atmosphere, . . . and situated [at the mouth] of a small river whose fresh, sweet, and limpid water, oxygenated by repeated rainfall and the rapidity of its flow, arrives perfectly pure to the sea.

Here, we have a collective variation on Michelet's seaside house: Michelet's crescent-shaped house whose convex side is exposed to the sea complements the crescent formed by the protecting mountains around the city, whose concave side is exposed to the sea. The dream of miniaturization (and therefore of control over the world) that is found in Michelet's *La Mer* corresponds to the abundance of mines and quarries of all sorts near Verne's city, just as both works share a vision of the

---

[49] Invoked by urban planners as well as architects of private dwellings, doctors, even by moralists, *hygiene* is one of the key words from the middle of the century. For but one sample out of a thousand of the hygienist discourse on the house and the city, see Jean-Baptiste Fonssagrives, *La Maison: étude d'hygène et de bien-être domestique* (Paris: Delagrave, 1873). See also *Le Magasin pittoresque, 1870–1871*, vol. 1, p. 102. Promiscuity, hygiene's greatest foe, was staged in literature by Zola in Gervaise's various dwellings in *L'Assommoir* and in the mining cottage in *Germinal*. On the importance of exposure to sun and on hygiene in nineteenth-century urbanist treatises, see Guy Ballange, "Phoebus embourgeoisé: les règles de l'ensoleilement de Von Camerloher" and Georges Ribeill, "Une Machination urbaine: les Aérodromes de Borie," in *Amphion* 1, 1987.

alliance of opposites (as in Verne's "oxygenated water"). Even the brick houses of France-Ville (as opposed to the compact stone of ancient monuments) permit the salutary ventilation of the interior of the walls and partitions, since they are pierced through with openings. Aside from the "total freedom allowed architects in matters of ornamentation . . . no house will be taller than two storys high, since air and light must not be monopolized by some to the detriment of others." Interestingly, the beneficial exposure of the site is accompanied by exposure to the beneficial laws of the city. Moreover, these two types of exposure can be read as metaphors for the "glass-house" style of writing, as well as for the salutary pedagogic communication of which the author dreams: "Upon arrival, each citizen receives a small brochure, where the most important principles for a life based on science [hygiene] are *exposed in simple and clear language.*"[50]

Such ideal sites, cities, or houses are not confined to the specialized discourse of science fiction, philosophical essays, nor architectural theory. The components of an "exposition mentality" (as opposed to Hugo's "church-portal mentality" in *Notre-Dame de Paris*) can also be found in literary texts. Sometimes exposition mentality is seen on a small scale in a character's momentary action, posture, pose, or pause; it can also be encountered at the level of a room or window some character or other will traverse. But as always, architecture remains the locus, the means, the metaphoric vehicle or pretext for organizing the world's itineraries, spectacles, scenes, classifications, and regulations.

Proust's work features many examples of aquarium-like dwellings and ambiguous belvederes. He created complex sites whose exposures are both contradictory and borderline by juxtaposing water and land, night/day, and private/public. He achieved these effects by making numerous comparisons to the exposition and by "mounting" several exhibition scenes. For example, his preface to Ruskin's *Sesame and Lilies* compares San Marco in Venice to an "exposition palace"; Bergotte's famous death-scene takes place at an exhibit of Dutch paintings while admiring "a little patch of yellow wall" in Jan Vermeer's *View of Delft.*

---

[50] Emphasis mine. The entire description of France-Ville, which acts as an antithesis of the other ideal city of the novel—Schultze's prismlike and obscure Stahlstadt—is haunted by an obsession with miasmas: "The principle task of the central government is to clean, to clean unceasingly, to destroy and annihilate as soon as they form the miasmas that constantly emanate from an urban agglomeration." Miasmas escape upon exposure to the atmosphere; they are the unseen, invisible agents produced by walls, and therefore the logical opposite of walls which allow visibility—the conservatory and the crystal palace.

The Guermantes's townhouse also brings to life images of a veritable painting exhibit in the narrator's mind:

> From the strange trigonometrical point at which I had positioned myself, . . .
> I watched from a little room, which had seemed to me to be a good lookout
> post, for the arrival of [the Guermantes's] carriage. . . . The extreme proxim-
> ity of the houses with their windows looking across at one another over a
> common courtyard makes each casement the frame in which a cook sits
> dreamingly gazing down at the ground below, or, further off, a girl is having
> her hair combed by an old woman with a witch-like face, barely distinguish-
> able in the shadow; thus each courtyard provides the neighbors in the adjoin-
> ing house, suppressing sound by its width and framing silent gestures in a
> series of rectangles placed under glass by the closing of the windows, with an
> *exhibition* of a hundred Dutch paintings hung in rows.[51]

We will see later on that this is an example of Proust's rewriting of a commonplace of lyrical exposition, which cuts across the literature of the entire century: The observer behind his window watching the ob-served behind her window. Elsewhere in Proust, the narrator's grand-mother's Balbec room transforms itself into a prism. The narrator's doctor has recommended that the boy not be exposed to "the blazing sun" while at the sea. Choosing to follow this advice regarding "hy-giene" he decides to accept invitations for excursions inland. While waiting, he goes to his grandmother's room, which he describes as an intermediary place between immobility and excursion. This site for as-sessing "different exposures" to different "sides" (*côtés*)—a key Proust-ian term if ever there was one—and for synthesizing space and redistrib-uting impressions, is described as a prism-like locus situated between single and multiple exposure.

> Hers did not look out directly on the sea as mine did, but was open on three
> of its four sides—onto a strip of the esplanade, a courtyard, and view of the
> country inland, . . . and at that hour when the sun's rays, drawn from differ-
> ent exposures, and, as it were, from different hours of the day, broke the
> angles of the wall, projected onto the chest of drawers side by side with a
> reflection of the beach a festal altar as variegated as a bank of field flow-
> ers, . . . warmed like a bath, a square of provincial carpet . . . this room in
> which I lingered for a moment before going to get ready for our drive
> suggested a prism in which the colors of the light that shone outside were
> broken up, a hive in which the sweet juices of the day, which I was about to
> taste, were distilled, scattered, intoxicating, and visible, a garden of hope
> which dissolved in a quivering haze of silver threads and rose petals.[52]

[51] Proust, *Remembrance*, vol. 2, 594–595. Emphasis mine.
[52] Ibid., vol. 1, 756–757. Let us note that coupled with the construction of an ambiva-lent belvedere architecture there is the reference, once again, to the other art of the body

This chamber functions like a camera's chamber by virtue of the metaphor in which the outside is imprinted as if it were fixed and reproduced inside the room on its lace and tapestries. Variations on this
theme are found not only in other rooms (notably Baldassare Sil-
vande's in *Les Plaisirs et les jours*) but in those objects or places of
exposure such as the "amphibian" sites represented by Elstir's sea-
scapes or the Duchess of Guermantes's opera box, which is described
as an "aquarium-theater" and a "cube of semi-darkness."[53] The mobile habitat of the train compartment is yet another variation on this; a
true trope or turn, it presents conflicting tableaux (sometimes diurnal,
sometimes nocturnal), responding to the random changes in exposure
that are provoked by the meandering route of the railway line—and
how can one avoid reading this line as a self-descriptive metaphor for
the Proustian sentence:

> the course of the line altering, the train turned, the morning scene gave place
> in the frame of the window to a nocturnal village . . . and I was lamenting the
> loss of my strip of pink sky when I caught sight of it anew, but red this time,
> in the opposite window which it left at a second bend in the line; so that I
> spent my time running from one window to the other to reassemble, to
> collect on a single canvas the intermittent antipodian fragments of my fine,
> scarlet, ever-changing morning, and to obtain a comprehensive view and a
> continuous picture of it.[54]

In such texts the inhabitant seems to take on the same characteristics as
the *camera lucida* of the habitat—a locus one looks out from, into, or
through—the person thereby becoming a *camera lucida*—a space for
recording and developing sensations. Or the inhabitant becomes a multi-
faceted prism with peripheral vision that apprehends the real in its
ongoing state of exposition. Even the most ethereal and evanescent
idealist–symbolist fin de siècle novels—novels that represent a stance
completely opposed to Verne's or the Goncourts's great novelistic store-
houses of human documents—novels that are at variance with Zola's
"crystal-clear sentences," or Proust's "cathedral opus," novels that generally eschew any systematic description of the modern city—even those
novels deployed in a landscape of windows, mirrors, gems, frozen lakes,

---

which is like the reversal of architecture, gastronomy. On Proust's fascination with transparent objects, see David Mendelson, *Le Verre et les objets de verre dans l'univers
imaginaire de Marcel Proust* (Paris: José Corti, 1968).
[53] Proust, *Remembrance*, vol. 2, 36.
[54] Ibid., vol. 1, 704.

and crystal, whose prismlike habitats refract the various abstract, disembodied stage settings of the Idea.[55]

As a result, there emerged a superabundance of the theatrical spaces and their accompanying forms of architecture designed for spectators who were themselves conditioned and multiplied by points of view created by industrialization: house windows, a train compartment's doors, or shop windows. The flâneur, immersed in a cosmopolitan city in perpetual architectural upheaval and perpetually on display, could lose himself in the profuse and discontinuous flow of trifling urban events and spectacles. Instead of the registered landmark, the monument, or building as the purpose for one's visit and as the object of the tourist's or Romantic traveler's reverie—with its obligatory tours and vantage points, its accompanying archaeological and historical discourse—architecture now became a *means*, a modern, urban reality in perpetual motion whose staging was continually being composed and decomposed. The prism (the title of a publication that accompanied the great anthology *Les Français peints par eux-mêmes*) or the kaleidoscope (the title of one of Verlaine's more beautiful poems about the city) are both good emblems of this conception of a world imagined as a juxtaposition of accessible visual images. This conception as we shall see can very well entail its unhappy opposite, which can have consequences for the status of the spectator—subject. By being ourselves, by living inside a prism, do we not risk decomposing, like light inside a prism?

Paris appeared as a city remodeled by and for spectacles. Its fashion-

---

[55] The apartments were those that Melancholy would choose if she ceased to be an ideal. No mantel pieces with painted cupids, no tapestries weaving a decor of hunters and horses, no frames entwining with golden snakes the mysterious attraction of portraits: only the images of virgin nature were abandoned there and art recreated the spectacle at the window for the forests and the sea entered the house through the picture window in order to beguile the walls with the illusion (of silk, wool, or pastel) of the inert magnificence. And those artificial waves and forests comparing themselves to their model in nature presented in contemplation singular sketches of rigid faces those innumerable and elusive faces that strive to emerge from the objects of everyday life. (Camille Mauclair, *Couronne de clarté, roman féerique* [Paris: Ollendorf, 1985], 6)

This typical and slightly irritating text should be compared to Proust's description of his grandmother's room as well as to a number of Mallarmé poems like "Sainte." See also Adolphe Retté's references to "glass cages" (18), "crystal towers" (23), "chambers" (107ff., 95ff.), "amber rooms whose translucent walls . . . allow one to make out the busy people coming and going in and out and as far as the eye can see" (110–111) in *Thule des brumes* (Paris: La Bibliothèque artistique et littéraire, 1891). See also references to the "world of glass and mirrors" in Adrien Remacle, *La Passante* (Paris, n.p., 1892), 125ff. In such texts glass-house mentality is not accompanied by "storehouse mentality" since there is no obsession for order and classification.

able arcades, balconies, conservatories, bow windows, sidewalk cafes, and glass canopies turned insides out. Theater was both in the playhouses and on the boulevards. Paris was indeed the "City of Light,"[56] an exposition city par excellence devoted to display and exhibition, a city that set the tone for expositions all over the world and for literature that exhibited its own objects of description. Logically, then, the Eiffel Tower of 1889 should have been the "sun-column" that Bourdais envisaged, a gigantic electric beacon 366 meters high, intended to illuminate all of Paris and to be seen by all of Paris in return, a monument that was also meant to contain "fresh-air therapy" rooms. By the middle of the century, everything revolved around Paris as if around the sun, in the literal as well as in the figurative sense. Alfred de Vigny's poem "Paris" ("Paris the pivot of France"), Hugo's introduction to the *Paris-Guide* published by Lacroix for the Universal Exposition of 1867, Michelet's *Tableau de France*, which served as the "exposition" to his *Histoire*, and innumerable Parisian novels of manners all made Paris the center, the beacon, the hearth, the crucible, the pivot, the hub, or the belly around which all thoughts, according to Hugo, or regions, according to Michelet, "turned"; and more prosaically, as though they functioned as a sort of architectural working sketch laid out like a ground network—the modern industrial equivalent of the garden design—the railway lines drew objects, raw materials, and inhabitants of the provinces to the capital like geometric rays.[r] Paris was a trope, a topos (a literary commonplace), an extended metaphor, and a tropism, in all the various senses of these terms. Glass-and-iron architecture, although not the only architectural styles of the era, can metaphorically serve as apt universal containers for the contents of any literary work. Lantier, the painter of *Le Ventre de Paris*, indulges in overly lavish praise of this modern architecture. Like the real-life architect Horeau—whose design for the Palace of the 1855 London Exposition lost out to Paxton's—Saccard, the real-estate speculator of *La Curée* (a character Zola had planned to include in a work before beginning to compose *Les Rougon-Macquart*) has symptomatic dreams of "putting all of Paris under a bell jar, turning it into a hothouse, multiplying the glass-covered arcades, raising the

[56] This expression is sanctioned, for example, in the title of Camille Mauclair's *La Ville lumière, roman contemporain* (Paris: Ollendorf, 1904), a novel similar to Zola's *L'Oeuvre* with its painters' milieu and their problems in getting exposure for their work in exhibits and salons.

[r] Hamon reminds us that *rayon* is a term that also refers to the exhibition architecture in stores, since it also refers to different "departments," "counters," or "aisles" as well as "rays."

shop rents tenfold and permitting everyone to walk around Paris without getting wet."[57]

The standard Romantic themes of the nocturnal or underground city, of the ruin in shadow, or of the behind-the-scenes world of hidden layers whose existence informs history as well as stories by providing the hermeneutic dimension of all novelistic plots,[58] these themes also traverse fantastic novels such as Féval's *La Ville-Vampire,* serial adventure novels such as Sue's underworld in *Les Mystères de Paris,* or socially conscious novels such as Hugo's *Les Misérables* with its sewers ("the intestines of the Leviathan") that had been brought to light in the catacombs photographed by Nadar and had been described by him in the chapter entitled "Paris Underground" in Lacroix's *Paris-Guide.*[59] "The intestines of the Leviathan" also resurface in the limpid, transparent architecture of Zola's "Bowels of Paris"—Baltard's Les Halles. Visitors to the 1900 Exposition were able to inspect and admire a house made entirely of glass, Ponsin's "luminous Palace." Georges Pérec would later describe it in *La Vie: mode d'emploi,* itself a "glass house" in textual form, like the one found in Zola's *Pot-Bouille.*

In sum, one might link the glass house to a sort of all-encompassing heliotropism—Baudelaire, in reference to heliography, spoke of the "new sun worshippers"[60]—or to a neurasthenia and erethism of the gaze and the spectacle—*gaze* and *spectacle* being two words quite common in an era fascinated by the "imperial brilliance of enormous edifices" (Rimbaud), two words that were also the fetish of realist and

[57] Emile Zola, *Les Rougon-Macquart,* vol. 1 (Bibliothèque de la Pléiade), 419. On the architect Hector Horeau (1801–1872) see the catalogue to the exhibit devoted to him in Paris in the supplement to *Cahiers de la recherche architecturale,* No. 3. See also in the same issue F. Boudon, "Horeau et les expositions universelles" (160ff.). Huysmans, in his "Salon de 1881" speaks of Horeau's *monuments sidérurgiques.*

[58] The clausula-sentence of vol. I, Book 8, chapter 2, of Hugo's *L'Homme qui rit*—the chapter entitled "Inferi" reads: "A reign is a dictation: the loud voice is the sovereign, the muffled voice is the sovereignty. Those who know how to distinguish this muffled voice in a reign and to hear what it whispers is the real historian" (*Complete Works,* vol. 6 [New York: Nottingham Society, n.d.], 214).

[59] Edouard Charton, *Dictionnaire des professions* (Paris: Hachette, 1880). In the entry "photographer," he writes: "[photography] allows the whole world to know a precious ruin that without it would only have been studied by bold explorers. Because of magnesium's light, photography can now do without sunlight. No necropolis is too obscure, no tomb is too deep, no inner recess too dark for photography to carry out its wonders." *Wonders* is a key term that occurs so often in the titles of that century.

[60] The first journal devoted to photography (which for a long time was called heliography) would be entitled "La Lumière" (light; 1851). Let us mention in passing Le Corbusier's famous definition of architecture: "Architecture is the skillful, accurate, and magnificent interplay of assembled volumes under the light." Here the term *light* conserves both its aesthetic, medical, and moral senses.

Map drawn by Zola of Les Halles in Paris, for the preparatory file of his novel, *Le Ventre de Paris* (1873).

A character-type of the modern city: the flaneur (in *Les Français peints par eux-mêmes*, 1843).

Inspecteur privé des travaux publics

Another character-type of the big city: the bourgeois observing major construction (caricature by Gavarni in *Le Diable a Paris*, 1845).

The frenzied exposition: Grandville (in *Le Diable à Paris*, 1845).

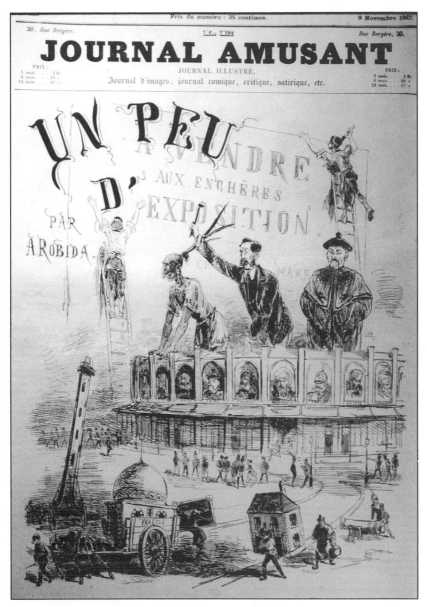

The exposition, or the collapsible city (caricature by A. Robida in *Le journal amusant* from November 9, 1867).

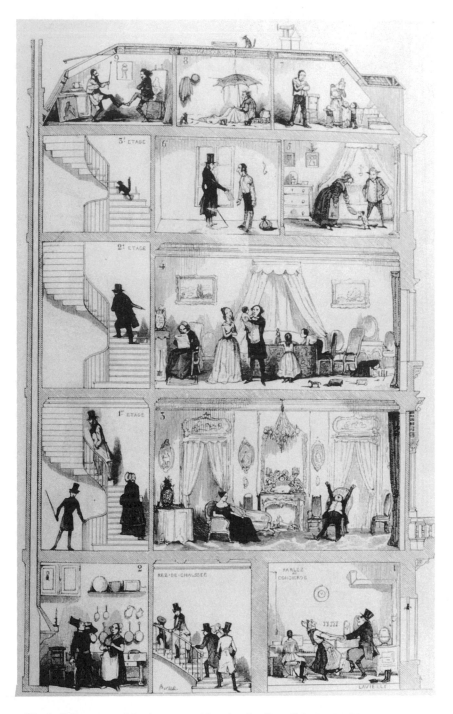

The building as social microcosm (drawing by Bertall in *Le Diable à Paris*, 1845).

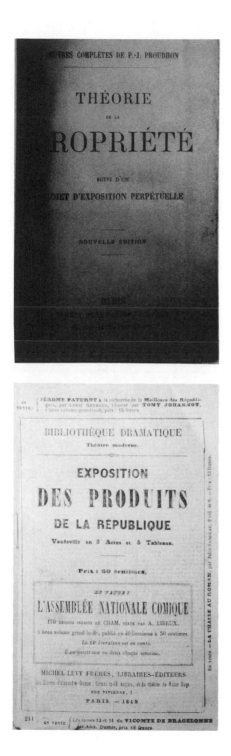

The serious exposition (top) and the comical exposition: Proudhon (1855) and Labiche (1849).

The first French comic-strip: Christophe, the Fenouillard family at the exposition of 1889 (in *Le petit français illustré*).

naturalist novelists whose camera-box architecture would be responsible for organizing their distribution. "We are violently enamored of gas and glass," observed Poe in *The Philosophy of Furniture*. As Walter Benjamin noted in "The Return of the *Flâneur*," everything "bears the sign of transparency,"[61] to such an extent that even the private dreams and fantasies of nineteenth-century individuals display its traces. Aside from the "diamond Babels" that Théodore de Banville dreams of in the poem "Décor," included in his collection *Stalactites,* one could cite the aforementioned "aquarium walls" and the various "prismlike habitats" found in Mallarmé and Proust. Baudelaire in his poem "Irrémédiable" dreams of being *"un navire pris dans le pôle / Comme en un piège de cristal."*[s] As he lay on the couch of Doctor Toulouse, Zola dreamt of what he thought was the most beautiful thing in the world: a *diamond steam-engine,* the energy-producing black box fused with the clear box of the prism, the century's most emblematic machine submitted to the expository transparency of analysis.[62] After all, this dream object did in fact concretely exist: all the great universal expositions contained exhibits of machines in running order, their cross-sections and cut-aways displaying their inner workings, in the great gleaming glass houses of the Gallery of Machines.

[61] Walter Benjamin, "The Return of the Flâneur," 1929 text (Fr. trans.). Let us remind those who wish to pursue the history and poetics of this metaphor of transparency that Ruskin divided his reflection on architecture into different lamps (of memory and of truth, for example).

[62] Emile Zola, *Docteur Toulouse: Enquête medico-psychologique sur les rapports de la supériorité intellectuelle avec la nevropathie. Introduction général par Emile Zola* (Paris: Société éditions scientifiques, 1896). In his preface to this inquiry, of which he is the subject, Zola writes: "My brain is like a glass skull. I gave it to all and I am not afraid that anyone should come to read it" (vi). It should be remembered that one of the preliminary titles of *La Bête humaine* was L'Inconscient (The unconscious). Of course, the principle scene of this novel, whose "main character" is a locomotive, describes the accident during which the locomotive literally explodes and exhibits its interior machinery. One of Zola's contemporaries, Raymond Roussel, takes "optical delirium" to the limit with his exhibition parks in *Locus Solus* and with his texts like *La Vue*. On the links between *fantasmagoria* (one of Walter Benjamin's key terms), *fantasy,* and the *fantastic* (the genre) in the nineteenth century, see Max Milner, *La Fantasmagorie: Essai sur l'optique fantastique* (Paris: PUF, 1982).

[s] "A ship caught in a crystal trap at the arctic pole" (Baudelaire, *Complete Verse,* 166).

# The Book as Exposition

A prospectus at the end of Louis Huart's *La Physiologie du garde national* (1841) announced a collective work that would soon become famous: *Les Français peints par eux-mêmes.* The book, advertised as "a moral panorama of our society" and hailed as an "encyclopedic publication," would consist of a "portrait gallery" in which "every sector of society ... would appear." Walter Benjamin quite correctly remarked that in a time of increasing numbers of expositions there was also a growing market for "exposition-books": "Contemporary with dioramas there was a dioramic literature. *Le Livre des cent et un, Les Français peints par eux-mêmes, Le Diable à Paris,* and *La Grande Ville* belonged to this."[1] Many other titles could be added to Benjamin's list. First of all, there were the various *magasins,* the best-known being *Le Magasin pittoresque* that Edouard Charton published from 1833 to 1913.[2] Some of these publications had the word *gallery* or *museum* in their titles. Systematic offshoots of the *physiologies,* these publications provided an alternative to the human-interest stories or gossip purveyed by the tabloid press and to the political commentary of the opposition newspapers. Whether didactic or encyclopedic in scope, this dioramic literature also set out to amuse and entertain. One can cite examples such as *Les Prisons de Paris,* E. de La

---

[1] Walter Benjamin, *Charles Baudelaire: A Lyric Poet in the Era of High Capitalism,* trans. Harry Zohn (New York: Verso, 1973), 161.

[2] This same Edouard Charton edited the *Dictionnaire des professions*(1842), cofounded the newspaper *Illustration* in 1843, and developed the *Bibliothèque des merveilles* and the collection of illustrated travel accounts entitled *Le Tour du monde* (1860). A former Saint-Simonian, Charton was active in lobbying for education reform.

Bédollière's *Londres et les anglais, Les Étrangers à Paris, Paris chez soi*—
a neighborhood-by-neighborhood description of Paris—*Asmodée à
New York, Paris pittoresque, La France pittoresque,* and finally a
guidebook—published in 1867, the year of the Universal Exposition, by
Lacroix, who also published both *Les Misérables* and *Les Rougon-
Macquart*—*Le Paris-Guide*. These copiously illustrated and often collaborative efforts included contributions by the great writers of the era.
Both functionally and structurally these publications engage the same as-
sumptions that underlie the expositions: to summarize; to compose lists
of sites, types, or objects; to offer a methodical overview of an entire field
of knowledge; to classify; to juxtapose scenes; to render things legible by
putting them on view; and to provide recreation and instruction.

Certainly, many of these dioramic or exposition-like books were first
and foremost books about expositions. Taken together, they form an
imposing mass of volumes, both literary and nonliterary, ranging from
the evaluations submitted by exposition juries and brochures issued by
expositions themselves to exposition guides and special newspapers
chronicling the various preparations for the event.[3] Literary works with
ironic intent also took on the exposition as a frame or pretext, such as:
Coppée and Verlaine's *Qui veut des merveilles?* (1867); Christophe's
cartoon strip of the Fenouillard family visiting the Exposition of 1889;
as well as the previously mentioned light comedy by the Douanier Rousseau. The latter is in fact also an example of a literary genre that approxi-
mates another genre so dear to the nineteenth century, the *revue*—a
theater production of juxtaposed scenes rehearsing contemporary hap-
penings in the form of a summary of the past year's events. This kind of
panoramic text was most often a theatrical piece along the lines of
Pottier and Mathieu's 1855 *Dzing! Boum! Boum!: Revue de l'Exposition,* in three acts and sixteen scenes, or the play *L'Exposition des
produits de la République,* a light comedy in three acts and five scenes
by Dumanoir, Clairville, and Labiche in which the actors presented a
satirical summary of the "social and democratic department store" of
the Second Republic's National Exposition.[4] Conversely, there was the

[3] For example, see *Les Merveilles de l'Exposition de 1878* (Paris: Librairie illustré et
Librairie Drefous, n.d.), *L'Exposition Universelle de 1867,* ed. Ducuing, in sixty install-
ments (Paris: n.d.), and *Le Moniteur de l'Exposition de 1889,* no. 1 (3 January 1885).
[4] Dumanoir, Clairville, Lahiche, *Exposition des produits de la République* (Paris:
Michel-Lévy Frères, 1849). In this play we find a cobblestone, a Tree of Freedom, a Republican Guard, a revolutionary street urchin, a *lorette,* the Constituent Assembly, Father Suffrage, a female parliamentary candidate, and a socialist. In the same satiric vein, see the
comic "counter-salons" of the caricaturist, Cham, that depicted the Official Salons.

*Paris-Guide;* although this collaborative work was published in the
same year as the 1867 Exposition and included a "Promenade à
l'Exposition," the guide was not strictly descriptive, nor was it simply a
lowly adjunct to the expositions. Instead, it set out to expose the city of
Paris methodically, in as many different chapters as there would by
pavilions in an exposition, neighborhood by neighborhood, function by
function, monument by monument. It intensified the effect of the exposition, since this exposition book dealt with Paris, the "exposition city"
and site of the Universal expositions. These books shared more than
their common subject matter with the expositions; they also shared a
structure. Mallarmé wrote in *La Dernière mode* of September 1874:
"Only Paris prides itself on being the sum of the entire universe, acting
both as museum and department store," Hetzel wrote in 1866 in his
foreword to Verne's *Voyages et aventures du Capitain Hatteras* that he
wished to publish a series of books that "summarized all knowledge,"
and Hugo wrote in the preface to the *Paris-Guide*: "The book is Paris";
it is hard to determine who or what is being exposed: the book, the city,
or the exposition itself. These various projects hoped to alter the structure of a predominantly descriptive text so that it could accommodate
the profusion of a real that had been previously structured by authority
(*pouvoir*)—in the form of "quarters," "districts," "aligned" streets, or
"registered" landmarks—or by knowledge (*savoir*)—in the divisions
and sections of the encyclopedia or the different branches of the sciences. The dream of these texts was to compose books as "presentations," "object lessons,"[5] or, in a metaphor borrowed from Hippolyte

---

[5] *Le Guide du Bon Marché* for the 1900 exposition is a department-store publication
(*magasin-zine*) that describes the great universal department store of the Exposition and
often uses the expression "object lesson" (5, 79, passim). *Le Petit Français illustré,* a
"newspaper for school children" was launched in 1889, the year of a universal exposition,
which the journal presented as a "lesson in objects" that schoolchildren should visit (137),
and as a "vivid summary of the march of progress" (172). As for that indefatigable
popularizer Louis Figuier, his publication, *L'Année scientifique et industrielle,* had the
subtitle: "*exposé* annuel des travaux scientifiques, des inventions, et des principales appli-
cations de la science" (My emphasis). Rimbaud cited the name of this great compiler in an
ironic clausula to his listlike poem, "Ce qu'on dit au poète à propos des fleurs," holding
up Figuier as a model of good writing:

> "Et pour la composition
> De poèmes pleins de mystères
> . . . Rachète
> Des tomes de Monsieur Figuier
> —Illustrés!—chez Monsieur Hachette!"

> ["As to the composition
> of poems full of mystery

Taine and that the Goncourts and Zola would both repeat ad nauseum in their respective prefaces and theoretical writings on the novel, to "warehouse observations . . . and collect human documents." (See Edmond de Goncourt's 1879 preface to his *Frères Zemganno*.)

This notion of the store or storehouse should not be confused with the clutter of bric-a-brac; rather it is an ordered place that demonstrates a given rationality. As the site for both spectacle and display, the store strives to entertain, distributing objects to seduce and manipulate visitors to pleasure- and consumer-oriented ends. There is an emotional delight associated with shopping, the "joy of the department store" (be it the joy of managing or visiting it) as evoked in the title of Zola's novel, *Au Bonheur des dames*, whose main character is a department store. It may be noted in passing that *Au Bonheur des dames* is the only novel in the whole *Rougon-Macquart* cycle with a happy ending. The joy of the store is found in the mastery of human activity, the harmonious circulation of objects that enter and exit the store's premises, the perpetually replenished stock, and the efficiency of their arrangement. The same sense of well-being is found in the department store in Verne's *P'tit Bonhomme*, a novel that recounts how an abandoned child finds a home as well as his fortune. In fact, Verne's well-managed, well-patronized, and well-stocked store where everyone finds his mate becomes a home in and of itself.

The modern city is a place of luxury, wealth, intensity, juxtaposition, and abundance, as all its visitors attest. Daudet, for example, in an interview granted to Jules Huret in 1895, summarizes his impressions of London:

> One characteristic of London is its abundance, a mad exaggerated abundance. Take their monuments: there are far too many of them. One has the sensation of an immense toy chest of monuments, emptied out haphazardly over a plain. Look here, a tower, two towers, ten towers. Do you like obelisks? Here's one, then another, and yet another as well as plinths, statues, palaces, colonnades, cupolas, church steeples, and none of them is ever big enough, tall enough, or ostentatious enough!

Like the store and the exposition, the city had to be organized in several ways in order to provoke such euphoria and delight. This was

---

... Buy
a few volumes by Monsieur Figuier
—Illustrated!—at Hachette's!" (trans)].

There could be an entire study devoted to Rimbaud's specific and parodic allusions to the works of Figuier.

done either administratively, through the imposition of an urban logic of districts and building lots; practically, through recourse to such user's manuals as guidebooks, maps, and tourist itineraries; or aesthetically, through the literary device of the work-as-storehouse or diorama.

The architecture of the store is devised for both storage and display. "The whole visible universe is nothing more than a storehouse of images and signs," remarked Baudelaire in his review of the Salon of 1859. A priori this insight could be applied to the Romantic tourist as much as to the Parisian *flâneur*—that enthusiast of modern allegories—or to the anthropologist/naturalist/novelist for whom images and signs would provide the raw material that would eventually be transformed into a structurally homologous textual store or warehouse. Such books would therefore tend to be revues, dioramas, or galleries, of scenes or tableaux and function as the balance sheet or summary of all knowledge on a given subject, or as a survey or itemization of a paradigm of places, classes and social types, objects, information, topoi, functions, or actions.

Such a book would both saturate and install the real in a methodical way—*method* being the operative word in naturalist theoretical discourse. Here the real would be conceived as a juxtaposition of a finite and manageable number of fields that come to be covered one at a time. In this way, both the real and each of its constitutive fields are thus assumed to have an actual or semantic closure.

This kind of total coverage is exemplified by two of Louis Reybaud's novels featuring Jérôme Paturot. On the one hand, his *Jérôme Paturot à la recherche d'une position sociale* (1843) runs through the lists of all the typical professions of the era that the hero would take up in succession. First he becomes a "retailer" (*industriel du détail,*[a] a term that could be applied to the realist writer himself) then a *garde national,* then a journalist, shopkeeper, poet and *deputé.*[6] Reybaud's *Jérôme Paturot à la recherche de la meilleure des républiques* (1848) in turn lists all the varieties of opinion that make up the French political spectrum of the period around 1848. The structure of these dioramic books—their juxtaposed scenes held together by the common thread of the hero's own social progress—recalls the basic paratactic structure of the revue, the picaresque tale, or the epistolary novel with a critical bent. An example of this is the remake of Montesquieu's *Lettres persannes* by the

[6] There is a long chapter in the first volume of the Paturot books about the relation between the hero, who wants to build a house, and his architect.

[a] The French word *détail* can mean either detail or retail.

Comte de Villedeuil entitled *Paris à l'envers* (1853). These dioramic works take off from the pocket-sized *physiologies* (of the bourgeois, the *deputé*, the student, the *lorette*, the garde national, among others), but their aims and organizations are far more encyclopedic. Thus, as with other more or less anthropological or novelistic projects (such as Francis Wey's *Dick Moon en France*, Hippolyte Taine's *Thomas Graindorge*, and Maxime du Camp's opus *Paris: Ses Organes, ses fonctions, et sa vie*), these works compiled lists of such typical Parisian places as the theater, the salon, or the boulevard. Many of Michelet's works, such as *La Mer, La Montagne, L'Insecte,* and *La Femme,* are simultaneously prose poems and encylopedia entries. The innumerable histories (of castles, farms, cities, or houses) by writer/architects such as Viollet-le-Duc and Narjoux, are nothing more than a summary of the conventions involved in constructing and using a building, recast into a more or less novelistic narrative form. These texts observe the exact structure of Homeric description as set forth in Gotthold Lessing's *Laocoon,* a technique of description that makes it possible to undertake the exhaustive inventory of a given object while at the same time seeming to tell a story. Jean Macé's *L'Histoire d'une bouchée de pain,* a didactic tale for children that sold widely in the nineteenth century, also makes use of this technique in order to exhibit in succession each of the different organs of the body and their functions. In such texts, the step-by-step survey of a particular subject matter provides a pretext that remains subservient to a description of a totality, to an inventory, to an assessment of the premises, or to a presentation of an issue.

These expository or dioramic books, whether they appear singly or as part of a series or cycle of publications, should not be confused with other types of cycles that do not share their all-encompassing and global projects, with their aspirations of covering a totality and their attempts of providing a final word or a methodological overview of a given field. This second type of publication—such as Paul Féval's *Habits noirs,* published as a cycle from 1863 to 1875—was open-ended, easily adjusted, or expanded as new developments arose. This category includes books that are various in nature: caricatures serialized in the "Panthéons Comiques"; the volumes of Joséphin Péladan's decadent *ethopeia*; Hugo's *La Légende des siècles,* his *L'Ane,* as well as his three historical novels; Zola's *Rougon-Macquart* series—of which there are twenty volumes, just as there are twenty arrondissements in the city of Paris—as well as his *Trois Villes* series; Eugène Sue's *Les Sept Péchés capitaux*;

Heredia's *Les Trophées*; Madame Tastu's *Le Voyage en France*; Auguste Comte's *Cours de philosophie positive*; Jules Vallès's trilogy; Flaubert's *Dictionnaire des idées reçues, La Tentation de Saint Antoine,* and *Bouvard et Pécuchet*; Bruno's *Le Tour de la France par deux enfants*; Jourdan's *Contes industriels*; and Verne's *Le Tour du monde en 80 jours.* All these books are structured by a cyclical or circular movement, proceed in zig-zag fashion (there were innumerable "ziz-zag tours" through France or through foreign lands) or by a review or survey of items, of places, of worlds, of moments, of topics, or of common places.[7] In a sense these books function both as wholesale stores (*magasin de gros*) by their recourse to exhaustive description, and as retail stores (*magasin de détail*) by their recourse to realistic effects (*effets de réel*) and references to things seen, to details, to technical information borrowed from scientific discourse, and to real examples drawn from case studies.[8] Alongside the great encyclopedias of the nineteenth century compiled by abbé Jacques-Paul Migne, Pierre Larousse, Maximilien Littré, and Berthelot, these various tableaux, magasins, and almanachs (whether undertaken in a serious or parodic register) all shared that same desire to seize reality in the form of lists.[9] A further example of this tendency is provided by periodicals such as *Le Voleur* which explicitly proclaimed its project of compilation and synthesis.[10] Many of these books—which by their very structure are at once *exposition* and *exposés*—in turn were items in a publisher's series or *collections* that were issued at regular intervals, as for instance the great literary or pedagogic collections of Hachette, Hetzel, or Calmann-Lévy. The issuing of these books as part of a publishers' series simply reinforced the encyclopedic dimension of the individual work.

[7] Jacques Neefs deals with Flaubert's *La Tentation de Saint-Antoine,* in "Exposition littéraire des religions," in *Travail de Flaubert,* Raymonde Debray-Genette, ed. (Paris: Seuil, 1983).

[8] Pierre Larousse's *Grand Dictionnaire* gives this definition for the noun *détail:* "an *exposition* of particulars," and for the verb *detailler* (to detail): "to recount, *expose* in detail" (My emphasis). See below for more about this notion of detail.

[9] According to Fournel "almanacs . . . have made enormous efforts to rise to the grandeur of this century; . . . nowadays they act as universal catalogues. Their contents condense the contents of an encyclopedia into a few dozen pages. . . . An entire period summed up and judged in the blink of an eye," *Ce qu'on voit dans les rues de Paris* (205). Even conversation or chit-chat, a socialized and informal linguistic practice, allowed itself to be captured in dictionary form (*Dictionnaire de la conversation,* 16 vol., ed. W. Duckett [Paris: n.p., 1832]).

[10] *Le Voleur*'s subtitle contained the adjective for the nineteenth century's greatest fetish: "Cabinet de lecture universel" (universal reading room). Its frontispiece showed a copyist at his work table with the caption: "He compiled, compiled, compiled." Flaubert, author of *Bouvard et Péchucet,* must have seen this frontispiece.

Symptomatically, a storehouse book such as *Les Français peints par eux-mêmes* opens with the description of the storekeeper par excellence: Balzac's *grocer* who is said to be an "encyclopedia in motion," for whom "life is distributed in drawers, in bottles, and sachets," and who is subjected to a close, monographic scrutiny in which Balzac pastiches the terminology of scientific taxonomy. Words like *gallery, scene, frame,* and *table* constitute the key terms of Balzac's 1842 foreword to *La Comédie humaine,* and underscore the classificatory thrust of texts of this type. The same tendency is at work in the framing devices found in so many short stories of the nineteenth century—a literary genre in which such authors as Barbey d'Aurevilly and Maupassant excelled. The interplay of inner and outer frames (i.e., the framing exposition or conclusion versus the framed tale itself) testifies to the desire to insert within a clear structure various exemplary cases of human mores, passions, or social behavior. The notions of the case (*chasse*)[b], social class, and classification provide both the means and the ends for the aesthetics of these kinds of literary texts.

It is understandable why the great Universal Exposition of 1867 exercised such a sway over contemporary commentators. Flaubert, who as a writer advocated expository display while bemoaning exhibitions as the century's "object of delirium," was at once fascinated and troubled by the 1867 Exposition. Writing to George Sand that same year, he remarks: "It is overwhelming. It contains splendid and exceptionally curious things. . . . Someone who had three whole months at his disposal to visit the Exposition every morning and take notes could spare himself the trouble of ever having to read or travel again."[11] Constructed by the architect and engineer Jean-Baptiste Krantz and rationally laid out by Le Play, the 1867 Exposition consisted of a series of

---

[11] Larousse writes in his *Dictionnaire* under the entry "exposition": "Just as in the history of all nations, there is only one prison called *The Bastille,* one religious reform movement called *The Reformation,* one political revolution called *The Revolution.* . . . Among all known *Expositions* there is only one which is called, and may forever be called, *The Exposition*—the Exposition of 1867." The design of this exposition, Larousse writes, offers "the advantages of two kinds of exposition: One is a collective exposition (i.e., the organization by nations) and the other is successive (i.e., a chronological display of the transformation of products). As in the work of Verne, Larousse must resort to an epideictic preterition and refers to the exposition book *par excellence,* the dictionary: "It is simply not possible for one to describe every item on display here which, depending on its merits and importance, has its own entry in the *Grand Dictionnaire.*" As for Louis Veuillot, someone on the opposite side of the political spectrum from Larousse, in his *Odeurs de Paris* he called the Exposition of 1867 "a temple of industrial bric-a-brac . . . ; Has there ever been such an enormous blood sausage with a parsley garnish rolled forth on a plate of such dimensions?"

[b] The term *chasse* means both reliquary and frame.

large circular galleries of iron and glass built in concentric circles inserted one inside the other. It was the last universal exposition to be held under a single roof; the subsequent ones were all organized into an outward "explosion" of many different independent pavilions. The 1867 Exposition presented itself as a summary or table of the various achievements of the era; structurally, it was laid out like an ideal two-way chart provided with two means of "entry." In other words, it could be read and visited along two axes: one for products, one for producers. The exterior circles displayed the more material and technical products while towards the center were found more spiritually rarified objects, such as the sections devoted to works of art or to weights and measures. Circulating "encyclopedically" through the same circular gallery, the visitor could survey one type of product—machines for example—represented by the various participating nations; moving from the periphery to the center, the visitor would instead survey the variety of products made in a single country. As a concrete model materialized by its very architecture, the 1867 Exposition represented a simple classifying procedure. On the one hand the circle, on the other the ray, or aisle: the design harkens back to Victor Fournel's *Paris futur* (1865), which had envisaged just such a design of radiating aisles.[12] Hans Christian Andersen, for whom the 1867 Exposition provided the setting for his tale "The Dryad," described its buildings as "an immense sunflower, whose petals are there to teach you geography, statistics, technological subjects, to elevate your mind to art and poetry, and to inform you of the relative size and importance of every country."

Literary exposition/description tended to follow the same logic in its various textual manifestations. Just as Haussmann's Paris tended to organize itself as "a city in the shape of a cross,"[13]—which brings to mind Baudelaire's "intersections of enormous cities"—so too did liter-

---

[12] See the discussion in the previous chapter of Fournel's city. As a hermetic and watertight variation on the theme of circulating fluidity (we have already seen a counterexample of this), see Herr Schultze's circular city in *Les Cinq Cents Millions de la Bégum,* whose "configuration . . . was a circumference whose sectors, determined by radiating fortified lines, were perfectly independent of one another, even though they were enveloped by a common wall and a moat." A similar logic governs both real and ideal architecture as well as negative and positive utopias.

[13] Françoise Paul-Levy, *La Ville en croix.* In chapter two of Zola's *La Curée,* Saccard speaks of the "great transept" (*la grande croisée*) while sizing up Paris from the heights of Montmartre—a rewriting of the famous scene at the end of Balzac's *Le Père Goriot*—dreams of carving up the city and making "notches" and "networks." Similarly Bouvard and Pécuchet surveyed the less grandiose universe of their garden, according to this principle of the augural and inaugural cross: "They went to the casement (*croisée*) to look at the view. . . . Two main walks, forming a cross, divided the garden in four parts."

ary description tame its ever-expanding and unfolding lexicons and lists—as in the "etc." of any descriptive system—by recourse to reticulated systems involving the distribution of *templas* like points on a compass (indicating "to the right," "to the left," "in front," "behind," "under," and "above") or by involving techniques of focalization that shift attention back and forth between the container and the contained or between the frame and the framed. This is readily apparent in the opening exposition of *Le Père Goriot,* where Balzac speaks of the "bronze frame which is the only one appropriate for this story." This outer frame in turn contains an entire series of inner frames which run—in descending order—from the city of Paris through the district of Montagne-Sainte Geneviève, the Vauquer boardinghouse, the boardinghouse garden, its interior, Madame Vauquer, and her dress to the petticoat beneath her dress. The circle and the aisle establish the trail the reader will follow; they provide ways of ordering or "shelving" various items and make it possible to make one's way through a latent lexical or thematic field. This kind of itemization lies at the very essence of any description and is particularly at work in the specifically literary practice of *exposition*—that is, the inclusion of an opening or inaugural passage at the outset of a work that, just like a universal exposition, provides an informative summary that prepares the reader's orderly progress through the material that is to follow. As that place where texts begin, the exposition is therefore structurally related to the fundamental gesture of the augur and the architect, that is, the inaugural tracing of the *templum.*

The formal and stylistic specifics of such expository practices should not be overlooked. *Exposition* comes into play in both literary and nonliterary works whenever the text shifts over into a *descriptive* dominant, in other words, whenever it starts filling out a *list* or nomenclature that it postulates as pre-existent somewhere outside the text and which is thus easily fleshed out, a list that is considered a useful means of compiling knowledge about the world, about language, or about the text that follows or precedes it. All this takes place regardless of the location of this list, the *nature* of its referents, their *quantity,* their *function,* their *finality,* or their *linguistic definition:* an exposition can be any length whatsoever; it can serve to render a story legible or simply function to jolt the reader or to provide the illusion of the real; and it can make use of any linguistic material it pleases, such as numbers, words, proper nouns, verbs, or adjectives.

The list of fish species in Verne's *Vingt mille lieues sous les mers,* or the comparable list of character portraits and histories in Balzac, the list of *phonemes* that Rimbaud parades by the reader in his well-known sonnet "Voyelles," the various lists of classes and fundamental notions included in the first lesson of Auguste Comte's *Cours de philosophie positive,* the lists of famous monuments (as in the celebrated coach scene in *Madame Bovary*), the list of France's regions featured in the "Tableau de France" that introduces Michelet's *Histoire de France,* the list of all the activities of a locomotive mechanic in Zola's *La Bête humaine*—all these lists are products of this expositional writing, whatever the particular *genre* of the text or the factuality or "fictiveness" of its component items. The textual practice of exposition thus takes sets of items and puts them into order (or, in the case of ironic texts, into disorder) calling upon the essentially paradigmatic semiotic competence of both the reader and the author, a competence that involves classification, heirarchization, actualization of lexicons, organization, equation, and imposition of formal or thematic closure.[14]

The practice of exposition can constitute a literary genre in and of itself (for example, the exposé, the Parisian tableau, or the descriptive prose poem). Or it can constitute a nonautonomous part of a larger textual whole that it is supposed to render more readable. But by excessively itemizing the various components of a given setting or milieu, or by providing a level of information that appears to exceed what is necessary to the preliminary understanding of the narrative's chain of events, expositions run the risk of either delaying that actual narrative, overelaborating the explicatory and ennumerative elements of the text to the detriment of narrative, or, to borrow Flaubert's expression, of overdeveloping the plinth of the statue to the detriment of character and plot. Many critics found fault with the lengthy expositions found at the outset of the works of Balzac and the Goncourts (Manette Salomon, the eponymous heroine of one of the brothers' novels does not appear until chapter fifty). Expositions tend to occasion an apologetic metalanguage

[14] For a typology which explains the function of descriptive systems, see Philippe Hamon, *Introduction à l'analyse.* According to de Beauzée in his article "Description" in *L'Encyclopédie Méthodique* (Paris: Panckouke, 1782), description is "a figure of thought by development that, . . . through a lively and animated exposition of . . . the most interesting properties and circumstances [of objects] makes something visible." In literary tradition, exposition refers to the inaugural part of a play, which involves "familiarizing the audience with the characters—whether they are speaking, spoken to, or spoken of—as well as the time and place of the action" (*Dictionnaire de la conversation*). In classical rhetoric, *hypotyposis* is the definition of a "jam-packed figure" (*figure comble*) and therefore is an ideal figure for description/exposition. Pierre Fontanier, defined it in these terms: "[It] paints things in so vivid and energetic a manner, that it puts them right before your eyes, and makes an image, a tableau, or a living scene of a narrative or description."

on the part of the narrator who steps forward to justify the very exposition he is engaged in. The first part of Balzac's *Le Père Goriot* ends: "The exposition of this obscure yet appalling tragedy is now concluded," and the first part of his *Ursule Mirouët* in turn ends: "If one must apply the rules of stagecraft narrative, Savinien's arrival, which introduces to Nemours the only character whose presence had as yet been lacking in this little drama, concludes this exposition." Such an apologetic posture can also be found at the beginning of a text, at the *threshold* where a *stage direction* or some explicatory comment always seems in order on the part of the author/architect who is guiding the reader through the aisles of the work. For example, in *La Vieille Fille*, Balzac writes: "To make [X's] importance understood . . . it is necessary to expose two serious incidents that were troubling the city." These laborious excuses often reveal something about the work involved in constructing the text itself. Such an example appears in Sue's *Latréaumont*. As the clausula of the third part of this six-part novel, he writes:

> Such is the long and perhaps overly meticulous exposition of the principle characters of this drama: LATREAUMONT, VAN DEN ENDEN, THE CHEVALIER DE ROHAN, AUGUSTE DES PREAUX, MADAME LA MARQUISE DE VILHARS, AND MADEMOISELLE RENEE-MAURICE D'O. Now although the events described in this exposition occurred five years before the events and outcome of this adventure, which is based on a true story, the author felt that this final and bizarre occurrence, aside from what we judge to be the historical reasons that demand its inclusion, would be of interest precisely because of its strangeness [the narrator then goes on to give a twenty line summary of the entire exposition]. . . . If the reader will allow an ambitious comparison (not with regard to the material facts, which I have attempted to outline, but rather having to do with the methods used to attempt this difficult work, which is too great a task for the author of these lines) . . . we can compare the first part of the story to a pristine river whose indifferent waters reflect here and there the various sites they visit in their vagabond course: poor cities and splendid palaces, rustic manors and feudal towers. . . . And then, extending the simile in the second part of the story, this river, after innumerable detours, grows ever more rapid and narrow, deeply gauging its bed between wild and desolate banks, will soon change into an impetuous torrent that leaps furiously through all kinds of rocks, debris, and ruins, finally engulfing itself in a bottomless abyss.

Like the work of Balzac, this somewhat awkward and overly modalized text ("perhaps," "the author judged," "felt," or "believed") refers to the vocabulary of the theater ("this drama"), the original source for the term exposition as well as for the terminology of transparency (which as we have seen, Zola uses extensively in his critical and theoretical metalanguage); in addition, it refers via the extended metaphor of the river, to problems involving the rhythmic dominant: exposition announces itself by a slower rhythm different from the main story even when it tells its own summarized story. The particular awkwardness of this passage also alerts the reader to a vicious circle of explanation: the initial delaying tactics of the exposition are accentuated by the fact that it is accompanied by a proliferation of self-justifying commentaries, and even by summaries that synthesize it if it is particularly long. This passage also locates the site of a sort of narrative competition; the exposition of causal and chronological antecedents runs the risk of being more engrossing than the denouement.

There is a great deal of architecture in the opening passages of nineteenth-century novels, particularly after 1850 when the realist and naturalist avant-gardes started to establish themselves. It is an architecture that provides both the means and the pretext for an expository text, an architecture that, like the crystal palaces that housed expositions, provides the background for some cardinal functions: laying out and displaying useful objects (i.e., information), putting items on view, and directing traffic through them. Moreover, the presence of such *composed* objects—which are also *composite* architected buildings and places—in the expositions of a given work, a chapter, or a sequence, conveys the very idea of the *composition* of the literary work itself. The expression: "The house is composed of . . . and of . . ." shows up frequently in the works of Balzac and others. Finally, a certain number of preferred technemes concentrated in expositions (such as partitions, walls, doors, thresholds, mirrors, or closed spaces that open up) permit the writer the most economical, swift, efficient, and above all realistic way of distributing a certain number of informational file cards in the very first pages, as it were, to air a number of items and make them legible. *Airing* can of course be a term of hygiene as well as classification: *the exposition/description is the circulatory and informational form of hygiene adopted by the naturalist text.* Thus it is enough to situate a character in an interior comprised of a chamber with a door or a window that opens out onto the world in order that this character be entrusted with the task of rendering his habitat via his very gaze. By recourse to familiar phrases like "he caught sight of . . . ," "she knew well . . . ," "before her eyes . . . ," "she contemplated . . . ," "before him lay the . . . ," "his gaze fell upon . . . ," and "at her feet she noticed . . . ," the text need only station the character by a window or threshold in order to situate the environment. A physical description of the character can be in turn arranged merely by having him or her pass before a mirror or before the eyes of a second character entering the room. Finally it is enough to bring characters into contact either with an object that prompts their memory or with other characters who share their memories in order to provide basic information about the characters' personal backgrounds or past histories. In realist novels, this kind of introductory topos, with all its various partitions, furnishings, entryways, and exits, often takes the form of a belvedere-like structure situated at the center of the environment that is being described, or it takes the form of a liminal space along the lines of a vestibule or a threshold. The analyses of both Barthes in *S/Z* and Serres in *L'Hermaphrodite* demonstrates how the boundary-like window in Balzac's *Sarrasine* distributes, via the gaze of the narrator who is positioned there, the contents and characters of the novella. There are further examples, such as the view from the "astrologer/poet's" "garret" in Baudelaire's poem "Paysage," which opens the "Tableaux Parisiens" section of *Les Fleurs du mal,* the view from the fifth-floor window "at the corner of the mansard roof" which sets into motion the exposition of Zola's *La Bête humaine,* or, in the opening passage of *Manette Salomon,* the "opened dome" of the "belvedere" in the Jardin des Plantes, a vantage point from which the painter Anatole exhibits the vast panorama of Paris to the tourists.

Thus situated in time and space, both the character and the reader become available to the events or the plot that will follow. The explanatory exposition is a novelistic procedure that situates its initial character in a kind of photographic box. This device allows the novelist to introduce a certain number of the novel's traditional components—portraits, biographies, and descriptions of interiors and exteriors. This operation can be carried out by relying on a stationary character who does not move from a particular observation post: Saccard at his restaurant window in front of the Place de la Bourse in the beginning of *L'Argent*; Roubaud at his window opposite the train station in *La Bête humaine*; and Gervaise at her window on the boulevard in *L'Assommoir*. The operation can also be carried out by characters in motion who insert themselves gradually into an unexplained world whose various sectors are invested with increasing significance as they make their way through the milieu by means of "ambulatory descriptions." This type of description, which was perfected by the Goncourts and by Coppée in his *Promenades et intérieurs,* progressively saturates the world to be described with partitions, thresholds, and rooms representing in material form the various subdivisions of the author's own card catalogue of society. Hence, the extraordinary yield of the theme of the character who has newly arrived on a given scene and whose naive and innocent eye over the course of the very first pages is homologous to the naive gaze of the tourist and the exposition visitor who discover and are in turn discovered by the world. The *homo novus* setting out to conquer Paris, the country bumpkin arriving at the capital, the Parisian in the provinces, the traveler entering a city for the first time, the new student in school or the new employee on the job—all of these types are illustrated in the literature of that century: the "newly graduated" Frédéric Moreau traveling up the Seine at the outset of *Education sentimentale*; Denise, the young girl from the provinces and new employee at the novelty shop in *Au Bonheur des dames*; Florent hired as the inspector of Les Halles in *Le Ventre de Paris*; Charles Bovary the new student in the class at the beginning of *Madame Bovary*; the anonymous traveler who arrives in Verrières "for the first time" in the opening pages of Stendhal's *Le Rouge et le noir*.[15] In the preface to *The Tragic Muse,* Henry James speaks of the "panoramic and processional" technique of some of his own novels such as *The Princess Casamassima,* whose preface describes how the city of London suggested to him a character who he refers to as the "pedestrian prowler."

The vehicle for an "ambulatory description" (the term is René Ricatte's) can be provided by the particular point of view or an interior monologue of the new arrival, or by the voluble voice of the effable, knowledgeable native guide who parades the scenery of these unfamiliar surroundings before the newcomer's, and of course before the reader's, eyes, for whom the character of the newcomer is a transparent intermediary. This is what Sue, in describing the good boss Hardy's phalanstery— whose buildings have southern and eastern exposures and lie on top of a hill—in *Le Juif errant* called "exposing dramatically." Other characters could be considered variations on the "newcomer"; among them the *abandoned child*, a roving character who appears continually among the dramatis personae of nineteenth-century novels. The abandoned child falls under the legal definition of the term *exposition*: the action of aban-

---

[15] For a systematic study of the protocol of introductions in expositions–descriptions of the realist and naturalist text, and notably of the realistic role played by certain places as well as by the gaze, words, and work of an inhabitant on his habitat, see Hamon, *Introduction à l'analyse,* 180ff. On the figure of the *vagabond,* the mobile character with no permanent address who was an obsession of the nineteenth-century bourgeois, see the excellent book by Jean-Claude Beaune, *Le vagabond et la machine* (Paris: Champvallon, 1983).

doning or exposing a child in a public place. Serials, romance novels, and melodramas would make considerable use of this character. Hector Malot's *Sans famille* (1878), Adolphe d'Ennery's *Les Deux Orphelins* (1894), Zola's *Le Rêve* (1888), and Verne's *P'tit Bonhomme* (1893) are the better-known examples. The narrative function of abandoned children goes beyond the emotional response and plot development generated by their quest for their origins or search for a home. Like their literary forebear, the picaro, they also serve to exhibit the world. In this tradition, Verne would exhibit Ireland methodically, city by city, region by region, through the travels of his hero P'tit Bonhomme, just as Zola would exhibit the decor of the cathedral through the movement and gaze of his heroine in *Le Rêve*. Similarly, Bruno's pedagogic *Tour de la France par deux enfants* uses just such a character as a pretext for linking the different tableaux that correspond to the different parts of France. A further variation on the child as traveler and voyeur, who takes stock of a given place would be Verne's young Robinson family as well as the *robinsonnades* (be they Swiss or French) of every sort that multiplied over the course of the century.[16] The Robinsons' island is rather like the Champ de Mars of the exposition for they share similar structures and functions: the methodical movement through space; the parading of natural or artificial objects chosen for their utility and importance; and the importance of both the gaze and the spectacle. Both undertake a project which is pedagogic and entertaining, involving the organization and labeling of a stockpile of items, the glorification of work, and the idea of mastering the world by closure and inventory. To repeat, these ambulatory expositions/descriptions have the advantage of distributing and diluting a stock of information throughout the whole of the text rather than *jamming* all of it into one single compact portion.

Thus there are no blind spots in such general expositions of the world

[16] The preface to Verne's *Deux ans de vacances* (1888) hoped to "show a band of children between the ages of eight and thirteen abandoned on an island." Among the great number of Robinsons created throughout the nineteenth century Rodolphe Wyss's *Robinson suisse* of 1813 holds an important place. *Robinson industrieux, histoire semée de détails sur la botanique, sur la physique, la geographie, les arts industriels, l'histoire naturelle* . . . by Abbé Jean Laurent contains an interesting preface on the pedagogic uses of this theme. Curiously, in one of Barbey d'Aurevilly's *Diaboliques*, "Le Dessous de cartes d'une partie de whist," the narrator in a parenthetic comment associates two meanings of the word *exposition*: to place something before the eyes, to exhibit something for the sake of appearance, as is done in this spa; and to expose a child. "An extraordinary breeze, almost like a stange breath, comes to wrinkle the smooth purity of the waters. Are not children left exposed in China, by the Yellow River or the Blue River? . . . French spa waters are rather like that river. Perhaps children are not exposed there, but one always exposes something for the benefit of impressing those who have never been there."

nor any "leftovers" or "untidy corners" in these stagings of the store-house of the real: glass houses should be indistinguishable from the store, just as this ordering should be indistinguishable from a certain transparency, both literally (to the eye) as well as logically. In 1868, following the 1867 Exposition, Zola comes up with the idea for the *Rougon-Macquart,* a *series* of novels that was to cover the natural and social history of the Second Empire. This family and series would in turn be based on a "closed circle," a circle of history closed by Napoleon III's defeat at Sedan in 1870.[17] The family chronicle would originate in a city, Plassans, that is itself circular with carefully differentiated districts,[18] and would distribute its cast of characters according to a certain number of equally differentiated social "worlds": merchants, workers, peasants, etc. Zola's very first outlines in 1868, foresaw "another world" to classify society's unclassifiable "prostitutes, murderers, priests, and artists."[19] Homais's dispensary, Captain Nemo's Nautilus, and the Green Box in *L'Homme qui rit*[20] all appear, alongside the

[17] In Zola's general preface of 1871 included in the first novel of his *Rougon-Macquart* series, he writes:

> For three years, I have been collecting documents for this great work. This present volume was in fact written when Bonaparte fell, which was an event as an artist I felt was necessary and which I had always inevitably seen at the conclusion of this drama, without ever having dared to hope that it would occur so soon, and which provided me with the terrible and necessary denouement for my work. This work is today complete; it stirs in a closed circle, and becomes the portrait of a now defunct reign." (*Les Rougon-Macquart,* vol. 1, 4)

[18] "The distinction between classes has long remained determined by the division between neighborhoods. . . . The neighborhoods are marked off by wide roads. . . . It is as if the city, in order to better isolate and shut itself in, had been surrounded by a belt of old ramparts. The population of Plassans is divided into three groups, each one had its own distinct neighborhood, each was a world apart." (Ibid., vol. 1, 37ff.) The term *déclassé*—meaning to be downgraded socially—recurs frequently in Zola's text to describe the cast of characters in the cycle.

[19] Zola's preparatory documents and preliminary drafts for the *Rougon-Macquart* cycle were published by Henri Mitterand in the Pléiade edition (vol. 5, 1,667ff.). Zola's outline was divided into "four worlds" and a "world apart" (1,734). When presenting his list of future novels to his publisher, Lacroix, Zola used in each case the term "framework": "the framework of this novel." On Zola and his system of classification, see A. Dezalay: "Zola face aux philosophes et aux classificateurs," *Cahiers de l'Association Internationale des Etudes Françaises,* no. 24 (1972). The nineteenth century was of course a century which attempted great rational systems of classification such as those of thinkers like Comte and Brunet as well as John Dewey and his decimal system. A number of Zola's research dossiers with their field notes, reading notes, and information gathered from specialists, compiled for each novel have also been collected and published by Henri Mitterand in *Emile Zola, Carnet d'enquête: Une ethnographie inédite de la France* (Paris: Plon, 1986).

[20] "No ship's equipment was as complete and precise as the Green Box. Everything in it had been stored, arranged, considered, and necessary" (book 2, 8). The Green Box can be compared to the house of Alphonse Daudet's Tartarin de Tarascon, which is a parody

*Rougon-Macquart* series, as mock-ups of the ideal work of art dreamt of by this type of literature, that is, a neatly arranged work without any overlooked corners.

Of course, these documentary texts may, despite their overall readability, contain zones of disorder and randomness. But the great storehouse texts manage to domesticate such zones by neutralizing their local disorder, either by recourse to a larger transcendental order or to the formal organizational structures afforded by seriality, myth, history, commentary, or a system of clichés or of overarching logic. The negative points of the system serve only as a foil; they always refer to some kind of superior ordering of the real. Thus in the perfectly ordered universe of the Nautilus where each object has its place and each person mans a station, only Nemo's library has gaps: "I did not see a single book on political economy; it seems they were strictly forbidden on board." The library also escapes order: "one curious detail, all the books were indiscriminately shelved, no matter what language they might be written in." Such gaps carry meaning and constitute an indirect but transparent ethopeia of the character who inhabits this place—Captain Nemo himself. He is, in this way, endowed with superior abilities: "this arrangement suggested that the Captain of the Nautilus could easily read from any book he happened to pick up no matter what language it was written in."

The same may be said of Zola's untidy places. In *Au Bonheur des dames,* the disarray that Octave introduces into the overly logical order of the department-store aisles in fact establishes a more subtle order that seduces and manipulates the crowd of customers by using many different display counters in the store:

> He was suddenly struck with the idea that the arrangement of the departments was inept, and yet, it seemed a perfectly logical arrangement, the stuffs on one side, the made-up articles on the other, an intelligent order of things which would enable the customers to find their way themselves. . . . Suddenly he cried out that they would "have to alter all that."[c]

For the Goncourts, the disorder of the artist's studio in *Manette Salomon*—a novel about salons and about the difficulties painters

---

of this storehouse-world, a house that included a "marvelous garden" and a study that contained his weapons collection: "Everything was in its place brushed, dusted, and labeled as in a museum" (*Tartarin of Tarascon,* intro. Jean-Pierre Richard [New York: E. P. Dutton, 1954], 2).

[c] Emile Zola, *Au Bonheur des dames,* 210.

have getting exposure—is a sign of a bohemian counterculture that contrasts with the well-ordered bourgeois interior. Just as in Zola's *L'Oeuvre* (another key work about salons) Lantier's unfinished paintings, or set pieces, serve merely as a foil for the total work of both the character Sandoz and Zola himself. Certain characters in Flaubert and Zola, such as Sénécal in *Education sentimentale* and Lantier in *L'Assommoir* whose personal libraries are full of incomplete sets of books and ill-assorted titles, represent a recurring realist and naturalist theme in which general knowledge and the poorly digested reading material of numerous fictional characters become seemingly significant when contrasted with the well-digested readings of other, more positive characters. A character's incomplete library can furthermore constitute an ironic barb (underscoring the distance taken by the narrator from the virtues of the encyclopedia) or can simply signify a contrast to the narrator's own well-ordered text. Such details brought out in the course of an "exposition/portrait" can also describe a character who lacks either psychological unity or functional continuity within the plot.[21]

Thus a distinctive trait of the textual storehouse—whose anthropological and sociological project coincide with the basic credos of realism and naturalism between 1855 and 1890—would be its ability to make use of elements that lie outside of its expository structure. This technique is borne out on the most local level of the text by the role played by the notorious detail, the most in-significant element of the work. Free-floating, decontextualized, indeed, beyond the domain of exposition, summary, or collection, the detail emerges as an absolutely singular occurrence, or *hapax* that cannot be correlated to any other element in the exposition, nor integrated into any class or shelved in any aisles within it. Resistant to any interpretation that would assign it a function,

---

[21] On unmethodical autodidacts, or readers that have not properly "digested" their reading material, see Philippe Hamon, *Le Personnel du roman* (Genève: Droz, 1983), 282ff. In Flaubert's *L'Education sentimentale*, Sénécal is described in this way:

> He annotated Rousseau's *Social Contract*. His head was stuffed with ideas from the Revue Indépendante. He knew the works of Mably, Morelly, Fourier, Saint-Simon, Comte, Cabet, Louis Blanc, that entire bunch of ponderous socialist writers who insisted on reducing mankind to a barracks-room existence, making labor sweat in shops or factories, and finding relaxation in brothels. With this hotchpotch he'd worked out his ideal of a democracy full of virtuous qualities, a blend of share-cropping peasants, and textile mills. (*A Sentimental Education*, 148–149)

Comparing the blend of this library with Nemo's, one notices references to the same types of buildings: barracks, brothels, factories, farms, and mills.

the detail is assigned the task of simply signifying that the text is displaying something that is without a doubt, "real."[22]

At this point, let us consider at great length the ambiguous and
contradictory status of the detail. The question of the detail which we
have already touched upon has polarized the theoretical and critical
discourse on literature since the end of the eighteenth century. Most
notably, it has played a crucial role in the various debates concerning:
(a) the relationship of parts to a whole within a single work (the example of architecture inevitably comes to the rescue in this debate); (b) the
relationship of the text to reality; (c) the relationship of the text to its
donor as well as to its recipient. In spite of the efforts to promote detail
to a higher status in the latter half of the eighteenth century within a
new descriptive genre of the literature of "gardens" that sought to
"enclose the world" (as in the writings of the Marquis de Girardin),[23]
neoclassical discourse ever since Boileau's *Art poétique* (I, 1.49–60) had
proclaimed that the detail was useless, and that it posed a threat to the
internal coherence of the literary work. This position continued into the
nineteenth century in official critical discourse, at a time when, from
Balzac to Proust by way of Flaubert, the Goncourts, Stendhal, and Zola,
an entire aesthetic of detail was being put into place, to the point where
many novelists would have undoubtedly accepted the label with which
Reybaud characterizes his hero Jérôme Paturot, namely, that of a retail
merchant (*industriel du détail*).[24] Scenographically bringing the detail
into play by way of a character's gaze is fundamental to the aesthetics of
representation at the heart of the realist and naturalist project of the
period: a mimesis or a transparency that hinges on a mathesis (a kind of
knowledge and system of classification) and thus triggers a "suspension
of disbelief."

[22] On detail see Roland Barthes, "L'effet de réel," *Communications,* no. 11 (1968);
Barthes, *Camera Lucida.* See also Philippe Hamon, "Thème, thématique, et effet de réel,"
*Poétique,* no. 64.
[23] See Joseph-François Michaud's "Quelques observations sur la poésie descriptive,"
which appears as a preamble to his poem *Le Printemps d'un proscrit* (Paris: Giguet et
Michaud, 1803).
[24] (Reybaud, *Jérôme Paturot, à la recherche d'une position sociale,* 184). Concerning
the debate surrounding this notion of detail in the nineteenth century, see Ferdinand
Brunetière, *Le Roman naturaliste* (Paris: Calman-Levy, 1896). See also Francis Wey,
*Remarques sur la langue française,* 2 vol. (Paris: Didot, 1845). For more recent work on
the subject see Naomi Schor, *Reading in Detail* (New York and London: Methuen, 1987).
In planning his *Vie de Henri Brulard,* Stendhal hoped to write a "detail novel" (*roman à
détails*). Conversely, Proust complained: "Those passages in which I was trying to arrive
at general laws were described as so much pedantic investigation of detail" (*Remembrance,* vol. 3, 1,098–1,099).

Therefore at a certain level, the exposition–description of the world may well have a quasireligious dimension to it. Larousse, in listing the different meanings of the term exposition, (see the epigraph at the beginning of this book) reminds us that, in addition to products of technical know-how such as machines and manufactured items and in addition to the testimonials to power such as the trophies of industry, other types of objects are also exposed for all to see: namely, the corpses or more specifically the *relics* of saints. For the Romantic antiquary who delighted in gothic ruins just as for the fin-de-siècle tourist enamored of Sandro Botticelli's paintings (for example in Francis Poictevin's *Ombres* and *Tout bas*), a journey always included the obligatory visit to the cemetery, the sepulcher, the shrine, or to the reliquary containing such sacred remains.[25] There is an element of pilgrimage to every journey. The shop is thereby transformed into a treasury, a crypt, or a mausoleum, just as the display windows are transformed into the transparent panes of a reliquary. A complex semiotic system informs the exposition of the remains and fragments of the bodies of saints, whose display often relies upon architectural objects or means. The shrine—a house made of gold, ivory, or glass—a little crystal palace within a larger house, or a small-scale model within a church is in a sense redundant within the habitat that contains it. The same redundancy can be true of the object contained

---

[25] One must remember that the cemetery with its crypts, an architecture of privacy in death which is often as "delirious" as pavilions at universal expositions, are essentially products of the nineteenth century. The prominent role of Père Lachaise in the literature of the century, including the works of Michelet and Balzac, as a site for reverie, and as an obligatory passage in many novels is well-known. On the "invasion of stone" and the proliferation of funerary architecture in which "the original myth of a return to nature is replaced by all the constraints of city setting for the dead," see Michele Vovelle, "Le corps montré, le corps caché," in the collective work, *L'Homme et son corps, de la biologie à l'anthropologie* (Paris: Centre Nationale de Recherche Scientifique, 1985). Furthermore, the descriptions of exposed and anonymous cadavers in morgues starting with *Thérèse Raquin* (published in 1867, the year of one exposition), became a literary commonplace of what would come to be called "putrid literature." Antoine Albalat—in his work *La Formation du style par l'assimilation des auteurs*, 12th ed. (Paris: Armand Colin, 1921), 173ff.—takes as an example of a "model" description the "Morgue de Mont Saint-Bernard": "The dead found buried in the snow were exposed there." For other examples of morgue descriptions, see in Maurice Rollinat's *Les Névroses*, his poem entitled: "La Morgue":

Noyés, pendus, assassinés,
Ils sont là, derrière un vitrage,
Sur des lits de marbre inclinés.

["Drowned, hanged, murdered,
They are there behind glass,
On slanted marble beds"—trans.],

or one of Villiers de l'Isle-Adam's *Contes Cruels*, "A s'y méprendre" based on parallel descriptions of the morgue with its displayed cadavers and the passage de l'Opéra.

within the shrine; reliquaries containing an arm are shaped like an arm, just as those shaped like a head contain skulls. The relic can also be an object analogous to the remembered figure—a mummy or the imprint of a body, as in the case of the Holy Shroud of Turin or Saint Veronica's veil. Or it may have a metonymic relation to the figure—a part of the body, a fragment of bone, or an extension of these as in the case of tools, fragments of utensils, or the shred of a garment. The relic both attests to the reality of a figure's existence and reconfirms belief in this figure. This is how the "martyr's bone in a carbuncle frame" functions in Flaubert's "La Légende de Saint Julien l'hospitalier." But the most beautiful and ironic exposition of relics undoubtedly occurs in the final chapter of the same author's tale, "Un Coeur simple," in which the altar erected for the celebration of Corpus Christi includes Félicité's stuffed parrot alongside "a small frame containing relics and a variety of other rare objects which caught the eye." The relic thus constitutes a *sign* granted a positive *value* and a *valence* (since it has a value equivalent to a reality that it represents), and inasmuch as this sign is *exhibited* it instigates or reconfirms the very act of belief. Relatively speaking, the relic is homologous either to the *ruin*—the remains of a building or monument that exposes its interior— or to the *item*—exhibited in the shop window or the museum display case. In either case architecture serves both as the means of staging and as the object that is staged.[26] Both in the way the relic triggers the process by which a certain reality is revealed (a term at once mystical and photographic) and in the way it stages a spectacle, the relic becomes homologous to the procedure whereby the realist text puts detail into play in order to insure the illusion of referentiality.

[26] See for example the description of Francis Poictevin's visit to Catherine of Siena in *Tout-Bas* ([Paris: Lemerre, 1893], 111), in her "hermetic crystal reliquary"; or this note: "If there is a relic that attracts one towards Italy, the fragrant cemetery, it would be in the treasure house of the Church of Monza where there are flasks of holy oil having burnt in the catacombs of Rome, and flasks of mystic transparency addressed as a token of apostolic heroism to Theodelinde by Saint Gregory the Great" (*Ombres* [Paris: Lemere, 1894], 76). Zola in *Lourdes* (1894) described at length the "store-like" and "exposition-like" aspects of this site of pilgrimage with its statues, images, its thanksgiving placques, and "souvenirs." He presents characters who are priests—such as Peyramale in *Lourdes*, Mauduit in *Pot-Bouille*, Faujas in *La Conquête de Plassans*, and Serge Mouret in *La Faute de l'abbé Mouret*—as the stage directors or architects of their churches. See also Coppée's prologue to his collection of poems *Le reliquaire* (1866). In *Au bonheur des dames* the department store is systematically described by way of a lexicon of religious architecture: chapel; altar; convent; tabernacle; temple; church; and nave. See also the novel by the portuguese Eça de Queiroz, *La Relique* (1887) which is a parody of "the Romantic voyage to the Orient." On the relation between the relic, detail, distance, and photography (connected by way of "exposition" and "revelation"), see the article by Georges Didi-Huberman, "L'Indice de la plaie absente, monographie d'une tache," in *Traverses* 30–31 (March 1984).

The *detail,* like the "bone of the martyr" in Flaubert's text, needs to be set or enclosed in a descriptive frame, that severs the continuity of the narrative and sometimes takes on the thematic form of a superfluous fragment (or a leftover, microscopic detritus, debris, part of a whole, relief, trace, scratch, or mark) that creates a *gap* in the text which exercises a fascination over the reader. By its very physical and semantic incompleteness, the detail triggers interpretation and almost automatically provokes acts of faith or belief in *what* the text exhibits (i.e., its subject matter) as well as belief in the person *who* is responsible for the exposition (i.e., its author or narrator), thus leading the reader to think: "This description is so precise that it could not have been invented by the author."[27] This particular response is created by the interplay of different kinds of belief: on the one hand the reader believes *that* what the text is saying via a particular detail is real; on the other, the reader believes *in* a narrator/exhibitor whose implicit image and credibility are borne out by a knowledge of the real. In other words, the reader is led to say, "I believe *that* because I believe *in*." These acts of belief implicitly go hand in hand with the notion of *believing with*—for belief necessarily presumes participation in a community that shares a common stock of credible clichés and received ideas which constitute its encyclopedia. Any detail has an element of stigmata to it; it is therefore an item that encourages the reader to *make believe* and places the realist discourse of exposition into the general category of a *discourse of manipulation* and thus of seduction, authority, persuasion, and pedagogy. The exposition at the beginning of a text—the descriptive passage that often (but not always) opens the narrative and in which the narrator tries to make the reader believe that what he is describing is indeed "true to life" and also "useful"—serves as the privileged site for the concentrated display of details. These relics of a reality the reader cannot help but believe in.

The universal exposition exhibited the effects, the results, the objects, and the sum total of the labor of all nations. The Paris Exposition of 1878 would even include a section devoted to the history of work. According to Zola himself, *Au Bonheur des dames* (1883) was to be the novel of modern activity par excellence. Zola in fact is forever rhyming the main character's name, Octave, with the adjective

[27] An approach well described by Diderot, as Charles Nodier reminds us in his article, "Du style typographique" in *Revue de Paris* 6 (1829), which deals with descriptive style. See also the thoughts of Bouvard and Pécuchet on the *effet de réel* found in Sir Walter Scott's descriptions: "Without knowing the models, they thought the portraits were perfect likenesses, and the illusion was complete."

*active*. The novel recounts the duel between two department stores:
The gloomy store, reminiscent of the store in Balzac's *Maison du chat
qui pelote* and represented in Zola's novel by "Old Elbeuf," contrasts
with Octave Mouret's retail novelty department store with its tall
display windows. But Mouret's store is above all presented as the
hyperbolic locus of proper and euphoric circulation. Money circulates
as do customers, who are subtly channeled from department to department; in addition, the gaze circulates, thanks to the new architecture
of iron and glass. (It is worth noting that, when writing his novel, Zola
conducted his research at the side of his friend Franz Jourdain, the
future architect of the Samaritain department store.) Moreover, the
store is also the locus of circulating information governed by the omnipresent sales pitch as well as the circulation of lexical and descriptive
systems that are carefully distributed throughout the novel in chapter
headings that correspond to each of the store's seasonal displays (*expositions*). See for example the description of the "white sale," where
Zola employs his great "symphonic" descriptions.[28] The Zolian text
therefore adjusts its textual exposition, as accurately as possible to a
real exposition. With its store that exposes and as an exposure of a
store, the novel even culminates in a scene in which the itemization of
its descriptive paradigm (descriptions are always the itemization of a
latent lexical system) coincides with the very activity performed by the
novel's characters—a store *inventory* in which every object is ac-
counted for.[29] Zola here takes up, more or less systematically, the

[28] In *Au Bonheur des dames* Zola writes that his hero even "attempts to exhibit
paintings" in his store (vol. 3, 612). Pierre Giffard in *Les Grands Bazars* ([Paris: Havard,
1882], 276ff.), a book that was of great use to Zola in writing *Au bonheur des dames*,
speaks of "the symphony of seasonal displays" (*symphonie des expositions*) in the department stores: "Nothing would prevent department stores from creating a calendar for their
lovely customers based on the theory of the special yearly sales events (*expositions*). They
could call February, White; March, Parasol; June, Chapeau; and July, Sales" (283).

[29] The novel's inventory scene (vol. 3, 646ff.) can be read as an extended metaphor for
the very operations of the naturalist method: classifying, enumerating, writing, and making lists.

> In the store, flooded with sunlight from the tall, opened bay windows, the employ-
> ees shut up inside had begun the inventory. . . . Every employee able to hold a pen
> had been drafted into service: the inspectors, the cashiers, the bookkeepers, and
> even the shop assistants. . . . "Five coats, cloth, fur-lined, size 3, at 240!" Margue-
> rite called out. "Four of the same, size 1, at 220!" the work continued. Behind
> Marguerite, three salesgirls were emptying the armoires, classifying the items,
> giving them to her in bunches. . . . While the man inscribed this, Joseph kept
> another list as a check. Meanwhile, Madame Aurélie herself, aided by three other
> salesgirls, kept a tally of the silk garments which Denise inscribed onto a sheet of
> paper. Clara was in charge of overseeing the piles, of arranging them and stacking

technique he first developed in *Le Ventre de Paris* in which he gives his hero, Florent, the job of inspecting the pavilions of Les Halles. The descriptive list—the textual figure that unfolds, displays, and exhibits or explicates certain vocabularies—can be used to justify the very activities of characters like inspectors, warehouse workers, or department managers, just as their activities in turn justify such a list. Even if such a descriptive inventory is entrusted to a fictional character or the narrator himself, its essence nevertheless consists of lexical ostentation, a flaunting of knowledge, a demonstration of onomastic competence, a tour through a card file or an intertext, or a filling out of the knowledge that would reveal an encyclopedic proficiency that is more or less shared with the reader. The longer the expository description lasts the greater the effect of an "increasing congruence," to use Michael Riffaterre's expression, and the greater the impression that it can reconcile term for term the storehouse of words with the storehouse of the world. In cases like these, metonymy works to reveal proximities and juxtapositions, just as synecdoche underscores the interlocking elements and detail that floats free of the entire structure (it serves no purpose) while it integrates these interlocking and contiguous networks, and offers the sought-after "realistic effects" (*effets de réel*). Expository description thus fulfills a very subtle function: Like the universal exposition, literary description must exhibit the effects of *work*, "to display the labor that went into its expression," in the words of Valéry,[30] and to demonstrate stylistic know-how as well as

---

them up. . . . "Seven cloaks, old style, sicilian, size 1, 130!" . . . "Three surah pelisses, size 2, at 150!"

This chapter constitutes the height of homeric description, the technique that permits the "airing out" of listed elements in a work sequence. Many nineteenth-century novels, such as *L'Education Sentimentale, La Dame aux camélias, Cosmopolis,* have exposition—inventory scenes describing a character's belongings that are about to be auctioned off.

[30] Paul Valéry, "Un problème d'exposition," *Oeuvres*, vol. 2, 1,150ff. See also his *Présentation du musée de la littérature* (1,146ff.). In these texts written at the time of the 1937 Universal Exposition in Paris, Valéry imagines (in regard to the labor of the mind, and most notably the writer's labors) "the visible display that could best suggest an essentially invisible labor." Zola asks the same question at the time of the Exposition of 1878. It is customary, in order to make the labor of style visible in any literary section of an exposition, to put the writer's manuscripts on public display. Thus by exposing the manuscripts with all their changes in their various drafts, a certain quantity of labor is rendered visible. The nineteenth century was not only the golden age of the manuscript, but also the time of the first attempts to create *stylistics* (the word and the thing appear at the end of the century) which would be founded on the study of the various drafts of writers' manuscripts (Antoine Albalat, *Le Travail de style enseigné par les corrections manuscrites des grands écrivains* [Paris: Armand Colin, 1903]). Charton in his *Le Dic-*

understanding of the world. If the writer and the architect indeed share this "problem of exposition" that Valéry speaks of, then *style* becomes precisely that distinguishable, objectivized, and concrete trace of the time and effort put into the work, just as description itself becomes the primary locus of the manifestations and display of such effort.[31] More specifically, inasmuch as it is the locus for the deployment of professionalized language (the vocabulary of botanists is brought to bear on the descriptions of gardens, that of sailors is applied to a port, that of architects is applied to buildings), description automatically becomes the place to exhibit the lexical work that has been carried out on language. Flaubert, as is well known, was hounded by the desire "to beat the bourgeois at their own game," to get the better of them in the very area where they think they are champion—the world of work— by exhibiting a quantity of labor that would legitimate Flaubert both as writer and as craftsman. The practice of description/exposition may well have allayed Flaubert's fears, in that it provided a definition of the artist at variance with the one offered by the *Dictionnaire des idées reçues*: "What they do can hardly be called work."

One final remark regarding the notion of work: many opening passages from nineteenth century novels that are devoted to an inaugural, informational exposition are in fact devoted to the description of an actual mechanical object. If the expositions of novels, as we have seen, often take on the attributes of a camera (as in the opening passage of *La Bête humaine,* which includes a window open onto the world, a room, a mirror at the back of the room, and a source of illumination) and thus become a sort of textual machine that "poses" and "develops" the real, these expositions also become the place where any number of machines make their appearance. The first thing that "dizzies" the "traveler"

---

*tionnaire des professions* notes in the article "Architect": "Whereas the painter can merely expose a painting and the sculptor can merely expose a model to express a joyful inspiration, to attract attention and from the start obtain a bit of celebrity, the architect can only expose to the gaze of the crowd blueprints unintelligible to the majority of people."

[31] "C'est là qu'il faut des vers étaler l'élégance" (Here verse must display elegance) writes Boileau in his *Art Poétique* (vol. 3, 259) speaking of description in epics. *Display* (*étalage*) can be seen, as far as exposition–description is concerned, in a figurative sense (the exposition is the "display case" of the writer's know-how and knowledge) but also almost literally as a sort of textual diagram that displays a latent lexical or thematic field. M. Cresson, an excellent observer and analyst of the stylistic processes of the impressionist period who speaks of "artist" phrases, makes what he calls the "fanlike phrases" (*phrases en éventail*) of descriptive passages of the period the syntactic prototype of a certain "unfolding" (*ex-plicare*) of a lexicon (*Le Style et ses techniques* [Paris: Presses Universitaires de France, 1951], 171).

arriving in Verrières (the perfect name for a *camera lucida*) in the opening pages of *Le Rouge et le noir,* is the

> din of a noisy machine terrifying in aspect. A score of weighty hammers
> falling with a clang which makes the pavement tremble, are raised aloft by a
> wheel which the water of the torrent sets in motion. . . . This work, so crude
> in appearance, is one of the industries that most astonish the traveller who
> ventures for the first time among the mountains that divide France from
> Switzerland.[d]

A few pages later, the "noise of the saw" from old Sorel's factory picks
up the din. The same machine noise appears in the opening passage of
Zola's *Germinal* (1885) and Georges Ohnet's *Maître de forges* (1882).
The first thing that Roubaud sees in the initial paragraph of Zola's *La
Bête humaine,* as he peers through "the glass canopies of the covered
halls" of the Gare de l'Ouest, are the smoking locomotives ready to
depart. The first thing that appears before the reader of *Education
sentimentale* is the boat that will carry Frédéric home to his mother:
"The *Ville de Montereau* was lying alongside the quai Saint-Bernard
belching clouds of smoke, all ready to sail . . . baggage was piling up
between the two paddle-boxes; and through all this racket the hiss of
steam could be heard escaping through the iron plates."[e] Just as in the
actual Gallery of Machines of universal expositions or in the actual
paintings on the walls of the official salons,[32] machines can be observed
at the thresholds of novels like star attractions of an exposition, exhibited as they run at a standstill, exposing their workings on the spot like
so many autoreferential metaphors of textual machinery, or of the narrative machinations to follow. The first chapter of Italo Calvino's *If on a
Winter's Night a Traveller . . .* nicely captures this standard way of
beginning novels: "The novel begins in a railway station, a locomotive
huffs steam from a piston and covers the entire beginning of the chapter,
a cloud of smoke hides part of the first paragraph. . . . There is someone
looking through the befogged glass door of the bar."[f]

The aesthetic of "warehousing observations" or of "amassing collec-

---

[32] *Exposer des machines* (literally, "to expose machines") means in the slang of artists'
studios and painters, to send to the salons paintings that are ambitious in format and
subject (which are usually historical). On the literary theme of the machine in the nineteenth century, see P. Noiray, *Le Romancier et la machine* (Paris: José Corti, 1981).

[d] Marie-Henri Beyle (de Stendhal), *The Red and the Black,* trans. C. K. Scott Moncrieff
(New York: Modern Library, 1926), 10.

[e] Gustave Flaubert, *A Sentimental Education,* trans. Douglas Parmée (Oxford: Oxford
University Press, 1989), 3.

[f] Italo Calvino, *If On a Winter's Night a Traveller . . . ,* trans. William Weaver (San
Diego: Harcourt Brace Jovanovitch, 1979).

tions of human documents," as Edmond de Goncourt defined it in 1879, can come into play at various levels and in various literary genres. The *tableau parisien*—which in the nineteenth century became what Lanson calls a "fixed prose form" and a preferred textual locus for the staging of details—would serve to designate texts that were broadly expository and descriptive (a cycle of novels, a series, a synthetic summary table, or an arcade thoroughly covering a large field of reality, as we have seen in the work of Balzac, Verne, and Zola) as well as short poems or brief moralizing texts such as "the calendar of sensations" that constituted the little tableaux in Souvestre's *Le Philosophe sous les toits* of 1850. Aside from the verse tableaux, there were the prose descriptions known as sketchbooks filled with *choses vues* (things seen) or impressions. Such prose tableaux could either constitute a portion of a longer text or stand on their own as autonomous shorter texts. A modern version of hypotyposis, the tableau in its autonomous, versified form appears as a sort of Western variation of haiku or as a poetic snapshot in which the detail is put on display and exhibited in all its unexpectedness and freshness. The tableau can be presented as existing independently from the allegorical or explanatory framework of narrative, or it can function in the opposite fashion as a sort of *exemplum* that signifies the very essence of modernity. This snapshot quality is captured by Coppée's famous "realist poems," or *dizains réalistes* composed around 1870 and so appreciated by Verlaine, Rimbaud, Nouveau, and Charles Cros that they inspired the savage parodies included in the *Album zutique*.[33] Here are three examples of Coppée's *dizains*:

> Croquis de banlieue
> *L'homme en manches de veste, et sous son chapeau noir,*
> *A cause du soleil, ayant mis son mouchoir,*
> *Tire gaillardement la petite voiture,*
> *Pour faire prendre l'air à sa progéniture,*
> *Deux bébés, l'un qui dort, l'autre suçant son doigt.*
> *La femme suit et pousse, ainsi qu'elle le doit,*
> *Très lasse, et sous son bras portant la redingote;*
> *Et l'on s'en va dîner dans une humble gargote*
> *Où sur le mur est peint—Vous savez? à Clamart!—*
> *Un lapin mort avec trois billes de billard.*[g]

[33] See also the collection *Dizains réalistes par divers auteurs* (Paris: Librairie de l'eau forte, 1876). One can compare Germain Nouveau's *Petits tableaux parisiens* to Baudelaire's. On the *tableau* see Karlheinz Stierle, "Baudelaire and the tradition of the tableau de Paris," *New Literary History*, 11, no. 2 (1980).

[g] "Suburban Sketch"

> A man in his shirt sleeves, his handkerchief placed under his black
> hat because of the sun

Le Cahier rouge
*L'école. Des murs blancs, des gradins noirs et puis*
*Un Christ en bois orné de deux rameaux de buis.*
*La soeur de charité, rose sous sa cornette,*
*Fait la classe, tenant sous son regard honnête*
*Vingt fillettes du peuple en simple bonnet rond.*
*La bonne soeur! Jamais on ne lit sur son front*
*L'ennui de répéter les choses cent fois dites!*
*Et, sur les premiers bancs, où sont les plus petites,*
*Elle ne veut pas voir tous les yeux épier*
*Un hanneton captif marcher sur le papier.*[h]

Promenades et intérieurs (XVIII)
*J'adore la banlieue avec ses champs en friche*
*Et ses vieux murs lépreux, où quelque ancienne affiche*
*Me parle de quartiers dès longtemps démolis.*
*O vanité! Le nom du marchand que j'y lis*
*Doit orner un tombeau dans le Père Lachaise.*
*Je m'attarde. Il n'est rien ici qui ne me plaise,*
*Même les pissenlits frissonnent dans un coin.*
*Et puis, pour regarder les maisons déjà loin,*
*Dont le couchant vermeil fait flamboyer les vitres,*
*Je prends un chemin noir semé d'écailles d'huîtres.*[i]

---

Merrily wheels around his little pram,
To air his progeniture.
Two babies, one asleep, the other sucking his thumb.
His wife follows, urges him onward, as well she should,
Weary, carring his frockcoat under her arm;
They are off to dine in some cheap hash house
That has painted on its wall—Do you know it? it's in Clamart!—
A dead rabbit and three billiard balls.—trans.

[h] "The Red Notebook"

The school. White walls, black tiered seats and beyond them
A wooden Christ decorated with sprigs of boxwood
A nun, pink under her cornet,
Leads the class, holding under her sincere gaze
Twenty little working class girls in plain round bonnets.
The good sister! Never could one read on her face
The boredom of repeating things said a hundred times already!
And in the first rows, where the littlest pupils sit,
She does not want to see all those eyes looking at
A captive june bug walking across the paper.

[i] "Strolls and interiors (XVIII)"

I love the suburbs with their fields lying fallow
And their old leprous walls, where some old poster
Tells me about neighborhoods long since demolished.
O, Vanity! The name of the shop keeper that I am reading
Probably now decorates a tomb in Père Lachaise.

As the only form flexible enough to adapt to the discontinuities of the juxtaposed, ever-changing, fragmented spectacles of the big city, this poetry that derives from the tradition of Restif de la Bretonne's "nocturnal tableaux" and whose foremost examples are found in Coppée's realist dizains, Verlaine's "Paysage belges," and Baudelaire's *Spleen de Paris* rivaled the photographic snapshots in exposing the real as though it were a collection of impressions to be set down. An aesthetic debate at the very core of the "exposition mentality" pitted the upholders of the encyclopedic form (or wholesale store)—represented by the novel cycle, the "gallery," or the *tableau des moeurs*—against the upholders of the shorter form (the retail store)—represented by brief poems, impressions, and sketches. Although it designates various textual and aesthetic realities, the term *tableau*, encountered in Balzac's aforementioned foreword to his *Comédie humaine*, Zola's preface to his first volume of the *Rougon-Macquart* series, as well as Baudelaire's work, signals a shared underlying project: accounting for modernity as a form of coexistence between inhabitant and habitat, and as the emergence of *urbanity* in every sense of the term. Baudelaire, speaking of paintings (tableaux) in his account of the Salon of 1859, deplores the absence of what he terms "big-city landscapes, that is, the collection of all the grandeur and beauty that has resulted from the powerful agglomeration of men and monuments, the deep and complex charm of an old capital aged and mellowed by the glories and tribulations of life." In his discussion of Charles Méryon's engravings, Baudelaire sketches out in a few lines the themes of the *tableau parisien* of which he dreams—a text where the *intensity* of the raw visual encounter with a "riot of detail" (an expression he used to describe Constantin Guys) would somehow blend together with the *exhaustiveness* of the collection, or the totality of agglomeration. Hence the multiple contradictions that traverse this urban tableau: depth versus the mottled surface of display; mobile and cyclical agents such as clouds, smoke, or seasons versus the immobile solidity of stone structures; the intense drama and pathos of humanity (stage and actors inevitably imply drama) versus the majestic impassiveness of

---

I linger. There is nothing appealing here
Not even the dandelions that quiver in a corner.
And then, to see the houses already far away,
Whose windows are enflamed by the scarlet setting sun,
I take a dark pathway strewn with oyster shells.

stone; opaque versus perforated material; the monumental versus the industrial; and the permanent versus the changeable:

> Rarely have I seen the natural solemnity of a big city represented more poetically. The majesty of accumulated stone, the steeples *pointing their fingers toward the sky,* industry's obelisks belching their accumulated gusts of smoke against the firmament, the great scaffolding of monuments under repair, applying to the solid body of architecture their own temporary architecture whose beauty is so paradoxical, the stormy sky, heavy with anger and resentment, urban perspectives deepened by the realization of all the dramas they contain—none of the complex elements which compose the painful and glorious stage scenery of civilization have been left out.

Exposition undoubtedly involves both the dream of putting an item in its proper place within a totality, such as the store, thereby giving it meaning, as well as the dream of bringing to light or putting on display, that which is hidden, to ex-plicate a complexity.

# Plaster, Plate, and Platitudes

Perhaps all of this is too good to be true. Like Baudelaire's "hysterical" character in "Le Mauvais Vitrier" who decides to perform an "earth-shattering" act by smashing the all-too-lucid panes of glass of the glazier's "crystal palace," we too can choose to throw stones at this glass-house world. The transparent world of the exposition whose quantitative, democratic, and bourgeois vistas replaced the Romantic world of lapidary inscriptions and monuments with a vision of the world-as-chart, glass house, or storehouse, displaying a reality mastered by sheer organization, may well have another, more disquieting aspect. To borrow from the lexicon of photography, "overexposure" threatens the ultimate "revelation" of an image. The "exposition mentality" of the world as storehouse arouses suspicion even in its most ardent champions. Could they exercise memory in this modern urban world, or even write about it, and finally could such a world produce monuments, signs, symbols, and works of art imbued with meaning?

A 1 May 1834 entry in Michelet's *Journal* provides an example. The historian recounts a walk that takes him across a symbolic boundary between a legible and an illegible Paris. He goes from Les Invalides—an "eternal monument where war and homeland are crowned by religion"—to the other side of the Seine to visit the Industrial Exposition on the Champs Elysées. This embryo of future great Universal Expositions, with its "charming stalls" and its "railroad," was a veritable "monument of the future" exposing industry's "brilliant trinkets."

Michelet goes on to write: "What saddened and frightened me upon entering the Museum of Industry was my complete ignorance of the processes, resources, etc., of this outwardly new, dazzling, and striking world that offers nothing but pleasure and profit." This can be seen as a sort of *exemplum*. By crossing this bridge Michelet allegorically goes from one age to another. He makes the passage from a period of stability and value to a period, as Walter Benjamin has shown, of arcades (*passages*) solely concerned with "exhibition value." Although the "modern" architecture of mid-century had its supporters, for many it functioned either as the cause or the effect of a general loss of meaning. The world of the Romantics, susceptible to hermeneutic readings and restorations, is thus replaced by what is felt to be an endemic semantic deflation. Actually one might ask whether Michelet's bridge even deserves the status of architecture. After all, while it was the preferred construction of nineteenth-century architects and engineers, the bridge like the arcade is purely a site of passage, and nonhabitation. Curiously enough, the leitmotif of the bridge over the Seine found in a number of other texts is also an *exemplum*. The metallic and industrial pont des Arts that coexists with La Cité, the Pont-Neuf, and the Louvre in the historic heart of Paris is often cited in such cases. To borrow the subtitle of Gustave Courbet's famous painting *L'Atelier,* the bridge is a "real allegory." On the one hand, it may euphorically suggest an eagerly accepted modernity. For example, for many years the newspaper that would come to incarnate the century, *L'Illustration,* featured a frontispiece depicting a bridge. The bridge is also the theme of the great "modern" painting that would be the death of the artist Claude Lantier in Zola's *L'Oeuvre.* But on the other hand, this leitmotif could also have negative connotations when used to represent the incongruous intrusion of iron architecture onto a treasured and ancient setting. Thus Francis Wey's *Dick Moon* describes the iron footbridge of the pont des Arts as "made of thin bars of iron, neither elegant nor solid, . . . devoid of any style capable of suitably connecting together the monuments on either side of the river . . . and strung up like an ugly spider's web on the wave between two buildings," thereby ruining one of Paris's most beautiful sites. The author goes on to say that this area

> presents one of the most charming tableaux to be found in the interior of the city, . . . [where] one lives in the midst of nature, politics and history, . . . [where] tradition's thread has not been broken, and [where] the past is not in

ruins: All these centuries are evoked, and shine in the sun, as each edifice follows its destiny.[1]

Contrary to what one might believe, the observers of this widespread staging of the city as spectacle *by* industrial architecture and *for* the objects of industry did not necessarily react according to their usual political or ideological stances. Although their diagnoses of the cause of this phenomenon may have differed, progressives like Michelet and Hugo and modernists like Baudelaire found themselves agreeing with a reactionary like Louis Veuillot, who wrote in *Les Odeurs de Paris*:

> Among the many passions of democracy, none is more prodigious and more widespread than the need for conspicuous display; and the baseness it inspires is its greatest success: pretentious signposts, *advertisements*, grotesque and impudent charlatanism, theater—all of this is of a piece; a nation of democrats is a nation of *ham actors (histrions)*.

In this passage the reactionary Veuillot sets forth what many outside his circle also saw as the disturbing symptoms of a world that seemed devoid of any substance. This world was in a state of perpetual representation (in the full theatrical, mimetic, and political sense of the term), as is apparent in Honoré Daumier's series of drawings entitled "Les Représentants représentés." The world of Michelet's "brilliant trinkets," of paper, signs, and advertisement was also a place where objects were beginning to lose volume and depth. In such a world the great projects of historical and philosophical synthesis and of the collation of the document and the monument no longer seem capable of deploying their principle of all-embracing legibility. Before Marx and Benjamin, Baudelaire's prose poem "Perte d'auréole" equated this incapacity with the loss of memory's or culture's "halo" or "aura."[2]

A new type of urbanism and architecture are directly related to the causes, framework, means, symptoms, and consequences of this loss. Of course, Veuillot and Michelet are not the only witnesses to this crisis of

---

[1] Francis Wey, *Dick Moon en France: Journal d'un anglais de Paris* (Paris: Hachette, 1862), 69–70. Further on in this chapter we will see the characters in *L'Assommoir* skimming rocks in this very same historic site. The same motif was photographed from the pont du Carrousel by Le Gray in 1856–1857. The Douanier Rousseau would increasingly come back to the theme of the metallic bridge in his paintings. Of course an entire volume by Félix Narjoux in the collection *Bibliothèque des merveilles* sang the praises of the bridge.

[2] On this point and on the metaphor of the loss of solidity see Berman, *All That Is Solid Melts into Air*. Berman's title refers to a famous phrase in Marx's *Communist Manifesto*, which was in turn borrowed from Shakespeare.

meaning: "Stone is more stone than ever. . . . We no longer understand architecture," writes Friedrich Nietzsche;[3] "Even stones are becoming stupid," writes Flaubert;[4] "At the rate Paris is going, it will renew itself every fifty years. Thus the historical significance of its architecture is erased every day," observes Hugo.[5] Proudhon notes that the Obelisk of Luxor transplanted from Egypt to the Place de la Concorde in 1836 had lost any "mnemonic purpose" and had become merely one more item in the urban "bric-a-brac"—Baudelaire's term in "Le Cygne"—a "sure sign of a people devoid of consciousness, whose nationality is dead."[6] Or, to cite Veuillot again:

> This new Paris will never have its own history, and it will surely lose the history it once had. All traces of the former city have been erased for those who are under thirty years of age. Even if the old monuments are still standing, they no longer articulate anything since everything around them has changed. Notre-Dame and the Tour Saint-Jacques are as out of place as the Obelisk, for they too seem to have been imported from elsewhere, like some sort of frivolous curiosity item.

Clearly Veuillot is not alone in thinking that the histrionics of ham actors had started to take the place of history.

The techniques of the exposition, which include transporting, transplanting, selecting, dismantling, and transforming everything into a spectacle, were perfectly acceptable within the confines of the store, the museum, or the fairgrounds themselves. Perhaps less acceptable was the use of these techniques to reorganize, sometimes quite drastically, the very framework of everyday urban life.[7] The city is henceforth no longer seen as a legible space which history has progressively layered into strata of patina or into concentric circles that grow from the oldest sections at the core to more recent sections at its periphery. Such a fundamentally illegible city can no longer be conquered neighborhood by neighborhood by

[3] Friedrich Nietzsche, *Human, All Too Human*, trans. Marion Faber (Lincoln: University of Nebraska Press, 1984), 130.

[4] Gustave Flaubert to Louise Colet, 29 January 1854.

[5] Hugo, *Notre-Dame de Paris*, Part 3.

[6] Pierre Joseph Proudhon, *Du principe de l'art et sa destination sociale* (Paris: Garnier, 1865), 339.

[7] The term *urbanism* appears after 1867, which is not only the date of one of the most important of Paris's universal expositions, but also of Ildefenso Cerda's *Théorie générale de l'urbanisation*, ed. Antonio Lopez (Paris: Seuil, 1979). On the variations of the image of Paris for writers of the nineteenth century, and particularly on the effect of two traumatic experiences (the public works of the Second Empire and the destruction of the Commune) for Parisians, see Marie Claude Banquart, *Images littéraires du Paris fin-de-siècle* (Paris: 1979); Marc Eli Blanchard, "In Search of the City: Engels, Baudelaire, Rimbaud," *Stanford French and Italian Studies* 37 (1985); and of course Walter Benjamin's notes for his great unfinished work on Paris, Baudelaire and arcades.

the likes of a Rastignac: in the absence of clear differentiations, how does one move from the Montagne Sainte-Geneviève to the Faubourg Saint-Germain? Instead, as an object of land speculation this city, where money brutally refashions the urban fabric, is merely a plot of land to be developed. Emile About's 1856 short story "Terrains à vendre" (in his collection *Les Mariages de Paris*) recounts the romance between a painter—a "first prize winner at the Universal Exposition"—and a young woman whose dowry consists of vast plots of land within Paris. In addition to Zola's story about the "bowels" of Paris—*Le Ventre de Paris*—and his story about the well-ordered store—*Au Bonheur des dames*—he also wrote a novel about the "disembowelment" and the "disorder" of Paris in *La Curée* (1872). Later, in 1906, one of Zola's disciples Céard, wrote a sort of disenchanted summary of the second half of the century, entitled *Terrains à vendre au bord de la mer* dealing with real-estate speculation on the coast of Brittany.

Meanwhile the paragons of intellectual and moral virtue, the models of the demiurge, architects, found their reflection being considerably distorted by literature.[8] Zola alone presents us with architects like Lazare Chanteau in *Joie de Vivre*, Louis Dubuche in *L'Oeuvre*, and Achille Campardon in *Pot-Bouille*. Other unflattering portraits include Duhamain in *Une Belle Journée* by Céard, and the architect hired by Reybaud's character Jérôme Paturot. These highly negative characters are either complete failures or incompetent and pretentious. In *Le Dictionnaire des idées reçues* Flaubert gives us this lapidary definition of the architect: "They are all imbeciles. They always forget to put staircases in houses." And Frédéric in *Education sentimentale* contemplates with horror the prospect of "burying himself in the provinces, playing cards, overseeing masons, and walking around in clogs." To this list might be added the Pecksniff of Charles Dickens's *Martin Chuzzlewit* (1844), not to mention the ludicrous and pompous Monsieur Bonneau in Champfleury's *Les Bourgeois de Molinchart* (1854) who is obsessed with the idea of measuring every monument in his department, using his umbrella as a yardstick.[9] These negative characteristics of the architect can

---

[8] On the status of the architect's profession and image in the nineteenth century, see the article in Charton's *Dictionnaire des professions* and Andrew Saint, *The Image of the Architect* (New Haven, Conn.: Yale University Press, 1983). The classical image of the architect is more or less interchangeable with the image of the orator as defined by Quintillus.

[9] See also chapter 10 of *Les Bourgeois de Molinchart* entitled "Delirium archeologicum tremens," a delirium Flaubert would remember. This disease, according to Champfleury, which began to infect many bourgeois "sometimes after 1830," caused them to shed "more tears over the demolition of an old shack than [if they] had lost a

be seen both as rewritings of the Romantic antiquary and devotee of grandiose edifices as well as a hyperbolic way of putting the very status of the *artist* into question.

The intrusion of the illegibility of modernity into architecture took on two possible forms: the building could either serve as a support for a proliferation of novel and indecipherable signs, signals, or insignias or the building could become illegible by the sheer fact of its transparency. Thus on the one hand there occurred a kind of semiotic hypertrophy, as the hieroglyphics of commerce and state multiplied, and on the other hand the transparency of the glass exposition halls seemed to create a radical absence of signification caused by the overexposure of the real. In other words, there was at once an excess and a void—at once too many signs on buildings (but meaning what? having what value?), and at the same time buildings that signified nothing. Clearly semiotics were at issue here, as were aesthetics (what were the literary forms and formulas that could capture a world devoted to exposition?), but perhaps even more important was the status of ethics. An "age of the fake" seemed to be establishing itself; Ruskin's architectural lamp of truth seemed about to be snuffed out.[10] These issues would be dealt with (either explicitly or implicitly) by the new set of objects, scenes, and characters that had begun to populate the literary texts of the era.

One such new object was the telegraph; Charles Chappe's optical telegraph, followed by the electrical telegraph with its wires and poles, would soon become an integral part of the real and literary landscape, in such texts as Rimbaud's "Ce qu'on dit au poète à propos des fleurs," where he speaks of "*la lyre au chants de fer*" (the lyre that sings a song of steel) as an emblem of the *siècle d'enfer* (hellish century) or Verlaine's "*télégraphe-paraphe*" (telegraph-initials) in "La Bonne chanson, 7." In yet another "real allegory," monuments could be reduced to mere semaphoric supporting structures for Chappe's device, thus creating a sort of semantic superimposition of a monument and a communication device. This juxtaposition was often felt to be incongruous, or perceived as a deviant and parasitic use of a picturesque site or a historical monument for the purpose of transmitting the incomprehensible messages of

---

limb"—a barb most likely directed at Hugo's *Notre-Dame de Paris*. In his novel *La Relique* Eça de Qeiroz would take up the character of the ridiculous antiquary measuring monuments with his parasol. A letter from Flaubert to Louise Colet attests to moments of saturation regarding the description of architecture in a certain type of travel literature: "*Do not describe the Acropolis' propyla.* Just think that we are up to our necks in architecture" (9 March 1853).

[10] Ruskin, *Seven Lamps*, 4.

the modern State. Victor Hugo speaks of the "tortured and grimacing telegraph" on top of Saint-Sulpice as an "accident" in *Notre-Dame de Paris*. Stendhal had originally planned to entitle his novel, *Lucien Leuwen, The Telegraph* since the device plays a major role in the political strategy and manipulations of the hero campaigning for office in the provinces. The telegraph appears as a "vile bracket" perched atop the old Montmartre tower in the first chapter of Emile Souvestre's *Philosophe sous les toits* (1850), and the narrating traveler of Hugo's *Le Rhin* continually encounters telegraphs whose "gesticulations" are like those of a "huge black insect." Flaubert and Maxime Du Camp notice telegraphs during much of their journey through the French countryside in *Par les champs et par les grèves*, and ask themselves about the "purpose . . . and meaning" of this device. For them it constitutes the "fantastic grimace of the modern world." In *Education sentimentale* it ironically dominates the already ironic scene that takes place in the historical site of Fontainebleau. Finally Lacroix's *Paris-Guide*, in a chapter entitled "Telegraphs," evokes "the mute and mysterious language which taunted our fathers' minds without ever betraying its secrets." If the semantic paradox of the telegraph—exposed to the eyes of all, and yet incomprehensible—contains some sort of state secret, what kind of secret can the omnipresent posters, signs, and commercial inscriptions of advertisement conceal? In an ironic twist on Hugo's "this will kill that" these texts had begun to practically devour the city's buildings. Since writers are always extremely aware of what is *already written* in the real, and what competes with the text in the surrounding context, what will be their attitude regarding this oversemiotization of the architecture of everyday life? In his travels Hugo had easily been able to integrate these rival written texts into his essentially philological and historical reading of the real. For example the title and pun of the last paragraph of chapter six of *Le Rhin* is: *"Ce qu'enseigne les enseignes"* ("What signs can teach us").[11] Later in his *Choses vues*, Hugo could still elicit a certain objective irony from the alignment of posters, strange juxtapositions of mural graffiti, or the indirect messages of political posters.[12] However, in *Mon coeur mis à nu* (a fine title for a work of

[11] "Where there are no churches, I simply look at signposts. Anyone who knows how to visit a town knows that shop signs have a great deal of meaning" (Hugo, *Le Rhin*, 90).

[12] French legislation attests to the invasion of the city's walls by the written word. A law known by most Frenchmen even today is one that is still posted on the walls of many buildings and monuments: *Defense d'afficher: Loi du 29 Juillet 1881* (Post no bills, law of 29 July 1881). For records of incongruous juxtapositions and *détournements* of posted texts, see Hugo's *Choses vues* in his *Oeuvres complètes*, Bouqins (Paris: Lafont, 1987), 1,110, 1,014, 1,057, 1,125.

self-exposure), Baudelaire speaks of the "overwhelming nausea brought on by posters." The only possible literary response to that nausea seems to be either irony, a second-degree discourse, or simply a "collage" of juxtaposed posters. These tactics alone enable the writer to mimetically reclaim the city. Jules Laforgue's *Grande complainte de la ville de Paris: Prose blanche* is just such a collage of "things seen" (*choses vues*), things overheard, and advertisements. Rimbaud's well-known, ironic *art poétique* in *Une Saison en enfer*—"*J'aimais les peintures idiotes, dessus de portes, décors, toiles de saltimbanques, enseignes, enluminures populaires*"[a]—or his poem entitled "Paris" in *L'Album zutique* makes a collage of the slogans and names borrowed from the advertisements on the city walls:

> *Al. Godillot, Gambier,*
> *Galopeau, Volf-Pleyel,*
> *—O Robinets!—Ménier,*
> *—O Christ!—Leperdriel!*
>
> *Kinck, Jacob, Bonbonnel!*
> *Veuillot, Tropmann, Augier!*
> *Gill, Mendès, Manuel,*
> *Guido Gonin!—Panier*
> *Des grâces! L'Hérissé!*
> *Cirages onctueux!*
> *Pains vieux, spiritueux!*
>
> *Aveugles!—puis qui sait?*
> *Sergents de ville, Enghiens*
> *Chez soi!—Soyons chrétiens!*[b]

[a] "I liked stupid paintings, door panels, stage sets, backdrops for acrobats, signs, popular engravings" (Arthur Rimbaud, *Une Saison en enfer*, trans. Wallace Fowlie in *Rimbaud Complete Works, Selected Letters* [Chicago: University of Chicago Press, 1966], 193).

[b]
> *Al. Godillot, Gambier*
> *Galopeau Wolf-Pleyel,*
> *—O Spiget!—Ménier,*
> *—O Christ!—Leperdriel!*
> *Kinck, Jacob, Bonbonnel!*
> *Veuillot, Tropmann, Augier!*
> *Gill, Mendès, Manuel*
> *Guido Gonin!—Basket*
> *Of the Graces! L'Hérissé*
> *Unctuous waxes!*
> *Old loaves of, spirits!*
> *Blind men!—but who knows?*
> *Policemen, Enghiens*
> *In your own home! Let's be Christians!*

(Rimbaud, *Complete Works*, 157)

This text can be compared to a *dizain réaliste* by Germain Nouveau in an anthology of such poems published in 1876:

> *J'ai du goût pour la flâne, et j'aime, par les rues,*
> *Les réclames des murs fardés de couleurs crues,*
> *La redingote Grise, et Mònsieur Gallopau;*
> *L'Hérissé qui rayonne au dessous d'un chapeau;*
> *La femme aux cheveux faits de teintes différentes.*
> *Je m'amuse bien mieux que si j'avais des rentes*
> *Avec l'homme des cinq violons à la fois,*
> *Bornibus, la Maison n'est pas au coin du Bois;*
> *Le kiosque japonais et la colonne-affiche . . .*
> *Et je ne conçois pas le désir d'être riche.*[c]

The confrontation between literary text and advertisement represents a crucial moment in the nineteenth century. Until then advertisement and hype (*puff*) had been confined to the workshop or the private home through subscription newspapers. Now it was descending into the streets and spreading over the city's facades. The street vendor's cry that could still make Proust dream was gradually making room for the "brouhaha" (*tintamarre*) of writing.[13] Thus the urban landscape becomes a sort of paper city, a capital—to quote Balzac in *Ferragus*— "clothed in billboards." The journalist and critic Victor Fournel described it in this way:

> Nowadays, Paris is nothing more than an immense wall of posters. It is studded from chimney to pavement with squares of paper of all colors and sizes, not to mention the graffiti. . . . In any street, arcade, or alleyway where there is . . . room on a wall, you can see the trophies of daguerreotypes

---

[13] *Tintamarre* is a word of the period. Along with *Le Charivari, Le Tintamarre* was a satiric newspaper (1843–1910) devoted to—as its subtitle indicates—"the critique of advertisement" and "the satire of hype." In this same vein there is a famous lithograph by Grandville "Les noces du Puff et de la réclame" (The wedding of Hype and Advertisement), or the chapter in Pierre Giffard's book, *Les Grands Magasins*, on "Puff and Krach" (Hype and Crash, 230ff.). The terms *toc, chic,* and *krach* which refer to a world of "emptiness," of "wind" and "void," or of "fakes" and lies, are formally monosyllabic and expressive onomatopoeias with negative connotations.

[c]  I like to hang about, and I like the streets,
The walls made up with advertisement of garish colors,
Grise's frockcoats and Mr. Gallopau;
L'Hérissé who beams from under a hat;
The woman whose hair is dyed different shades.
I have more fun than if I had a fortune
With the man of five violins at once,
Bornibus, the House is not at the edge of the Bois de Boulogne;
the Japanese kiosk and the column of ads . . .
And I have no desire to be rich.

reflecting myriads of bourgeois of all ages and forms, spread out with an intolerable complacency.[14]

In Andersen's "The Dryad" the first thing the heroine sees upon arriving in Paris for the 1867 Universal Exposition are "great inscriptions in letters one yard tall, figures painted on the walls from ground to cornice, . . . a wall plastered with posters and notices in front of which people stood immobile." The widespread practice of the exposition generated a widespread accompanying discourse—a voice posted and exposed. This collusion seemed to fascinate literature since it too is a writing practice devoted to exposing the real and propagating itself. *Au Bonheur des dames* provides an account of this fascination with words that flow freely and efficiently:

> Never had a store stirred up the city with such a publicity splash. *Bonheur* had spent almost six hundred thousand francs a year in posters, advertisements, and appeals of all sorts; four hundred thousand catalogues had been sent out, over a hundred thousand francs worth of fabric had been cut for samples. It was the ultimate invasion of newspapers and walls. Like a monstrous brass trumpet, ringing without respite in the ears of the public at the four corners of the earth, the store sounded the commotion of great sales. Henceforth, mobbed with people, its facade, with its bespangled, gilded magnificence, its huge windows for displaying the poetry of its women's fashions, and its profusion of signs, painted, engraved, and cut in stone became a living advertisement. From the marble slabs on the ground floor to the sheets of iron rounded off in semicircles above the roof, unfolding their gilded banners on which the name of the store could be read in letters bright as the sun.[15]

A borderline case of posted advertisement is found in a Villiers de l'Isle-Adam's story "L'Affichage céleste" (Celestial publicity; 1873)

[14] *Ce qu'on voit dans les rues de Paris* (Paris: Delahaye, 1858), 299, 397. See also John Grand-Carteret, *Vieux papiers, vieilles images: Cartons d'un collectionneur* where the author dreams of constituing a "story of paper" and speaks of the street as a "permanent open-air exposition, ever changing like a kaleidoscope" ([Paris: Le Vasseur, 1896], 428); and E. Maindron, editor of the official catalog of the 1889 Exposition, who published in 1874 *Les Murailles politiques,* a collection of posters from 1870–1871. Of course it is in the first modern megalopolis—London—that literature encounters the world of "vermillion signs" (enseignes vermeilles) (Verlaine, "Sonnet Boiteux," Book 7). See also the seminal treatment of advertisement in William Wordsworth's *The Prelude,* Book 7. In the twentieth century, Michel Serres confirms Hugo's famous phrase from *Notre-Dame de Paris* in a somewhat disenchanted way: "In principle transparent, glass walls are covered up and blinded by advertisement. This has killed that. Writing has killed architecture" (*Les cinq sens* [Paris: Grasset, 1985], 20).

[15] Zola, *Au bonheur des dames,* 348. Octave Mouret, who is a *calicot* [meaning both a "fabric clerk" and a "banner"—trans.], is therefore secretly homologous—that is why he is so fascinating—to that other type of "man-of-letters and paper"—the writer. Both are experts in the manipulation of signs, both produce "fictions" inscribed on public supports.

where the writer ironically proposes the possibility of a lumnious advertisement projected onto the sky. This futurist writing process of "universal exposition" would also be evoked in Verne's *La Journée d'un journaliste américain en 2,889*. Thus advertisement, an omnipresent discourse multiplied and made redundant which exploits all the possibilities offered by semiotics—signs, paintings, drawings, letters, symbols, sculpted allegories, orders, acronyms, brands, images, and brand images—can also paradoxically manufacture nonsense and illegibility. This is due to its overwhelming focus on an element which has no meaning in a language system—the proper noun. Moreover, advertisement's use of representational drawings and images, often of a synecdochical nature, can remain enigmatic since it is not always clear that a certain eye represents a specific optician or that a certain frock coat represents a specific tailor.[16] Perhaps because Hugo could appropriate any support—whether of stone or of paper—merely by initialing or signing it, he knew how to find meaning in any inscribed graffiti or proper noun. Flaubert, on the contrary, saw this wave of names left behind by tourists and merchants as a symbol of universal platitude. Flaubert, who had been so irritated upon finding "so many imbeciles' names" written all over the monuments of Egypt, associated the proper noun—an "asemanteme" to use Guillaume's term—with something else that has no meaning, namely stupidity. As a bearing structure that displayed objects, the wall seemed to have become the final destination for any work of art. This, in turn tends to change semantic status of the work of art which goes from being a sign to be understood, to a signpost to be recognized or a consignment for a purchase. An account of this evolution can be found in Henri Murger's *Scènes de la vie de Bohème*, which tells of Marcel, a painter whose masterpiece is refused several times by the Salon and is therefore deprived of exposure. His painting, initially entitled *The Crossing of the Red Sea* (*Le Passage de la mer Rouge*) is successively renamed to reflect the ever-changing trends of the art world: It is baptized *Crossing of the Rubicon*, *Crossing of the Berezina*, and then *The Arcade of the Panoramas* (*Le Passage des Panoramas*)—a title which would have no doubt delighted Walter Benjamin—before ending up as a sign for a fine-foods shop. A

---

[16] Renée, the heroine of *La Curée*, contemplates the boulevard below from a window of the café Riche: "Her eyes rested on the advertisements on a kiosk, harshly colored like Epinal prints on a pane of glass, in a yellow and green frame; there was the head of a laughing devil, with his hair standing on end (*hérissé*)—a hatter's advertisement that she failed to understand" (*Les Rougon-Macquart*, vol. 1, 450). This rebuslike advertisement is based on the same proper name, "Hérissé," mentioned in Rimbaud's collage poem "Paris" and Germain Nouveau's "Dizain realiste" ("J'ai du goût pour la flâne").

similar story occurs in *Ventre de Paris* where the painter Claude Lantier, who is also perpetually being refused exposure at the Salon, creates his "masterpiece" when he arranges the display window for the Quenu-Gradelle charcuterie. In a chapter entitled "Expositions au Louvre," in *Le Diable à Paris,* Bertall drew a caricature of a rejected artist painting a sign for a grocery store with the legend: "Mr. Oscar Patouillet, having had little success with paintings in the religious genre, is launching himself into a career painting monuments." These absurd itineraries reflect the victory of the streets over the Salon, and of the shop window over the picture frame.[17] In this sense the nineteenth century often seems nothing but a battle of expositions.

Many nineteenth-century works reveal literature's attraction to or repulsion of advertisement. There are texts, for example, that incorporate advertisement by recording and describing it. By copying what is *already* written or inscribed in the real, these works have truly accomplished the realist project. After all, language can only truly copy language; and in this sense a collage poem like Rimbaud's "Paris" is a *completely* "realist" text since it is a word-for-word transcription of a wall. However, writers who are committed to the values associated with the symbolic or the imaginary understand that what is at issue regarding space is no longer the problem of furnishing inhabitable volumes, or of interpreting monuments, but rather spatiality has become a succession of flat plots to be sold or divided into lots or vertical facades to be plastered with advertisements. By merging or exchanging functions, the wall and the book—two very different and privileged supports of production and preservation of meaning—run the risk of canceling each other out. Thus while the edifice becomes nothing more than a support for ephemeral advertisement or an exhibition "hall" for the exposition of objects or the exhibitionism of sub-

---

[17] Huysmans would often "thunder" against the paintings of historical subjects—"abominable window dressing for charcuteries"—that cluttered the cyma of the official Salon. These were not, he maintained, the equal of

those industrial posters featured on street walls and the boulevard's public urinals, which represent corners of Parisian existence: the flutter of the ballet, the work of clowns, English pantomimes, and the interior of circuses and racecourses. As far as I am concerned I would prefer that all exposition halls be plastered with [Jules] Chéret's chromolithographs or those wonderful sheets of paper from Japan worth one franc each, instead of seeing these walls stained with this heap of pitiful things. ("Salon de 1879," in *L'Art moderne/certains,* 28, 59)

The great competitor of the art object—the poster—can, as we see, serve as its model as well as its foil.

jects, the book becomes a mere article within the larger layout of the newspaper, an installment in a serial intended to boost circulation, or a mere pedagogic and documentary store-house (*magasin*).[18] Clearly, both the book and the wall which displayed (*étaler*) goods or knowledge were undergoing a symbolic loss of volume. In the section entitled "Etalages" of his work *Quant au livre,* Mallarmé evokes with some trepidation, "the architecture" of "piles or columns of books" that overflow from stores onto the sidewalks.

Of course, it is not surprising to see that all the great radical utopians, nostalgic for grand lapidary typography and free-flowing, lively speech, strictly prohibit this written and commercial voice from the walls of their ideal cities:

> Your gaze would never be offended by all that *scribbling,* those drawings and writings that sully our city walls and cause us to lower our eyes. . . . You would not have the pleasure or the bother of seeing so many *signs* and signposts above the doorways of houses, nor so many commercial notices and *posters* which almost always make buildings ugly; instead you would see beautiful *inscriptions* on monuments, workshops, and stores as well as useful notices magnificently printed on multicolored paper posted by the Republic's official bill posters in specially made frames so that these posters themselves would contribute to the city's overall beautification.[19]

In the eyes of most writers, the disrepute of the building was not the direct result of its role as a bearing structure to a universalized advertisement. Rather it is discredited as an edifice itself—as an architectural object. After 1850, fierce debates polarized around the urbanism of building lines so dear to prefects, on the one hand, and the "new"

[18] Curiously enough, the two buildings that are the most representative of the century are related to writing, the book, and the work of art: Garnier's Opéra on the one hand, a temple of lyric song, and the Bibliothèque Sainte-Geneviève designed by Henri Labrouste, on the other—the first building to systematically use iron and cast iron. The former was constructed to be a place that serves texts; the latter a place to store them. The Labrouste library facade and, according to some, its columns and ground floors (rez de chaussée) imitate the most characteristic texts of the century: the dictionary and the newspaper. Designed around 1838–1839 and built between 1843 and 1850, the fact that its facade seems composed "like a written page" with its vertical list of writers' names and its "serial" (feuilleton) at the ground-floor level, was pointed out by such contemporaries as Théodore de Banville in Lacroix's 1867 *Paris-Guide.* On the intersection of Hugo, Labrouste, *Notre-Dame de Paris,* and the Sainte-Geneviève Library, see Neil Levine, "The Book and the Building: Hugo's Theory of Architecture and Labrouste's Bibliothèque Sainte-Geneviève," in *The Beaux-Arts and Nineteenth-Century French Architecture,* ed. Robin Middleton (Cambridge, Mass.: MIT Press, 1982).

[19] Text by Cabet quoted in "Les symboles du lieu: L'habitation de l'homme," *L'Herne* (1983), 417.

architecture of engineers with its iron, cast iron, and glass, on the other. Paradoxically, for all its transparency this new type of architecture was deemed opaque by many writers. Because it was industrial, it was also seen as repetitive and therefore without style. Because it was polyvalent, its purpose or function was not readily identifiable; and because it was easily dismantled, it no longer had a privileged and fixed location. As a framework within which objects and styles from around the world were juxtaposed, it promoted eclecticism as a universal stylistic value. Finally, since the new transparent architecture lacked great walls, it no longer harbored great official depictions of the city's narrative, which unfold in prestigious frescos, stained glass, and paintings.[20] Thus this amnesiac, asemantic and unthinkable architecture's transparency was not felt to be conducive to the optimal organization of a space destined to insure and facilitate good connections between the objects on view and the spectators. What could be seen as its ability to welcome and arrange was on the contrary felt to block the practices of interpretation, meditation, and memory. All of these exacerbated the animosity of the belletrist who had always been troubled by the *semiotic* status of the building—was it sign, signal, symbol, signature, or insignia? For example, the Eiffel Tower—that empty symbol of an ephemeral exposition— only exposes and posits its own presence. Not until Guillaume Apollinaire, Robert Delaunay, the cubists and the surrealists at the beginning of the twentieth century would it be reclaimed as a plastic and symbolic object that acted as a signature for the city of Paris. As early as his 1890 self-portrait, the Douanier Rousseau was one of the few artists to integrate the Eiffel Tower into his work without any critical or satirical intent. Be that as it may, Charles Garnier, François Coppée, Charles Leconte de Lisle, Alexandre Dumas-fils, and Armand Sully-Prudhomme

[20] Hugo in *Notre-Dame de Paris* notes "[Architecture] no longer expresses anything, not even the memory of the art of another time. . . . The windowpane has replaced the stained-glass window." When speaking of the Paris Bourse he writes:

> Greek in its colonnade, Roman in the depressed arches of its doors and windows, Renaissance in its great segmental vault, . . . crowned with an attic storey such as Athens never knew, . . . we can hardly marvel enough at a monument which might equally well be a king's palace, a house of commons, a town hall, a college, a riding school, an academy, a warehouse, a law court, a museum, a barracks, a sepulcher, a temple, or a theater. For the present it is a stock exchange.

Thus for Hugo the monument manifests an excess of arbitrariness or eclecticism as well as a lack of motivation, since there is no relation between the container and the contained. He lays out the evidence of what, for the writers of the nineteenth century, would become the essential illegibility of their time.

came together in 1887 to sign a petition in the name of "humiliated monuments and belittled architecture" protesting this "useless and monstrous tower" that emerged from the "imagination of a machine-builder."[21] Michel Serres writes that before its widespread acceptance, the Eiffel Tower was seen as an antimonument:

> Three hundred meters that were not dedicated to the glory of a god, did not celebrate any victory or productive invention, three storys with no traditional, religious, military, or economic function. Apart from its symbolic use without any shining torches or heads, it is foolish yet wise, given the time when its engineer planned it. As transparent as it is devoid of meaning, its emptiness shows through its useless, derisory crossbars. . . . Without having any other meaning it exists solely for the purpose of being there. Static, built to stay erect, *posed*, . . . empty, translucent, almost theoretic, entirely explicit without any mystery or secret, perfectly metric, more formula than form, it *exposes* certain static theorems.[22]

Clearly this edifice is the apex of "exposition mentality." This borderline monument, which (unlike Hugo's) is not really meant to be viewed or questioned, serves merely as a means to an end. A mere support for an elevator, the Tower acts as a pedestal for tourists, raising them to a point from which they can deploy and exercise their gaze.[23] However, this ideal belvedere, like a solid version of the famous captive balloon of the 1867 Exposition, or Nadar's equally famous balloon that reduced Paris to photographic "plates," is a point from which the world reduced to dabs and lines is flattened, loses its depth, and is effaced.

These buildings, as both objects of spectacle, and means to a spectacle, along with their problematic semiotic status as legible structures, must also contend with new techniques and industrial materials. Coating and plating materials that lack depth such as zinc, macadam, plas-

---

[21] This petition is cited in *Le Moniteur de l'Exposition de 1889*, 20 February 1887, no. 112. Also cited is the response written by the then Minister of Commerce and Industry, Edouard Lockroy, who was also organizing the Exposition which was not exempt from political implications.

[22] Michel Serres, *Statues* (Paris: Edition Bourin, 1987), 128–129 (emphasis mine).

[23] In his enthusiastic description of the Eiffel Tower in his *Année Scientifique et industrielle de 1889*, the popularizer Louis Figuier presents it as an "observatory" like a "captive balloon" with "a splendid view" but which "flattens out heights." Montmartre is seen as a "white dab," the domes of the exposition are "shining dots in the sun" where the pathways are "lines," the streets "clear furrows on a brown and monotonous background." Figuier adds: "No noise rises to this height: the city so feverish and active, seems like the resting place of silence and immobility. It is a heap of stones, from which no noise emerges" (470–473).

ter, repetitive bricks—notably glazed bricks that become so popular after the 1878 Exposition—and industrial glass, all become obsessive literary themes and metaphors. This is particularly the case for plaster, that ersatz of stone which has the same status as the *temporary* exposition pavilion. In fact, Abel Hermant, referring to the Universal Exposition of 1900, writes of a "Cosmopolis of lumps of plaster." Hence, plaster becomes the insistent vehicle of an extended metaphor with strong moral connotations. Like a cosmetic layer applied to a facade, plaster masks, hides, and misrepresents the mediocre edifice underneath. "Our fathers had a Paris of stone; our sons will have a Paris of plaster," writes Hugo in *Notre-Dame de Paris* (bk. 3., chap. 2). Memnon, the mythic hero of living and singing stone, no longer had a place in this world of plate and lies. This suspicion is expressed by Ruskin in his chapter "Lamp of Truth" when he criticizes the "falsely represented materials" on the facades of modern cities: "This only results in throwing suspicion on the real stones underneath and on every piece of granite that we subsequently come across. After which, we even begin to doubt in Memnon himself." The practice of deceptively "whitewashing" facades with plaster and plate is frequently mentioned in literature throughout the second half of the century. Hugo and Delacroix (in his *Journals*) write repeated diatribes against the whitewashing of churches and houses, while in the novels of Balzac, Flaubert, and Zola innumerable plaster statues fill their characters' gardens and vestibules. Paris itself is presented in the "exposition" of *Le Père Goriot* as an "illustrious valley of lumps of plaster, on the point of collapsing into rubble at any moment." Moreover, Parisian novels of manners abound with "painted" ladies known as *filles de plâtre,* and *lorettes,*[d] or as Balzac calls them in *Béatrix,* "pioneers of fresh plaster." For example, *Les Filles de plâtre* is the title of an 1856 best-selling novel by Xavier de Montépin. Zola entitles a collection of critical essays *Marbres et plâtres* in 1867, and throughout his novels, where this material has more the status of stigma than of sign, the symmetrical characters of the old rogue and the young dead beat (*crevé*) in frock coats smeared with

---

[d] *Filles de plâtre* are literally "plaster women" and *lorettes* are women of ill repute living in the neighborhood around Notre-Dame de Lorette. Both terms refer to women staying in newly renovated apartments leased at low cost by men who kept their mistresses there during the long period of time it took for the plaster to dry.

traces of new plaster picked up while in the company of these women of the streets.[24]

Many writers were preoccupied by this new one-dimensional universe which brought with it an entirely new generation of habitats and inhabitants. "Solids no longer exist," for these writers.[25] In literary as well as critical texts the themes of flatness and loss of volume along with their accompanying lexical field of negative synonyms—platitude, posturing (s'afficher), effacing, face, facade, lay out, display, surface, superficial, dab, plaque, plate, panel, flattening, and film—come up over and over. Juxtaposition and abundance immediately imply the eclecticism and neutralization that obstructs any totalizing synthesis. Metonymy impedes metaphor. By exposing everything and anything, an individual's salon becomes the Salon, boulevards become theaters, and walls become picture frames, and the whole world is transformed into an "imaginary museum" where exposed objects and works stifle one another and where the imaginary itself cannot be exercized: "Everything ends up on a wall or in a display window. . . . *We are becoming superficial*," writes Valéry in 1923 in an article entitled "Le Problème des musées." This text can be compared to another that we have already discussed—"Un problème d'exposition"—where Valéry attributes the death of architecture, once the master of other arts, to this "system that juxtaposes works that devour one another." The "church-portal mentality" as expressed by Hugo in *Notre-Dame de Paris,* and "storehouse mentality" as presented by the Goncourts, Zola, and Verne had now both yielded to a fascinating and disquieting "cliché" or "platitude mentality." For these writers the juxtapositions of the bric-a-brac or

[24] In *Au bonheur des dames* the store expands by progressively consuming the neighborhood which is falling in ruins, "under a cloud of plaster" (vol. 3, 588); one of the characters declares, "We were being eaten away by plaster" (591). "Paris was rotting in a cloud of plaster," writes Zola in Chapter 3 of *La Curée,* and he described Maxime, the son of Saccard the real-estate speculator, as leading "the most nomadic life in the world, living in his father's new houses, choosing the story that he liked best, moving each month . . . he smoothed out [*essuyait les plâtres* literally means "to dry or wipe the plaster," but also means to "smooth out" or "iron out" problems encountered in the initial stages of a project—trans.] any problems in these new dwellings with a few mistresses by his side." (*Les Rougon-Macquart,* vol. 1, 168–169). In *Nana* among other works, we find the motif of the black frock coat smeared with white plaster, a motif which takes the popular expression *essuyer les plâtres* literally. As to the opinion that Flaubert attributes to his heroes in Chapter 4 of *Bouvard et Pécuchet*—"They deplored vandalism, thundered against whitewash"—it could be read as a parody of Hugo in particular and antiquaries in general.

[25] This phrase, typical of a certain post modern discourse of the 1980s, is definitely comparable to what was being written in the second half of the nineteenth century. It is taken from Paul Virilio, *L'Espace critique* (Paris: Christian Bourgois, 1984), 13.

pavilion style of exposition, which had replaced the great organizational style represented by Le Play's plan for the 1867 Exposition, are the negation of the efficient horizontal organization of the store. Similarly, plate, imitations, and gaudy fancy goods (*article de Paris*) negated the vertical symbolic and material plenitude of the authentic work of art. This was no longer a world of interlocking volumes or proportional scenography, a world of differentiated levels where the real, traditionally associated with the hidden, would allow itself to be apprehended *behind* screens or from within more or less impenetrable hiding places. Whereas Romantics like Hugo, in his preface to his *Odes* of 1822, could hope "to see more than the thing in things," it was no longer possible to do anything but see the thing itself. The black box of the ruin, an envelope waiting to be hermeneutically developed by the antiquary and a volume that exposed its meaning and stories by soliciting an active visitor/reader, had been replaced by a world of exposed and posted images. The laminated sheets of history had yielded to a sheet of plate. The windowpane, the facade, and the surfaces of things in general, were nothing more than windowpanes, facades, and surfaces that exhibited and exposed only themselves; they were merely exteriors that had become synonymous with artificiality, falseness, and stupidity. The new architecture seemed incapable of restoring this deeply felt loss of meaning, substance, and dimension—despite the knowledge that architecture was and should have been the exemplary art of adding dimension to a space by establishing limits, height, envelopes, volume, and depth in order that it be livable and thinkable.

The visit of Hugo's narrator in *Le Rhin* to the Belgian city of Liège is an excellent example of this conception of a world reduced to platitude. (It is perhaps worth noting that Belgium is also the site and symbol of all platitude for Baudelaire, Rimbaud, and Verlaine.) The description of this industrial city acts as a foil to Hugo's descriptions of other historic cities. He portrays an emblematic face-to-face encounter between on the one hand an industrial city that seems to have been ravaged by war, where "everything is being effaced by factory smoke," and on the other hand "a stupefied bourgeois" contemplating this spectacle without really seeing it, "as he reads *Le Constitutionnel* on a terrace sheeted in zinc." This typifies what would be a common scene in the "literature of suspicion," namely the conjunction of stupor and effacement. The noble inscriptions and historical monuments of ancient architecture had been replaced by the flatness of printed advertisements and newspapers, the plate of a zinc-covered terrace, and the platitude of a reader and his reading material. We are a long way from the mountain-top ruin, the monument in the hills, and the Gothic gables of the Romantic landscape with its architectured sites that are at once charged with meaning and polyaesthetic. These sites that were visited, surveyed, drawn, admired, combed through, smelled, and touched had made way for Hugo's staid (*assis*) bourgeois in a stupor who was a far cry from the cultivated antiquary questioning monuments whose symbolic and allegoric transcendence prompted the use of memory. By becoming merely an object to be viewed, losing its volume, and becoming purely an exposition of an appearance that serves to promote commercial or political manipulation, the real had seemingly lost its propensity to excite the imaginary. Plaster, zinc, facades, and display windows were only one aspect of this widespread semantic deflation. "Fakes, electrotype, and imitation gold" is the phrase that Verlaine and Coppée ironically place as the epigraph to one of the scenes of their revue, *Qui veut des merveilles?* performed in 1867, the year of what Larousse called the "great exposition." Of course the word *wonder* (*merveille*) was a fetishized term for exposition mentality. It would also serve as the title for the famous series by Charton published by Hachette entitled "La Bibliothèque des merveilles." In this case the revue acts as a sort of "counter-*bibliothèque*" or "countercollection" by parodying in textual form what the real lays out quite seriously.[26] For certain writers, a whole series of objects, habitats, and inhabitants were taking on the appearance of a vast flatland: The dioramas at the expositions; store displays (a century later France's large merchandizing marts would be referred to as *grandes surfaces*); daguerreotype plates that replaced real memory with paper memory disconnected from the subject and which, according to Baudelaire, "spreads a disgust for history among the masses" (according to Barthes,

[26] The epigraph of Verlaine and Coppée's epilogue reads: "Paris in 1868, in a supreme honor to electric light—immense and radiating boulevards in all directions—superb barracks—trees wrapped in detachable zinc collars—many photography establishments." "Imitation gold" (*similor*) is the name of one of the characters in Paul Féval's series *Habits noirs*. Everything in Tom Lévis's store is also imitation and fake, and plastered in advertisement, in *Le Roi en exil* (chap. 5) by Daudet. Electrotype (Garnier speaks at length about this as well as zinc in his book *A travers les arts*) is a procedure "which consists in coating, through the use of electric current, metal dissolved in a liquid, so that the surface of the object is smooth, and reproduces all the details of the original plate" (*Dictionnaire général des sciences théoriques et appliquées* [Paris: Privat-Deschanel and Focillon, 1877]). Fournel in *Paris nouveau et Paris futur* (294) often returns to the subject of the preferred material of the new Paris, "stucco, . . . plaster of Paris, . . . tinsel, . . . silver-plated metal (*ruolz*), . . . and imitation gold (*chrysocale*)." Chrysocale appears also in the first pages of *Education sentimentale*. The nineteenth-century text expresses considerable anxiety and suspicion towards construction materials.

"with photography we enter into a flatness of death"); the new aligned buildings whose facades displayed the wealth of their inhabitants (the *Paris-Guide* of 1867 describes them as "lapidary parvenus"); the bourgeois strolling in uniform, demonumentalized suburbs and spouting platitudes (Flaubert writes in *Madame Bovary,* "Charles's conversation was commonplace as a street pavement");ᵉ the poster (a flat sheet easily contrasted with the volume of the book, structurally resembling the serial that is but a slice of a novel) covering entire cities with ephemeral messages. These dull yet engrossing hieroglyphs of stupidity are the signs of a world where the visible and the legible, the exposed and the sacred, and the image and the imaginary are no longer conjured.

Once the building and the monument had been reduced to plate and facade they lost not only the attributes of works of art but their paradigmatic status as models for any "good" work of art. Actually, by the middle of the century the art form that would most benefit from this status was music, which was perceived as the only extant art involving a "volume" into which a spectator/listener could "enter." Because of municipal constraints that mandated the alignment of facades, city streets were traced as "straight as a die"; a verse from Verlaine's *Sagesse* (pt. 3, section 18) speaks of the resulting "long ennui de vos haussmanneries."ᶠ Thus, even the street had lost its scenographic function of delineating a system of mansions that included cafés, boulevards, salons, and even the Bois de Boulogne, all of which were evenly distributed for the purpose of permanent social rituals and spectacles. They too were reduced to a flat mosaic—a two-dimensional system of squares on a playing board. Anticipating Nadar's balloon trip over Paris, Victor Hugo wrote in *Notre-Dame de Paris*: "I do not despair but that one day a balloon's eye view of Paris will offer us that wealth of lines, that opulence of detail, that diversity of aspects, that somehow grandiose simplicity and unexpected beauty which characterizes a checkerboard."[27] In comparison to the great Romantic lapidary model the competing model of the well-ordered and well-stocked store had already been deemed deficient. This was even more true of the plated delirium of fin-de-siècle expositions. Thus Paxton's Crystal Palace yielded to New York's 1902 Flat-

[27] Hugo, *Notre-Dame de Paris* (bk. 3, chap. 2). Let us note in passing that *La Mosaïque* is the title of an encyclopedic and pedagogic magazine of the period.

ᵉ Gustave Flaubert, *Madame Bovary,* trans. Paul de Man (New York: Norton, 1965), 29.

ᶠ "The drawn-out tedium of your haussmanneries."

Iron Building;[28] the *flâneur* made way for tourists and shoppers; balance sheets were replaced by bric-a-brac; brilliance by tinsel; and what used to be a delight to the eyes became a gaudy eyesore. But perhaps the most important of these changes involved the replacement of art object by kitsch—an object defined by the perversion of such fundamentally architectural practices as the alteration of scale or the transformation of function.[29] The frequent appearance of kitsch in Flaubert's work is striking: the napkin rings turned by Binet; Charles Bovary's cap; Emma Bovary's tiered wedding cake; the church porch in Carnac, Plouharnel's hat, Fontevrault's cap, and structures on Semot's grounds at Clisson in *Par les champs et par les grèves*; the descriptions of the Chinese baths and the Alhambra in *Education sentimentale*; and finally all of *Salammbô*.

For the most demanding writers, the real, like a photograph that was either over- or underexposed, was no longer capable of lending itself to a readable reproduction. Two different types of illegibility ensued. There was either an excess of distinct moments such as a host of flashing lights or the pulverulence of an image. In the late nineteenth-century literary text, this is exemplified by the proliferation and juxtaposition of "useless details" in descriptions. In such cases the image displayed only a network of separated points that lacked a cohesive global principle. The second type of illegibility was derived from the production of a surface which was on the contrary completely undifferentiated and unmodulated from within—a surface that was little more than a dab (*tache*). Thus emerges the theme of effacement already encountered in Veuillot's diatribe and Hugo's scene in Liège. It is also present in *Notre-Dame de Paris*'s chapter, "A Bird's Eye View of Paris": "Present-day Paris . . . is a collection of specimens from several centuries, and the most beautiful have vanished (*s'efface*)." In a similar vein Taine's character Graindorge writes: "There are too many expositions,[30] news-

---

[28] Not until the twentieth century are flat buildings—historically and *effectively* a consequence of Haussmann-like urbanism which had increased the number of acute-angle buildings at the intersection of new streets—integrated into the imaginary and literature. Roger Caillois's *Apprentissage de Paris* (Paris: Fata Morgana, 1984) retraces his strolls in the fifteenth arrondissement of Paris. He asks himself, when confronted with these flat buildings and their acute, beveled edges, what mysterious beings could live there— ectoplasmic extraterrestrials, or ghosts of no dimension. The motif of the building on the corner can also be found on paintings like Gustave Caillebotte's *Rue de Paris, temps de pluie*.

[29] Kitsch displayed in a crystal palace would be the century's emblematic combination of aesthetic attraction and repulsion. On kitsch see Abraham Moles, *Psychologie du kitsch, l'art du bonheur* (Paris: Mame, 1971).

[30] The themes of eye strain and clutter in expositions is a commonplace of the Salon as a literary genre. Denis Diderot develops it for example in 1767 in his *Salon*, about Hubert

papers, and articles. . . . The five thousand paintings of the Exposition overwhelm your attention, and efface any possible beauty." Notions revolving around the "dab" (*tache*), the "dot" (*point*), and "flatness" clearly are leitmotifs in the aesthetic debates relating to painting after 1860. This was particularly notable in early stages of impressionism— the 1866 Manet Affair for example—and later postimpressionism when tachism, pointillism, and cloisonism—as well as the term referring to the Italian impressionists, *macchiaioli*—begin to create paintings where the surface overshadows the content (the sacrosanct subject of the work). These paintings also gave precedence to color over the modulation of values and over the rendering of an image which turned objects within paintings and gave the works depth.[31] These same terms come up in literary criticism's polarizing debates about *description*—that part of a work which is in charge of exposing the real by explaining it in detail. Description of course is considered a dangerous part of the text, since by laying out too much knowledge and know-how, the author, according to critics like Boileau, can compromise the global coherence of the

---

Robert, where he speaks of "eyes strained and dazzled by so many different objects." Balzac develops the same theme in the exposition of *Pierre Grassou* (1839) where he presents the Salon in this way: "Instead of a tournament, you have a riot; instead of a glorious exposition you have a tumultuous bazar; instead of choice, you have totality." Charles Blanc sharply criticizes the excess glare and daylight let in by these great glass walls (which would disappear by the time of the 1900 Exposition) that flatten or efface the exposed objects:

> The blinding light that the glass coverings pour out is so unfavorable to the exposition of an art object that it is necessary to use a prodigious quantity of canvases and false ceilings and cut panels acting as baffles to filter and temper the light. . . . The interior decorator thus becomes the indispensable ally of the architect, and we know how dear this type of help can be! As to sculptures exposed in gardens, with this harmful light pounding on them, wrapped in reflected light, they no longer are *model forms*—they have light shining on them where the artist had planned for shadow, and they only offer *flattened forms,* with *no accents,* because the *relief* is not supported by any vigor. (Cited in *Les Merveilles de l'Exposition de 1878* [Paris: Librairie Illustrée et Librairie Dreyfous, n.d.], 18–19.)

31 The influence on impressionism of the flat, compartmentalized forms of Japanese prints, which were discovered at the Universal Exposition in the middle of the century, is well-known. Writing about Manet in 1866–1867, Zola speaks in terms of "dabs" (*taches*). Maurice Denis in a famous definition of the painting (developed towards 1888 with roots in Zola's art criticism) says: "Remember that before being a war horse, a naked woman, or a certain anecdote, a painting is essentially a planar *surface* covered in colors and arranged in a certain order." It would be interesting to verify in what way the fascination of a text for cloisonné objects, for example the stained-glass windows in the legend of Saint Julian the Hospitalier, in Flaubert's story (and the colored glass that worked as a foil for a literature of the transparent "glasshouse") mimetically creates a text that is itself partitioned off into brief, separated paragraphs.

work. All of this occurred at the very moment that terms like *dab, dot, speck,* and *panel* had become almost obligatory literary leitmotifs.[32]

Of all these writers of the second half of the century, Flaubert was probably most acutely aware of and most easily exasperated by a reality which aesthetically and ethically had dwindled to a filmy residue. This is clear in his montages of composite and heterogeneous architectural objects. But it is equally apparent in his textual montages of platitudes (such as those exposed in the scene at the agricultural fair in *Madame Bovary*), as well as the proliferation of a one-dimensional cast of characters—as we will see in the following chapter—on display within the novel itself. Perhaps more importantly this platitude is seen in Flaubert's relentless composition of urban and natural landscapes through the juxtaposition of reference points that are completely void of volume or depth. Thus he gives us a panoply of lines, dabs, dots, profiles, pools, and panels as well as things that are layed out, spread out, and outlined as well as on display. He presented a world of flowerbeds (*plates-bandes*), pavements, suburbs, and open-work fences where even the trees—espaliers against the wall—are flat. Here are some examples taken from *Bouvard et Pécuchet*: "Torpor spread through the air"; "the unchanging road stretched out uphill towards the horizon"; "there were yards upon yards of rocks, the ditches were full of water, the country-side was layed out in wide slabs of cold, monotonous green"; "the Canal Saint-Martin, enclosed by two locks, showed in a straight line its ink-black water"; "between the houses the clear expanse of the sky was cut up into plates of ultramarine; and as the sun beat down, the white facades, the slate roofs, and the granite quays glowed dazzlingly."[g] Depth is mentioned only in an antiphrasal and nonsignifying way. It is either a voluble flow of words coming from an off-stage prompter or it comes in the form of a cliché severed from its origins. In the latter case it is like the perforation of a stencil (*poncif*)[h] which after all is a way of reproducing a line by using holes of a previously cut form. In *Fusées* Baudelaire writes of the "immense depth of thought in common sayings,

---

[32] The dab is regarded by a certain literary modernity as a distinctive and identifying trait. (Think of Baudelaire's "riot of detail" in reference to Constantin Guys.) An example taken from one of the most famous literary descriptions of the naturalist school is a description of Paris, in *Une Page d'amour* by Zola: "She made out passersby, an active crowd of black *dots*, carried in a swarm of movement; the yellow bodywork of an omnibus threw off a *spark*; . . . and along the grassy embankments among other strollers a maid in a white apron stained (*tachait*) the grass with brightness" (my emphasis).

[g] Gustave Flaubert, *Bouvard and Pécuchet*, trans. Earp and Stonier (London: John Cape, 1936), 17, 33, 34.

[h] *Poncif* means "stencil" as well as "commonplace" or "cliché."

holes dug by generations of ants." Of course depth can be silent or dumb like Charles Bovary's cap, which was "of a composite nature" and "whose dumb ugliness has depths of expression, like an imbecile's face."[i] (The term *composite* is of course an architectural reference, thus this passage can be compared to Hugo's description of the corn market resembling "an English jockey's cap.") Faces, facades, flatness, and plates are all elements of an overexposure that revealed only a void while becoming the criteria for gauging other beings and milieux. Thus we are told that Yonville is a "hybrid land where language has no accent, just like the landscape has no character." Emma Bovary believed that "other lives, however flat, had at least the chance of some event."[j] In his preface to his friend Louis Bouilhet's work, Flaubert notes: "His hatred of the commonplace ruled out any sort of platitude." He goes on to emphasize the significant relationship between political disillusionment and a more generalized reign of shallowness: "[After 1848–1852] imaginations had gone particularly flat." Hugo echoed this sentiment when he wrote in *Choses vues,* that the regime coming out of the coup d'état was "violent and flat," while in *Les Châtiments*—in the poem "Forces des choses"—he contends that "History has gone flat and grown ugly." Of course the Stendhalian hero's greatest fear was flatness and the adjective *flat* was considered a supreme insult. For Rimbaud it became a predicate describing the entire universe. In his poem "Soir historique" he writes: "*Un petit monde blême et plat, Afrique et Occidents, va s'édifier,*"[k] and he begins his poem "Bruxelles" with the word "flowerbeds" (*plates-bandes*). This vision of the world is equally true for Laforgue who begins his poem "La cigarette" with the statement: "Oui, ce monde est bien plat."[l] Zola, who authored a now lost work entitled *Recueil de vastes platitudes,*[33] wrote in *La Curée* of the "new regime's superficial peace." Finally, Céard's novel *Une Belle Journée*

---

[33] *Recueil de vastes platitudes* was mentioned by Henri Mitterand in his notes to Zola's *Oeuvres complètes* (vol. 15, 847). It is worth noting that the middle of the nineteenth century saw an end to the publication of collections of "poetic clichés" like "Gradus," collections of clichés from before the "age of suspicion" of platitudes (cf. Carpentier, *Gradus français*, 2d ed. [1825]; or De Wailly's 6th ed., ed. De Wailly [1875]; or *Le Génie de la langue française* by Goyer-Linguet [1864]). These first-degree manuals would be replaced by ironic and distant collections like *Dictionnaire des idées reçues* by Flaubert or Rigaud's *Dictionnaire de lieux communs* (Paris: Ollendorf, 1887); or Léon Bloy's *L'Exégèse des lieux communs.*

[i] Flaubert, *Madame Bovary*, 2.

[j] Ibid., 45.

[k] A small, white, flat world, Africa and the Wests is going to be erected," Rimbaud, *Complete Works*, 251.

[l] "Yes, this world is quite flat."

(1881)—practically a pastiche of a Flaubert novel—is a veritable collection of platitudes. The heroine of this work, who as coincidence would have it is married to a mediocre architect, is a devotee of Sunday strolls in sinister suburbs that are as flat as her husband's blueprints. On one particular day ruined by rain, she bungles a nascent love affair with a man who is as much of a nonentity as her husband. This pleasure party in the town of Bercy, "emptied out because it is Sunday," remains "platonic." They find themselves in a restaurant whose "flowered wallpaper" is meticulously described, located on a "pale embankment" with scenery resembling "photographic plates." Despite her prodigious and inordinate vision of her husband's abysmal incompetence and of the "continuous uniformity (*plat*) of his existence," and despite her desire to escape marriage's "flat horizon" and a life that was "unrelentingly flat," she does not commit adultery. Instead they kill time in the restaurant by reading newspapers, advertisements, and even the telephone directory, while exchanging clichés. By the end of the novel, as if captivated by insignificance and allowing herself to be "absorbed in platitude," the heroine returns to the conjugal home where she finds her husband absorbed in his newspaper—*Le XIXème Siècle*—and unconsciously reciting its phrases.[34]

In the realist and naturalist text, the petit bourgeois on a country outing in the suburbs—a "space belonging to no particular gender, a neuter space" according to Balzac in *Ferragus*—like the worker on a spree or on vacation often become the bearing structure for a systematic and ironic rewriting of the great Romantic travel scene in which the antiquary deciphers stones and their inscriptions, collects relics and fragments, and listens to history's rumblings and echoes while reactivating its cultures, symbols and myths. An important scene in Zola's *L'Assommoir* that centers around Gervaise's wedding can be read in exactly this way. In this chapter the couple's friends, relatives, and neighbors took a stroll in the heart of historic Paris before their

[34] Céard's expression "to be absorbed in platitude" functions like an ironic oxymoron. Certain literary characters of the second half of the nineteenth century would be intoxicated with platitude, like a vertigo, which coincided with a two-dimensional universe. Jean Lehor, who is part of the stable of writers employed by Lemerre, a publisher whose address—Walter Benjamin would have appreciated this—was *passage* Choiseul, writes in the poem "Le monde heureux des songes" included in his collection *L'Illusion: "Donc ne plus rien vouloir qu'adorer la surface / Adorable parfois de tout cela qui passe"* (Thus to want only to adore the surface / Sometimes more adorable than that which passes by). In *Education sentimentale* Frédéric hesitates between music (an art which like architecture creates volume and envelops the body), "which alone seemed capable of expressing his inner turmoil," and painting: "Or sometimes the surface of things spoke to him, and he wanted to paint."

celebratory meal. On the boulevards the members of the wedding party themselves became a spectacle by displaying "their ill-assorted and out-of-fashion clothing. . . . Other strollers quickened their pace to see them, while several amused shopkeepers stood behind their windows." The group resembled a tachist painting: "The couples of the procession set startling dabs against the grey wet background of the boulevards." When they enter the Louvre, they visited the collection of ancient sculpture: "With chins raised and eyes blinking, the couples slowly advanced between the gigantic stone figures. . . . Stone carving was a great deal better nowadays. Then an inscription in Phoenician characters amazed them. No one could ever possibly have read that scrawl!" They moved on to paintings that they did not understand: "Centuries of art passed before their bewildered ignorance. . . . The wedding party was shuddering and was thoroughly bored." Once again, in this prestigious site of exposition, the group became an object of spectacle: "News must have spread that a wedding party was visiting the Louvre, for painters hastened up with broad smiles on their faces, and inquisitive people installed themselves on the benches, so as to be comfortable when viewing the procession." Once outside the museum the group took shelter from the rain under one of the arches of the Pont-Royal:

> In the meantime, the men amused themselves by shouting so as to stir the echo of the arch. One after the other, Boche and Bibi-La-Grillade swore at the void, crying out: "You, swine!" with all their might, and laughing heartily when the echo returned the word. Then with their voices growing hoarse, they entertained themselves by skimming smooth pebbles on the water.[35]

Thus we clearly see what has become of the lapidary motifs and accessories of the Romantic traveler. Flattened stones are merely playthings to be skimmed across water. Echoes reverberating off architecture are no longer true echoes, the voices of the dead, or the rumblings of history, rather they are carriers of coarse and insulting language. The architectural structure itself is not only reduced to purely a means of passage, but also to a mere shelter from the rain. In another scene in the same chapter of *L'Assommoir*, the members of the wedding party, having climbed to the bronze belvedere at the summit of the Vendôme column,

---

[35] Zola, *Les Rougon-Macquart*, pt. 2, 442–448. In *Education sentimentale* Frédéric also skims rocks on water "still (*plate*) like a mirror" where water lillies "were layed out" in Nogent (part 2, 5). Skimming rocks that bounce off water is a game identifiable with a flat universe. In *Les Français peint par eux-mêmes*, A. de Lacroix portrays the urban *flâneur* in contrast with the passive gawker "who invented the sport of fishing and ingeniously passes the time by skimming rocks and making concentric ripples in the water."

are completely uninterested in picking out monuments, but instead seek out "the wine-shop where they would be dining that evening."[m] By systematically and prosaically flattening out their component parts, scenes like this one, invert or divert (*détourner*) the elements of the Romantic spectacle.

In a universe that has lost dimension and volume, no connections can be established between containers and contained or between habitats and inhabitants. Moreover, for texts devoted to describing this one-dimensional world, it is the very narrative organization of the work which may well be incapable of finding its place, given that its time is fragmented into moments and its space is fragmented into juxtaposed tableaux. Perhaps there is no way for literature to reclaim this flat world except through the use of irony or mimetic parody. The literary text can either imitate the eclectic juxtapositions of the exposition by means of its own juxtapositions, collages, and montages (such as the scene of the agricultural fair in Madame Bovary or Rimbaud's poem "Paris"). Or it can exaggerate (or, to use Rimbaud's term, *outrer*) the naive, shattered, and flat aspects of the real reduced to plastered images—as illustrated by Rimbaud's *Illuminations,* also referred to as "painted plates," or the title of one of his poems: "Eclatante victoire de Sarrebrück, remportée aux cris de Vive L'Empereur! (Gravure belge brillamment coloriée, se vend à Charleroi, 35 centimes)."[n]

One last point regarding typography. The great Roman, Gothic, or hieroglyphic lapidary typography of official inscriptions encountered by the Romantic traveler while visiting monuments (and which provided the very model used in recording memories of these visits) was clearly being effaced by two other, more ephemeral types of writing: graffiti and advertisement. This left room within the realist and naturalist text for a typography of "suspicion," *italics,* which was not hieratic, but almost always signaled the author's disengagement from the clamor of society.[36] Stereotomy is replaced by its foil, the stereotype, which is by definition words set in form and meaning, but not set in a bearing structure, and therefore lacking a sole proprietor or identifiable origin. One overwhelmingly architectural example of the use of italics is the exposition—

---

[36] On Flaubert's use of italics see Claude Duchet, "Signifiance et insignifiance: Le discours italique dans *Madame Bovary,*" in *La Production du sens chez Flaubert Colloque de Cerisy,* ed. Claudine Gothot-Mersch (Paris: Union Générale d'Editions, 1975).

[m] Emile Zola, *The Dram-Shop* ed. Ernest A. Vizetelly (New York: Albert and Charles Boni, 1924), 67–74; translation modified.

[n] "Resounding victory at Sarrebrück, won to the cries of "Long Live the Emperor! (Brilliantly colored Belgian engraving for sale in Charleroi, 35 centimes.)"

description in *Madame Bovary* which introduces the reader to Yonville.
In Flaubert's flatly retranscribed description of an overly semiotized reality, these italics insert themselves into a competing proliferation of signals, signs, and signposts. Next to Homais's shop sign and his pharmacy
plastered with advertisement and inscriptions; the notary's gleaming cop-
per signs and ornamental plaster Cupid; the natural sign in the form of a
bundle of twigs tied to a broomstick swinging from a window; the tavern;
and the church with its French flag, its pews labeled with the names of
parishioners, and its "painted copy entitled 'The Holy Family,'" Flaubert
presents the City Hall, "a sort of Greek temple" with the "Gallic cock
resting one foot upon the Charter and holding in the other the scales of
Justice." At this point the italics appear—the city hall it seems was constructed *after the designs of a Paris architect.*[o] These italics are a signal of
both proximity and distance. On the one hand they are used to cite a
phrase probably repeated over and over by the locals, and which may
very well be inscribed on the building or written in a guidebook; on the
other hand they signal an unbridgeable distance between this utterance
and the novelistic enunciation. Of course, with an nth degree of
autoreferential enunciation, they could signal that this distant "architect
from Paris" could very well be the author himself. Yet this polyphonic
enunciation, by producing several unattached and reverberating echoes
of different discourses and thereby dislocating any unique and univocal
source, does not re-establish any unique and reliable source. Instead of
focusing on volume and perspective—Flaubert often attributed the commercial failure of *Education sentimentale* to the novel's "lack of
perspective"—it offers a heterogenuous and flat intertextuality, an indefinite network of enunciatory disconnections, an overexposure of unattrib-
utable discourse. Such borderline platitudes can be fatal. A "purely"
insignificant surface, like the small "patch" (*pan*) of yellow wall in front
of which Proust's Bergotte dies while visiting an "exhibition of Dutch
paintings" is at once a fascinating, dumbfounding, insignificant, and
even precious fragment. The patch negates the great totalizing spectacles
embodied by architectural objects such as the *Pan*theon, the *pan*orama,
and the *pan*opticon as well as the exposure afforded by belvederes, stores,
museums, and glass houses. Thus when reduced to its simplest form of
expression, this scene on view, can only be a "punctum"—to use
Barthes's term—a site where meaning is collapsed. This poignant site

[o] Flaubert, *Madame Bovary*, 49–50.

that neutralizes the distinctions between past, present, and future, emerges as a place of absolute nondifferentiation, insignificance, and death. It is as if in this world devoted to the overexposure of mere surfaces, the component parts of legibility each assume their independence and proliferate in dissociation from each other. These component parts are made up of: (1) a planar and stable material support; (2) an act that makes a notch, mark, imprint, or inscription; and (3) words and phrases. They are rendered dysfunctional by (a) dabs, plates, and panels that do not offer a surface upon which significant marks or traces can be inscribed; (b) the scratches, notches, slits, cracks, and traces—microscopic stigmas of many site descriptions in realist and naturalist texts—that do not qualify as words because they are not endowed with meaning; and (c) the words and phrases of the clamor of society, clichés with no origin and diffuse slogans that lack both material support and meaning.

Even mimesis, a symbolic activity that according to Aristotle produces both pleasure and knowledge, no longer seems possible. Moreover the very gap created by maintaining distance, difference, and incompleteness between the original and the copy, words and things, or stage and spectator permits the exercise of reason, memory, or the imaginary. Mimesis also permits an active reappropriation of the real: the pleasure of comparing on the one hand and the pleasure of completing on the other, which was so important to Aristotle's successors from Batteux to Quatremère de Quincy (a theoretician both of architecture and of mimesis at the beginning of the nineteenth century). The exposition's objects, at once slavish, industrial, and repetitive copies as well as eclectic and kitschy juxtapositions, only give the impression of being fakes and *facsimiles*. This theme abounds throughout the literature of the period. Not only is Saccard's townhouse in *La Curée* a specimen of the Napoleon III style—an "opulent hybrid of every style"—but it is also a reproduction of Lefuel's new Louvre, itself a pastiche of the old Louvre.[37] Belgium, that flat country, where even vice is counterfeit, is according to Baudelaire a nation of "apes," who "pastiche" or act as "stand-ins" for original French talent. In Yonville people come to see the City Hall, which is a reproduction, the church contains reproductions of paintings, and Homais's name is repeated on his shop's walls. The petit bourgeoisie has busts of Napoleon III made; tableau-vivants reproducing the paintings exhibited at the Salon are a fashionable form

[37] Zola, *La Curée*, vol. 1, 332. *Cosmpolitan, hybrid,* and *composite* are the adjectives that come up most often in the works of contemporaries of Garnier's Opera.

of entertainment in salons;[38] and as Marx pointed out, history repeats itself in the form of farce when Napoleon III plays the role his uncle had previously played. In Maupassant, where these mimetic difficulties are the plot's driving force, women and men, the demi-monde and high society, housewives and women of the streets, and children and their parents all alternately mimic one another with catastrophic results.[39] And finally Anatole, the painter in *Manette Salomon,* is referred to as an "ape-man" and has a pet monkey in his studio. Thus a world of signs (*signes*) is replaced by a world of apes (*singes*) or—as Flaubert might say—of "parrots."

The same verb *to ape* appears in Balzac's description of post-1830 architecture in the exposition of *La Fausse maîtresse.* This interesting passage juxtaposes ethical considerations of what is real, fake, or trompe-l'oeil; aesthetic considerations of eclecticism; technical considerations of the sacrifice made to functionalism and to utilitarian *distribution* of space; and social considerations of class, promiscuity and the effacement of social distinction:

> Great fortunes had dwindled in France, the majestic town-houses of our fathers are continually being demolished and replaced by phalansteries of sorts where a peer of France lives on the third floor over some recently wealthy empiric. Styles are mingled in confusion. As there is no longer any court, or any nobility, to set the tone no harmony is to be seen in the productions of art. Architecture has never found such economical tricks for aping what is genuine, and solid, nor displayed more ingenuity and resourcefulness in its arrangement. Ask an artist to landscape a strip of the garden of an old town-house now destroyed, and he will build you a little Louvre crushed under its ornamentation; he will give you a courtyard, stables, and if you insist, a garden; inside he contrives such a number of little rooms and corridors, and cheats the eye so effectually, that you fancy yourself comfortable; in fact, there are so many bedrooms that a ducal retinue can live and move in what was only the bake-house of a president of a law court. . . . On a small plot of ground the miracle wrought by a Paris fairy called Architec-

---

[38] *La Curée* ends with a scene depicting tableaux vivants which have an important symbolic function for Zola as a *mise en abyme* of the novel.

[39] For an analysis of Maupassant's short story "Le Signe" which constitutes a checklist of these types of mimetic disturbances, see Hamon *Introduction à l'analyse,* 246ff. A noneuphoric conception of mimesis, very different from the Aristotelian tradition that realist and naturalist literature anticipates, is found in the work of such sociologists of the end of the century as G. Tarde (see his 1882–1888 texts assembled in 1890 in *Les Lois de l'imitation*), whose analysis is sometimes quite similar to certain analyses by René Girard, or Bourdieu who sees mimesis as a "general leveling" force that "effaces distinction."

ture produces everything on a large scale. . . . To sin there would be impossible: there are too many pretty trifles.[40]

Clearly, stylistic differentiation was being ravaged by the heterogeneous juxtapositions of kitsch, the effacement of difference made possible by industrial reproduction, the rapid circulation of codes, copies, and fashions—"Doesn't fashion come out of the Salon?" asks Mallarmé in *La Dernière Mode* of 6 September 1874—the exhibition of fake or plate surfaces, and the *inversion* of exposition's actors and functions. What Walter Benjamin argued about the arcade's propensity to invert private and public as well as interior and exterior certainly holds true for many sites where the spectacle of the modern was fashioned; these architectured sites invert spectacle and spectator as well as the relation of viewing and objects viewed. Baudelaire, for example, in "Notes sur la Belgique" finds the theater's chandelier much more intriguing than the performance on stage. For many contemporaries, the monumental staircase of Garnier's Opéra was the edifice's true stage. Mallarmé—once more in *La Dernière Mode*—wrote in the column "Chronique de Paris": "On this gala evening, the real performance was not illuminated by footlights but by house lights." Regarding the inauguration of this new opera house he went on to ask himself what type of play could be performed there: "a vast fairy-tale spectacle, good for breaking in the stage while the audience watches each other. This is the ultimate idea that the perspicacious genius of Architecture, having long ago completed its work, bequeathed to anyone who would exploit it." In Andersen's "The Dryad," the fish behind their glass wall in the exposition's aquarium, are turned into the true spectators watching the humans that they see exhibited on the other side of the pane. Finally, the traditional layout of the city—with its oldest sections at its center and the newer suburbs on its outskirts—is inverted, as is obvious from the criss-cross of the adjectives in Baudelaire's poem "Le Cygne": "Palais neuf . . . vieux faubourgs."[p] All these inversions seem to point to a neutralization of differences that would in turn, as Rimbaud wrote in "Nocturne Vulgaire," "confuse" (*brouiller*) erected "partitions." Two significant phenomena emerge. First, the era of the great universal expositions, in which the art and products from different nations were brought into

---

[40] Honoré de Balzac, *The Imaginary Mistress*, trans. Clara Bell, vol. 8 (Philadelphia: Gebbie, 1900), 335.

[p] "New palaces . . . old suburbs."

contact with one another, was also an era of heated debates on commercial and industrial plagiarism. After all, exposing makes something public, facilitating its reproduction. Second, this was also an era of equally significant debates about the establishment of a universal language, such as Esperanto, which would abolish differences between states and individuals.[41] If it is true, as Michelet and Benjamin believed, that each era dreams the one that will follow, it is noteworthy that metaphors of buildings, windows, transparency, and screens, which still had positive connotations for the supporters of the storehouse concept of the literary work, but had begun to carry negative connotations by the time of Flaubert and Céard, will turn up in an exacerbated form a hundred years later in certain analyses of the "postmodern" city and society. In this postmodern environment, the screen becomes even more dematerialized, and takes on the guise of a computer terminal's window—a cathodic, telematic, televisual display unit that eliminates spatial pathways and distinctions, reducing all space to a machine's response time, and leaving the city, in Paul Virilio's words, "overexposed."[42]

[41] On this question of a universal language see in *Le Moniteur de l'Exposition de 1889* (nos. 112) the articles by Emile Dormoy. (See pp. 614ff. on the international language *volapük*.)

[42] See also Jean Baudrillard, *Simulations* (New York: Semiotexte, 1983) and Paul Virilio, *L'Espace critique*. According to the latter, in the electronic and overcomputerized megalopolis that

> was formerly preoccupied with the opposition between private and public, the differentiation between habitat and circulation is replaced by an overexposure that does away with the distinction between near and far. . . . The representation of the contemporary city is no longer determined by the ceremonial opening of the gates, the ritual processions, and parades going from one street or avenue to the next; . . . the interface between man and machine replaces building facades and the surfaces of plots of land. . . . Time that passes chronologically and historically is replaced by time that *exposes* itself instantly. (14–15)

# CHAPTER IV

# Characters Exposed

But how does this theme of flatness relate to characters in novels? What are the consequences for the casts of nineteenth-century novels who are part of a world reduced to insignificant platitudes? The Romantic traveler's encounter with the monument represented the conjuncture and collaboration of two plenitudes: on the one hand a general culture and on the other, a landmark, either one restoring, adjusting, verifying, or completing the other. Elsewhere, as in the works of Zola or Verne, the reader's or fictional character's trip through the storehouse of the world offered a corresponding reward of experience or knowledge. It could even result in pleasure—the recreation provided by Hetzel's collections or the epideictic jubilation of Verne's characters when confronted with the world's wealth and wonders. Hypotyposis, preterition (as when an author asks, "How can one describe this?" and then goes on to do so), charts and tables, presentations, and inventories all became specific rhetorical figures for developing a more or less monumentalized world of envelopes or boxes that are themselves more or less light or dark (which brings to mind Serres's cybernetic metaphors). What was at issue was a filling out, or accumulation of knowledge whose efficient circulation was always assured, whether this entailed a movement from fuller to emptier containers, from the monument to the antiquary, from teacher to pupil, from the document to its decoder, from the old hand to the neophyte, from the shopkeeper to the consumer, or from the city to the flâneur. From this perspective of the world as museum or store, an empty (*vide*) character is only an avid (*avide*) character, or else someone momentarily open to acquiring new knowledge via the descriptive text's ostension of its wonders. The empty character can also be the reader's medium of expression, assuring the proper exposure of these "human documents," to use the Goncourts' and Zola's term. Expositions, both real and textual, with their stock and architecturally ordered lighting and traffic, aimed to be at once exhaustive and pleasurable for either exhibitor or visitor, while describing, teaching, and displaying. And needless to say, the exposition was always presumed to be beneficial to somebody.

Yet staging—in the term's most literal meaning—a character's search for knowledge and spectacle does not always boast such positive attributes. The receptiveness of the newcomer, confronted with a world that is itself made up of novelties, such as Michelet's "brilliant trinkets" or the notions for sale as in *Au bonheur des dames,* may never translate into pleasure, general culture, or experience. The Robinsons and the enthusiastic explorers that people the works of Jules Verne, like the working shopkeepers, artisans and artists of Zola's novels ("Let's get to work!" is the concluding sentence in *L'Oeuvre*), rubbed shoulders with a more disturbing fictional brotherhood in the second half of the century. When one void confronts another, when one fake meets another, when a newcomer encounters new architectural styles, or when a one-dimensional character in a flat habitat is merely subject to "exhibition value," the result is a hyperbole of vacuousness, a two-fold semantic deflation. A population of stupefied, one-dimensional, and corroded spectators without volume, memory, or culture, seems to invade literature.

In a scene from Hugo's *Le Rhin* that is emblematic of the real's loss of volume, the author recounts a visit to the industrial city of Liège which culminates in the conjunction of a bourgeois "in a stupor" and a city whose former architecture has been overtaken by industry and imitation. Everything in this city is being erased: smoke has replaced patina, the terrace sheeted in zinc has replaced stone and habitat has become confused in every sense of the term. Narrations on such conjunctions of vacuousness begin to appear as a recurrent theme with telling frequency in the literature of the end of the century. A perfect example is the wide-eyed Mr. Fenouillard and his family standing before an empty and functionless monument full of holes: the Eiffel Tower. Thus self-satisfied characters obsessed with appearances and filled with a lot of hot air confront a real world cluttered with unreadable buildings and monuments. Metaphors of transparency—that had positive connotations in the works of some of the authors previously discussed—now take on a negative aspect when describing a population of specific character types: the joker, the gawker, the actress, the deadbeat, the bourgeois, the fine-goods artisan, the amnesiac, the exile, the parvenu, the sales representative, or the representative of the people. These were the sorts of characters who appeared as variations on a particular theme and who moreover specialized in this spectacular embodiment and management of void, flatness, hollowness, the prompter's voice, or any superficiality. Having been flattened out, emptied of retrievable meaning, and reduced to a succession of facades suitable only for appearances—or for the posting of "advertisements"—the world could only be livable for one-dimensional people without imagination, culture, or body, people more devoted to carving the world up into lots than to delving into their own lot in life. Such people posture in public rather than maintain their privacy, and are thus destined to cyclothymic and metonymic disintegration (metonymy being the key figure, according to Roman Jakobson, of realist writing).

Within this cast of characters there are however borderline cases of relatively familiar and picturesque figures: the *sandwich man* provides an inverted and prosaic rewriting of the Romantic traveler or the Baudelairean *flâneur*. He is the wage-earning wanderer of the city—for whom the boulevards provide no spectacle because he himself is the object of spectacle—his body covered with advertisements. They are the literal "poster boys" of Taine's *Thomas Graindorge*[1] or the heroes of the long,

---

[1] Taine, *Thomas Graindorge*. Thomas Graindorge is characterized as an "American Huron" that by crossing through the Paris of the Imperial Festival is consequently a hero typical of the narrative structure of the revue, in the genre of Montesquieu's *Lettres persanes,* or of the picaresque novel that is characteristic of many dioramic books of the period. Graindorge is an oil and salted-pork merchant. In his "Complaintes du pauvre chevalier errant," Laforgue would ironically compare himself to a "sandwich man" whom he calls a "man-of-letters":

> J'ai beaucoup parader, toutes s'enfichent
> Et je repars avec ma folle affiche
> Boniment incompris, piteux *sandwiche*: Au bon chevalier errant
> Restaurant
> Hôtel meublé, Cabinets de lecture, prix courants.

> [However much I parade around, they are all bored
> And I go off with my crazy board
> Misunderstood humbug, pathetic sandwich:
> At the Good Wandering Knight
> Restaurant
> Furnished Hotel, Reading rooms, current rates.
> —trans.]

one-dimensional poem by Coppée, "L'Homme-Affiche," from *Les Paroles sincères*:

> *Portant ses deux châssis de toile*
> *Sur lesquels étaient peints, souriant et debout,*
> *Un joli chapelier grand comme rien du tout,*
> *Qui tendait au public, d'une mine fringante,*
> *Un gibus colossal marqué huit francs cinquante.*[a]

Kaspar Hauser, a historical character, was an even more distressing example: from the moment he appeared on a Nuremberg street in 1828, he became for many writers the disturbing emblem of the inhabitant of the modern world, a stupefied exile in his own environment. An abandoned, "exposed," child with an ironic name (*Haus* meaning "house"), disoriented, incapable of piecing his scattered memories back together, and dispossessed of his own history and space, this haggard, anonymous, gawking flâneur, incapable of mastering the multiple surprises and the discontinuous and variegated spectacles of the modern city, could perceive it only in its most fragmentary form. The naive tourists in Rimbaud's "Soir historique," like the Verlaine of "Paysages Belges," "Sonnet boiteux," and "Kaleidoscope," assimilate themselves to this charade both implicitly and explicitly:

> *Je suis venu, calme orphelin,*
> *Riche de mes seuls yeux tranquilles,*
> *Vers les hommes des grandes villes,*
> *Ils ne m'ont pas trouvé malin.*[2,b]

According to contemporary witnesses, Kaspar Hauser had difficulty in growing accustomed to the spectacles observed from his window, and in

[2] Verlaine writes in his epigram to the fourth section of the third poem in *Sagesse,* "Gaspard Hauser chante" ["Kasper Hauser sings"—trans.]. On Hauser see the article devoted to him in Larousse's dictionary. Is it purely coincidental that the French equivalent of the name *Kaspar*—Gaspard—is in the title of Aloysius Bertrand's collection of prose poems, *Gaspard de la nuit* (1842)? These poems feature many rooms framed by a window or a stained-glass window. The epigram of one poem in Bertrand's collection, "La viole de Gamba," is a quote by Théophile Gautier which mentions another great artist of naive exposition, the Pierrot portrayed by the mime Jean-Gaspard Deburau from the Funambulists.

[a]         Bearing these two canvas frames
            Upon which are painted, smiling and upright
            A handsome hatter tall as anything
            Who extends to the public, with a dashing air
            A colossal top hat marked eight francs fifty.

[b]             I came, a calm orphan
                Enriched by only my own tranquil eyes
                Towards the men of big cities
                They did not find me clever.

particular, in getting a sense of volume and perspective. Anselm von Feuerbach, the father of the philosopher Ludwig Feuerbach, made Kaspar the subject of a report; in it he recorded Kaspar's own account of this problem:

> When I would look out the window, it was as if a panel had been pressed against my eyes and a dauber had then taken a paint brush and smeared a splotch of many colors against this panel. . . . I could not recognize spheric or triangular objects from the painted circles and triangles.

Feuerbach went on to add:

> The painted horses and people in his picture books were seen as entirely the same as horses and people sculpted in wood. Everything had the same degree of relief or flatness.[3]

Kaspar Hauser was in effect a sort of "drunken boat," a negative variation on the character of Robinson Crusoe, who progressively masters the world that he explores. He also provided a contrast to the cultivated tourist who perpetually rediscovered memories as well as the abandoned, exposed orphan who simply served as the pretext for encyclopedic and methodical tours in the great texts that grew out of storehouse mentality, such as Bruno's *Tour de la France,* or Verne's *P'tit bonhomme.* In a world increasingly devoted to the eye-catching, Kaspar Hauser as evinced in Feuerbach's report embodied an "ocular defect," to borrow Zola's expression, just like Zola's painter Claude Lantier in *L'Oeuvre.*

> The various objects that comprised the vast landscape and the narrow band of sky that filled the space of his window must have appeared to him as a series of visions laid out one right next to the other up close, the whole view resembling a painting in which indistinct objects of varying sizes and different colors could not appear to him except as a shapeless, variegated blob.[4]

---

[3] A. von Feuerbach, *Gaspard Hauser,* preface by Françoise Dolto (Paris: Vertiges, 1985), 57–58. Hauser's new type of gaze can be compared to the type of gaze that Baudelaire attributes to Constantin Guys—the gaze of an "eternal convalescent," of a "manchild" who "sees everything as if it were *new*" and "is assailed by a riot of details," but which in this painting conflicts with the synthetic demands of a powerful memory (which differentiates him from the poor Gaspard). This text by Baudelaire, like his text on photography, must take its place in the context of intense discussions that shook the art world on the relation between memory and pictoral practice (Lecoq de Boisbaudran: *L'éducation de la mémoire pittoresque* [Paris: A. Marel, 1879]).

[4] Feuerbach, *Gaspard Hauser,* 60. Gaspard Hauser's tachist vision can also be compared to the claims of impressionist writers and painters a century later. Their previously discussed descriptive themes included the reduction of the real to a series of dots, dabs, and patches. Let us cite two examples, one from Jean Richepin who describes the street as a "crowd of strollers, a swarm of cars, and political posters that make the walls look like

Two contemporary historical events—Napoleon's coup de'état and the Paris Commune, which both lead to urban transformation and the exile of political opponents—brought into being an interesting literary type, namely the exile who, upon returning to Paris after having escaped or being amnestied, no longer recognized the transformed city—Florent of *Le Ventre de Paris* along with the anonymous hero of Louis Ulbach's *Mémoires d'un inconnu* are among the finest examples. Such dispossession of memory and place here translates into visual fright that could be either the result of real ecological or ideological trauma or simply the aesthetic and textual result of the fluttering quality of impressionist and tachist expository descriptions. (Walter Benjamin noted that the Parisian felt like "a stranger in his own city," and Rimbaud remarked in "Villes II:" "Pour l'étranger de notre temps, la reconnaissance est impossible.")[c] Zola's text describes Florent (as well as a good number of other Zolian characters immersed in this kaleidoscopic world) as "lost" in Les Halles, "his eyes wide with fright, racking his brains, overwhelmed, blinded, drowning, ears ringing."[5] Observations of this type often recur in Zola's portrayals of characters burdened with an excess of memories (who nonetheless fail to recognize this new world), as well as characters suffering from amnesia (who are also unable to find anything familiar in such a world). These two types of "exiles from within," dispossessed of their surroundings and their very selves (for example, the amnesiac Serge in Zola's *La Faute de l'abbé Mouret*) provide a further variation on the "ghost" from beyond the grave as seen in Balzac's *Le Colonel Chabert* and Edmond About's *L'Homme à l'oreille cassée*. The question of memory became indissociable from Michelet's dreamed-of "science of accli-

---

an impressionist's palet." (*Le Pavé*, 2d ed. [Paris: Dreyfous, 1886], 36.) The second example is from C. Mauclair's, *La Ville-lumière*, a novel about a painter who, upon arriving in Paris and seeing the spectacle in the streets, feels his "impressionist instincts stir. . . . A single desire quickly became clear, and it was impossible to think any differently, the desire, after having exclusively painted objects, was to now paint people. He yearned to mix light and dark shades to give the illusion of living among this swarm of thinking dabs of voluntary atoms—these city dwellers" (26–27).

[5] Zola, *Les Rougon-Macquart*, vol. 1, 596–633. See also the white sale of *Au bonheur des dames* which "exhausted the gaze" (vol. 3, 797). L. Ulbach's book is dedicated to the period's great exile, Victor Hugo. See also Baudelaire's poem "Le Cygne"—also dedicated to Hugo—which contains many allusions to famous exiles such as Ovid, Andromaque, the swan, and the poet in the modern city. The first poem in Banville's collection *Les Exilés* (1867) is entitled, "Les torts du cygne." The Andersen story "The Dryad," which as we have mentioned takes place during the 1867 Exposition in Paris, is literally the story of uprooting, since it revolves around a tree that is uprooted and transplanted in the city.

[c] "For the foreigner in our day, reconnoitering is impossible" (Rimbaud, *Illuminations*, 243).

mation." The amnesia victim (Kaspar Hauser) or the exile (Florent) were borderline cases; others are more familiar. Thus the elements of the scene that Hugo sets in Liège (the dazed bourgeois, the newspaper, the flat and illegible city) are strikingly close to what Flaubert defined, with a term made famous in *Bouvard et Pécuchet,* as "in-significance" itself—stupidity. In their final incarnation as psychologists, Bouvard and Pécuchet acquire a pitiable faculty: "able to recognize stupidity, they are no longer able to tolerate it." "Insignificant things filled them with despair, newspaper advertisements, the profile of a bourgeois, or a foolish comment overheard in the streets." Like the cliché (a foolish comment) and newspaper advertisements, the profile is also a negation of volume (in chapter one, Flaubert writes that Pécuchet's face "seemed entirely in profile"). Each is flat—nothing more than paper or hot air; each negates semantic depth—they represent insignificance itself.

Another article by Balzac in *Les Français peints par eux-mêmes* describes the *rentier,* the bourgeois of independent means. As a counterpart to his more active *grocer* (the man of drawers and classifications, the encyclopedia in motion), the rentier is the idler and gawker par excellence, one who rambles through the city dumbfounded by its sights. Balzac's description is nothing but a variation on the theme of the platitude and "reading":

> He reads the newspapers, print ads, and posters, which would be useless without him. . . . As for literature, he monitors its movements by looking at posters. . . . [He] resembles a goldbeater who laminates trifles, expands upon them, changing them into great events covering a vast surface. He spreads out his actions across Paris, and gilds the smallest incident with an admirably useless, widespread, but shallow joy. . . . The rentier exists through his eyes. . . . The giraffe, the new museum acquisitions, painting exhibitions, and the products of industry—everything is a feast for the eyes, and equally amazing.

Some of course would see this laminated world, both managed and haunted by one-dimensional characters, as an exercise in democratic or socialist leveling, "the slow, grey, methodical conquest of socialism, devoid of lyricism and external beauty, advancing day by day . . . [with] the implacable, mathematical, and terrible force brought on by the conviction that value only exists in utility, . . . a terrifying rolling mill . . . in which all beings and all social forms will be beaten flat as metal."[6]

---

[6] Mauclair, *La Ville-lumière,* 159–162. Féval's Pierre Blot is the incarnation of the nineteenth-century man corroded by ideology, and is described in this way: "Pierre's sorrow was *shallow* in nature: nothing could liven him up . . . there was no other word: it was shallow" (*Les Etapes d'une conversion: Pierre Blot, second récit de Jean,* 16th ed. [Paris: Palmé, 1880], 220–221).

Balzac's gawking rentier is not the same as a flâneur; the latter is an active wanderer, still retaining something of the Romantic antiquary and immersed in the "sinuous folds" (to use Baudelaire's phrase), or in the "waves of brick" (to borrow Apollinaire's) of the metropolis. The flânuer is a positive character with the capacity to interpret the many spectacles of the city symbolically or anthropologically and to create something meaningful out of this discontinuous spectacle: "Strolling while musing like a flâneur is the best way for a philosopher to spend his time," writes Hugo in Les Misérables.[7] According to Alphonse de Lacroix, in Les Français peints par eux-mêmes the flâneur resembles, or is perhaps a model for, the writer.[8] He resembles Gavroche more closely than the gawker who is, after all, little more than his passive and "stupefied" caricature. Hugo writes: "Paris begins with the gawker and ends with the urchin, two beings that no other city is capable of producing; one is the embodiment of passive acceptance, satisfied to look on, the other, the embodiment of inexhaustible enterprise."[9] The flâneur can act as the city's memory, given his wide recall of all transformations and events. The image of photography or daguerreotype, while usually having negative connotations in literary texts, can be applied to the flâneur in a positive way; the flâneur serves as a highly sensitive photographic plate on which the real leaves an imprint, which is developed after exposure:

> Such a man is like a mobile and impassioned daguerreotype that records the slightest visible traces, and through which the ever-changing reflections of the course of the city, the multiple physiognomy of the public's mind, beliefs, hatreds, and the admiration of the the crowd is reproduced.[10]

Yet, inasmuch as the flâneur exists, "through his eyes," according to Balzac—which are usually bulging (as in the fantastic drawings of Grandville)—the gawker by contrast is at once the origin and the consumer of a world of pure exhibition; the sidewalks, display cases, and stores (the moving sidewalk of the 1900 Exposition was in fact its drawing card) would be the sites that solicit his wide-eyed gaze. In Gaudissart II (1844), the monograph of the store clerk, Balzac writes: "One must simply please the most avid and most blasé sensory organ that has been developed in man since Roman times, and whose demands

---

[7] Hugo, Les Misérables, part 3, 492 (translation modified).

[8] "Literature can claim the elite group of flâneurs. . . . They are belletrists because they are flâneurs" (A de Lacroix, "Le Flâneur," 115).

[9] Hugo, Les Misérables, part 3, 491.

[10] Fournel, Ce qu'on voit dans les rues, 261.

have become limitless due to the efforts of the most refined of all civilizations. This organ is *the Parisian's eye.*" According to Ruskin in "The
Lamp of Truth" from *The Seven Lamps of Architecture,* the greatest
ambition of the decorative inflation of store facades is to "catch the
eye." "To catch the eye" is the aim at the heart of the aesthetic project
of the painters in Paul Féval's *Coeur d'acier* set in 1842. Laforgue in his
"Complainte des crépuscules célibataires" speaks of passersby as:

> Tueurs de temps et monomanes
> Et lorgneurs d'or comme de strass
> Aux quotidiennes devantures.[d]

At times, all nineteenth-century texts seem nothing more than mono-
graphs of mono-organed visual monomaniacs. This gaze when turned
away from the shop window has the obsessive habit of training itself
on public works projects, particularly on the construction of new
monuments.

Thus the gawking bourgeois rentier watching works in progress provides a further variation on the conjuncture of two voids. There is
something in this scene that is both symbolic and self-referential with
regard to the literary work—as there is each time the literary text
chooses an architectural object as its referent. The new edifice under
construction is the ideal development, the ideal progressive exposition
of an architect's project that is concretized little by little under the
vacant stares of the gawking onlookers. The construction site is the
permanent autopsy of the very act of production and creation of an
unfolding project; it offers itself for viewing like a developing embryo
with its increasingly complex envelopes, as it passes from flat floor plan
to three-dimensional building, from the latent ideas in the blueprint to
the patent view of the facade, or from the amorphous to the intimate.
This accelerated pace contrasts with the slow and imperceptible movement of the Romantic ruin, which is itself symmetrical to the deconstruction and decomposition used by the antiquary in trying to understand it;
yet there is no symmetry between the Romantic antiquary and the
rubber-necked bourgeois, the work inspector who lacks the ability to
create allegories out of the blocks of mute, insignificant stone, as did the
narrator of Baudelaire's "Le Cygne." The gawking rentier, a familiar
type in Balzac's writings, is a character he compares not only to the

[d]              Time killers and monomaniacs
                 And oglers of both gold and strass
                 In front of everyday displays.

demolition expert but to the stone itself (notably in his "Monographie du rentier" from *Les Français peints par eux-mêmes*), it is as if *spectacle* and *speculation* are in some way linked:

> The rentier stops . . . in front of the houses being demolished by the Tribe of Speculators. Like his fellow gawkers, he is planted there with his nose in the air as he watches a stone, which, while being moved with a lever by a mason, falls from atop a wall; he doesn't leave his spot until the stone has fallen, as if he had made a secret pact with the stone. When it has reached the ground, he goes on his way, excessively happy.

In *Les Employés* (1836), Balzac describes Poinsot, a particularly dull Parisian office clerk

> interested in everything happening in Paris, who devoted his Sundays to surveying new constructions. He asked questions of the invalid responsible for keeping the public from entering the fenced enclosure, and worried about delays in the construction due to the lack of materials or money, or about the difficulties the architect encountered. He could be heard to say: "I saw the Louvre emerge from the rubble, I watched the birth of the place du Châtelet, the quai aux Fleurs, the markets!"

Among the representative types of the era drawn by Gavarni in *Le Diable à Paris* in the chapter devoted to the bourgeois is the caricature of the private inspector of public works. Champfleury, in his *Bourgeois de Molinchart* (1854) seems to ratify Balzac's type: "Monsieur Creton du Coche was walking along the ramparts, as is his habit, after lunch. . . . He had left the house at exactly noon to *go see the construction work*. . . . He frets over the cost of the labor, wearies the road workers with his questions, furnishing his brain with some motifs for conversation."[11] There is the further example of the Charbonnels, provincials who go up to Paris in Zola's *Son Excellence Eugène Rougon*, dumbfounded by the spectacle of the big city: "The Charbonnels, their eyes wide open"—Zola often made this note to himself in his preliminary sketches, as though they were written instructions for a leitmotif. Another example is Monsieur Chèbe, the prototype of the worthless low-level clerk in Alphonse Daudet's *Fromont jeune et Risler aîné*.[12] All of these texts set up encounters between the gawker's face and the

---

[11] Champfleury, *Bourgeois de Molinchart* (Paris: Dentil, 1878), 14. While this bourgeois does not show enthusiasm for buildings—these solid forms—he does become enthusiastic over instability, wind, void, ephemeral nature, clouds, and meteorology.

[12] "The whole time they were constructing the boulevard Sébastopol, he would go twice a day to see 'how it was proceeding' " (Alphonse Daudet, *Fromant jeune et Risler aîné*).

building's facade without any extended depth between them. *La Curée,* a novel about demolition and speculation in Paris, focuses on the vacuous Parisian doll, Renée, and her masculine equivalent, Maxime, the young deadbeat, as well as the incapacity of information to circulate between habitats and their inhabitants.[13] Fournel, at the beginning of his *Paris nouveau et Paris futur,* has Monsieur Prudhomme from atop the Vendôme Column present the city displayed before his family's feet: "an august and majestic city, aligned at a right angle, stretching out in a straight line."[14]

The scene of a vacant habitat standing before a vacuous inhabitant, or of a solid habitat before a hollow inhabitant, simply rehearses all the variations on the same theme of dispossession: "The man and the surrounding world . . . become strangers to each other, . . . intimacy cedes its place to the illumination of details," wrote Walter Benjamin in his commentary on the fin de siècle photographs of Eugène Atget that invoke an inventory of the remaining old sections of a seemingly deserted Paris. In *Education sentimentale,* Frédéric and Rosanette simply exchange such banal observations in front of the chateau at Fontainebleau as: "that brings back memories!" The movements of the city provoke a kind of vertigo in them: "Frédéric and Rosanette did not speak, stupefied by the sight of all those constantly spinning wheels around them." The return from the Bois de Boulogne, the obligatory scene of social ritual in which characters display themselves, also becomes the moment of confrontation of social classes that become spectacles for one another. Since they are incomprehensible to one another, this figures as an encounter between indifference and imbecility: "People studied one another, indifferent gazes fell upon the crowd from the carriages emblazoned with names; eyes filled with envy shone from the rented cabs . . . their gaping mouths expressing their imbecilic admiration." While waiting for Madame Arnoux, Frédéric, "for lack of anything else to do," starts to "pound the pavement" and "study the storefronts":

13 The adjective "empty" comes back as a leitmotif in Zola's entire novel, both to describe Renée ("Renée looked with a fixed stare as if this enlargement of the horizon [the new, artificial Bois de Boulogne] . . . would help her feel more vividly the emptiness of her being."—*La Curée*), as well as to describe the disemboweled houses of Paris and Maxime: "A characteristic of his was his eyes, two blue holes clear and smiling like a coquette's mirror behind which one could glimpse the emptiness of his mind" (ibid.). See also René Ghil's poem "Les pas des ahuris" in his collection *Légendes d'ames et de sangs* (1895).

14 Fournel, *Paris nouveau et Paris futur,* 12. At this point Fournel's text suggests an *analogy* between inhabitant and habitat. For an identical scene of a group of spectators at the top of the Vendôme column, but described from the perspective of radical difference, see the previously discussed scene from Zola's *L'Assommoir.* This climb to a belvedere that overlooks Paris is an obligatory scene of the nineteenth-century novel.

He considered the cracks in the pavement, the mouths of the sewers, the lampposts, the numbers above the doors. The smallest objects became his ironic companions: and the identical facades of the houses seemed unpitying. . . . He felt himself crumble, overwhelmed. The sound of his footfalls shook his brain. . . . He felt dizzy. . . . In the distance of this perspective, on the boulevard, a jumbled mass of people flowed past him.[15]

This scene of urban stupor recurs in many novels. There is the example of the haggard wanderings of Germinie Lacerteux, the eponymous heroine of the Goncourts' novel, in the zones at the edge of the city limits, demonumentalized "custom's-barrier" zones consisting of:

> lopsided buildings, shabby structures, large moldy *portes cochères*, fences that enclosed plots of wasteland with the disquieting paleness of stone at night, the corners of the masonry with saltpetrous stinks, walls fouled with shameful posters and shreds of torn bill stickers where rotten advertising was like a leprosy. . . . She dragged herself mechanically to where there was still gas burning and stood in a stupor before the flickering storefronts. With dazed eyes, she sought to suppress her impatience by stupefying it. . . . She lingered over old advertisements for lottery drawings plastered at the back of a wine shop, promotions for a coffee laced with liqueur, an inscription in yellow letters, announcing, "New wine, genuine, 70 centimes." . . . Growing weak, she was incapable of any more thought.[e]

It is as if literature itself is fascinated by the confrontation between the idle inhabitant and the habitat's growing number of extraneous architectural features, such as decorative details, or knick-knacks in display cases. Thus Baudelaire describes the emblematic confrontation between "the eyes of the poor" open wide like "entrance gates" (portes cochères) and the "sparkling," "brand-new café on the corner of a new boulevard, still full of debris but already ostentatiously exhibiting the glory of its unfinished splendors"—its "gas lights," "blindingly white walls, the daz-

---

[15] Gustave Flaubert, *Education sentimentale*, 302–303. The montage of this scene which opposes a habitat with no meaning (*sens*) reduced to details and fragments, or to "confused masses" and a "dissolved" inhabitant, goes beyond the illustration of a mere, limited psychological sketch depicting the wait before a lovers' rendez-vous. In *Madame Bovary* the famous scene in the coach can also be read as an empty network of lines of sight and interference between spectacle and spectator, or opened and closed boxes. Léon and Emma, after having heard without listening the explanations of the verger showing them the wonders of the cathedral, close themselves up in an illegible cab and pass in front of all the monuments of Rouen without seeing them, "bourgeois . . . stared in wonder at this . . . cab with all the blinds drawn . . . more tightly sealed than a tomb" (Flaubert, *Madame Bovary*, 177).

[e] Edmond and Jules de Goncourt, *Germinie Lacerteux,* trans. anon (New York: Société des Beaux Arts, n.d), 200–201, translation modified.

zling expanse of its mirrors, and the gildings of the moldings and the cornices"—where one consumes multicolored, obelisk ice-cream.[16,f]

Exhibitionism, the exhibition of objects or subjects, the overexposure of the world, or its *over-exhibition*—all carry a sort of *inhibition,* a stupefied vision that blocks the normal functions of memory, imagination, or even speech: a wide-eyed stare usually goes hand in hand with dumbfoundedness, or at least with a cliché, which is a form of non-speech. Such a gaze clearly has little to do with a Romantic gaze (which was an instrument of hermeneutic inquiry) or with the gaze of such Vernian engineers and explorers as Captain Nemo, whose eagle eyes always offered the basis for *action, enablement,* or *knowledge.*

Other characters would join this wandering, spaced-out populace of the overexposed city, providing other variations on this confrontation of two vacuums or two plenitudes. There is first and foremost the actress who in her professional role can be considered a character on exhibit. Ross Chambers has described her as all surface "versatility" and "falsity," displayed against a vacuous backdrop.[17] She is the character who best embodies a century of spectacular expositions, while personifying the staging of modern life in general. She functions as the feminine double of the parvenu and the *blagueur,* two perpetual performers who also live by appearances and speech. In addition, the figure of the actress inevitably becomes a focal point for the various metaphors involving habitat, posturing, display, facade, the glass house, and staging, which are negatively deployed in literary descriptions of the female performer. The Romantic actress, such as Dea in Hugo's *L'Homme qui rit,* personifies an oxymoron, for while she is an actress—an object for the gaze of others—Dea is herself blind. She is however a particularly rich character in that she possesses complete lucidity, and is thus granted an additional symbolic dimension through her capacity for interpretation and prediction. Nana and Rosanette are on the contrary characters defined by emptiness, prosaic superficiality, and transparency—all of which are most clearly

[16] This spectacular scene is also a meticulously constructed montage of lines of sight: The narrator, gazing into "the green eyes" of his companion in order to read her thoughts, expects to see that she is touched by the "idiotic" pleasure expressed by this "family of eyes," only to find incomprehension and repulsion. Baudelaire describes a couple seated at a café terrace in a painting by Constantin Guy in this way: "These two beings don't think. Can we even be sure that they look? Unless like Narcisuses of imbecility, they contemplate the crowd like a river that reflects their image."

[17] Ross Chambers, *L'Ange et l'automate, variations sur le mythe de l'actrice de Nerval à Proust* (Paris: Lettres modernes, 1979).

[f] Baudelaire, *Paris Prowler.*

revealed by their bad taste. Nana is significantly linked to the architecture of arcades and the objects they shelter:

> She adored the passage des Panoramas, still obsessed by the passion she had felt in her youth for fancy goods, fake jewelry, gilded zinc, cardboard made to look like leather. She could not tear herself away from the shop windows any more than when she had been a street-urchin, lost in wonder in front of a confectioner's wares, or listening to a music box in a neighbouring shop, and above all going into ecstasies over cheap, gaudy knick-knacks, such as nut-shell boxes, rag-pickers' baskets for holding toothpicks, and thermometers mounted on Vendôme Columns and obelisks.[g]

Nana is moreover portrayed as a double sign: in the initial exposition of the novel she acts as a "sign post" for the work, while she is also featured on theater posters—the site of stucco, pasteboard, and fakery described in this scene:

> In the crude gaslight, on the pale bare walls skimpily decorated in the Empire style to form a peristyle like a cardboard temple, tall yellow posters were boldly displayed with Nana's name in thick black letters. Some gentlemen were reading them, as if accosted on the way. . . . And there was a din of voices, in the midst of which Nana's name sounded with all the lilting vivacity of its two syllables. The men standing in front of the playbills spelt it aloud, . . . a pet name which rolled easily off every tongue. . . . The name of Nana was on everyone's lips.[h]

This expository scene foreshadows later scenes of Nana exhibiting her body as a prostitute and picking up gentlemen as well as her career as an actress in the false society of the Second Empire (the gas lamp, the poster, the cardboard temple). As a character she is simply the doubling of a written name on a poster that is multiplied by rumor into "the name on everybody's lips." Thus, before circulating from bed to bed, Nana's name circulates from mouth to mouth; and it is as the object of widespread rumor that she in turn appears nude and mute on the stage. Thus her character (*personnage*) doubly lives up to its etymology since *persona* means a theater mask and *prostituere* means to expose, show, or exhibit oneself. Nana furthermore assumes the particularly apt role of Mélusine,

> a real star attraction, consisting as it did of three poses representing a silent and powerful fairy queen. . . . In the crystal grotto . . . she did not say a word; the authors had even cut the line or two they had given her, because they were superfluous. No, not a single word: it was more impressive that

---

[g] Zola, *Nana*, trans. George Holden (London: Penguin Book, 1972), 215.
[h] Ibid., 20–24.

way, and she took the audience's breath away by simply showing herself. . . .
Around her the grotto, all made of glass, was as bright as day . . . and amid
the transparent atmosphere and flowing spring water, which was pierced by
a ray of electric light, she shone like a sun with that rosy skin and fiery hair of
hers . . . like the Blessed Sacrament.[18,i]

Similarly, in "La Saignée," a short story collected in the 1880 *Soirées
de Médan,* Céard describes the actress and demi-mondaine Madame de
Pahauën:

> In tableaux vivants, wearing her flesh-colored silk tights that were flooded
> with oxyhydrogen light, she displayed the width of her hips, the fullness of
> her bosom, and from her heels to her smile, the fat and provocative immod-
> esty of her statuesque body. A lady bountiful, she could be seen at sales
> events for the poor, readily showing off all the skin her clothing could reveal.

The passage presents the same aesthetic of the crystal palace, albeit
slightly out of hand. In this instance, the objects of industry destined for
exhibit have been replaced by obscene bodies flaunted as though they
were shocking machines, yet nevertheless unable to speak or move on
stage, and even denied the mimetic powers that had so enchanted audi-
ences who came to see Debureau and the popular Pierrot character at
the Théâtre des Funambules around 1845.[19] The "machine" body of the
fin de siècle actress transposed into a poster, statue, or a tableau vivant,
has little in common with the Romantic body. Whereas the latter was
constellated with signs to interpret (scars, freckles, pallor, tears, wrin-
kles, tints, birthmarks, or bruises), the fin de siècle body was more like
an under-the-counter pornographic transparent slide or like Manet's
tachist painting of Olympia (of which Georges Bataille wrote: "She's
nothing")—in short, a body reduced to a Parisian luxury item, dis-

---

[18] Zola, *Les Rougon-Macquart,* vol. 2, 1,471–1,476.

[19] The craze for tableaux vivants pervades the Second Empire. See the chapter—which
is a short story in itself—entitled "Ma tante en Vénus" in G. Droz's *Monsieur, Madame,
et Bébé* (Paris: Ollendorff, 1900) or the tableaux vivants in which Renée participates
naked at the end of *La Curée,* which causes her to suddenly realize the emptiness of her
existence. In *Les Odeurs de Paris,* Veuillot in his own way addresses issue of the disappearance of language in theater: "Actors are nothing more than . . . stage hands, soon there
will be no more dialogue. . . . The principle scenes will be transformed into dioramas."
The naked woman is the supreme horror: "I am not speaking of the horror felt by the soul
when confronted with this prostitution I am speaking simply of the horror experienced by
the eye." This can be compared to the naked woman in such Romantic works as Hugo's
*L'Homme qui rit.* Already transformed into a museum by the enthusiasm for collecting,
the bourgeois salon is transformed into a theater with this fashion of the tableaux vivants.
This is an example of the widespread invasion of exposition. For the uncompromising
Sénécal in *Education sentimentale,* tableaux vivants "corrupt the daughters of the prole-
tariats" and "display an insolent luxury" (pt. 2, chap. 2).

[i] Ibid., 454–460.

played solely for its exhibition value. With the passing of the visual fantasmagoria of the fantastic or the Romantic text, there was no longer any reason to think that there might be some secret sliding panel or mysterious hidden hand, as in the sophisticated sets that stage the pseudo-body and pseudo-voice of the actress soprano La Stilla in Verne's *Le Château des Carpathes*; the backstage wings of the theater in *Nana* were transparent and open to the public who filed past them on their way to their seats. Just as in the universal expositions, light and glass sufficed. But this form of spectacular overexposure necessarily involves negation of any *arrangement* of space in a hierarchy or in any series of volumes. Surface effectively kills the backstage wings.

This population of strass oglers [*lorgneurs de strass*], in the words of Laforgue, finds its complement in both pasteboard characters as well as characters who, as a result of working with paste, turn into strass themselves. In *Fromont jeune et Risler aîné*, Daudet described the Parisian worker Sidonie Risler:

> Something remained at the tips of her fingers of the fake pearls she had worked on for so long, a bit of fake mother-of-pearl, something of their hollow fragility and superficial brilliance. She too was a false pearl, round, brilliant, well-set, its vulgarity had taken hold in her. . . . She was indeed a product of Paris, this jeweler of fakes, who had a thousand charming and brilliant useless things at her disposal, but which were hardly solid, oddly matched, and carelessly attached: a genuine product of the small-time trade of which she was a part.[20]

The influence of habitat upon its inhabitants, and of habits upon outer attire (*habits*), which regulates the circulation of information within naturalist and realist novels, also generates a world of characters who embody pure display, since they have lost all corporal depth or volume. Whereas Homais's pharmacy is described as covered with advertisements and brightly lit, the pharmacist himself is but a shadow behind his storefront. Thérèse Raquin, the eponymous heroine of Zola's novel, is presented in the exposition which also mentions an arcade, the passage Guénégaud—the same one that Benjamin would cite in his notes for his *Arcades Project*. She appears as a pure profile, simply a dab positioned behind the window of her notions shop. She serves as the sign for her store in both the novel and for the text, since her description appears in the opening passage: Nothing more than "the woman's name

---

[20] Zola, *Au bonheur des dames,* 117. In *L'Assommoir* Nana's first job was making artificial flowers. The *article de Paris*, whether it is a bauble or a newspaper article, is a synonym of "pretty," "plate," and "fake."

on the store-front window," she is bodyless, since "her body was not visible." She is reduced to a "pale and serious profile of a young woman," her lips compressed into two "thin traces," whose "profile alone appeared of a matte whiteness." Her "matte" coloring, her "profile," the "thin dashes" of her lips, and her "paleness" here echo the pictorial techniques of painters like Manet, whom Zola had introduced to the public in his *Salon*. In much the same way, Geneviève Baudu, the heroine of his department-store novel *Au Bonheur des dames,* is transformed into a mannequin, resembling the "headless women" of the display cases, or the "waxwork women seen in the physiologist's office at the barrière du Trône, who breathe mechanically through their breasts and stomach, in glass cages."[21]

The same term, *glass cage* is used in Balzac's work to designate the salon in Esgrignon's townhouse in *Le Cabinet des antiques*. Its tall windows offer passersby a view of mummies, and rare artifacts that are representatives of earlier societies. The same image of the "glass cage" is seen in Lisa Quenu's *charcuterie* display in *Le Ventre de Paris*, as a larger-scale, voluminous variation on the flat presentation by carefully situated profiles, blurs, and fragments, which are well set, yet a variation that serves as spectacle, suggesting such a transformation of bodies into signs.[22] Another more disturbing variation is found in Verne's *Cinq cents millions de la Bégum*, in which Herr Schultze is glass-enclosed and transformed into an object observable in vitro. The character is first invisible, then frozen in his laboratory, and then observed by the hero Marcel Bruckmann through

the thick glass of an *oeil-de-boeuf* fitted in the center of the floor ... as though it had been a dioptic apparatus of a lighthouse. . . . In the middle of the room in this glaring atmosphere, a human form enormously enlarged by

[21] Remy de Gourmont, "L'Automate" in *Histoires magiques et autres récits* (Paris: Union Générale d'Editions, 1982), 65–66. Zola describes Denise: "She had to obey, she had to let Marguerite drape that coat over her, as if she were a mannequin. . . . She was embarrassed to be changed into a sort of machine that was being examined. . . . She felt assaulted, stripped bare, with no protection" *Les Rougon-Macquart*, vol. 3, 496ff.

[22] Lisa's first appearance is made in *Le Ventre de Paris*'s exposition in the first chapter: "A woman standing in the sun on the threshold of the shop" (vol. 1, 637). She is then presented as "fractured": "In the mirrors she was reflected from the back, from the front, from the side; and he [Florent] even found her on the ceiling. The shop was filled with a crowd of Lisas . . . and her thick-set profile with its tender curves and swelling bossom formed the fleshy image of a queen, in the midst of this suet and raw meat" (ibid., 667). The woman is multiplied and exposed like a product of industry. She can be compared to the barmaid in Manet's *Bar aux Folies-Bergères*, a painting that poses several problems for critics: is there or is there not a mirror behind the barmaid? The Musée Grévin, a Parisian wax museum that opened in 1882, placed famous women—whether murderesses or queens—on display.

the refraction of the lens, something resembling a sphinx in the Libyan desert, was seated immobile as marble. . . . It was Herr Schultze, . . . asphyxiated and frozen by the terrible cold.

All these characters are presented in carefully specified architectural settings. Furthermore, they are described through the use of metaphors that rely on architectural terms, specifically metaphors of the window, the theatre, the store, and the glass house. In *P'tit bonhomme,* Verne describes an actress who has taken the young hero into her home: "They were not the noisy performers who demand walls to maintain their privacy. No! These actresses would cause rents on glass houses to rise the day architects learn how to build them."[23] The same metaphor appears in Zola's *Les Mystères de Marseille* in which he describes the parvenu Sauvaire "dreaming of kissing his mistresses in glass houses." The other parvenu of the Rougon-Macquart series, Saccard, lives in a townhouse whose windows are "so tall and so clear . . . [they] resembled the windows of modern department stores, placed there to display to the outside world their inner splendors." Saccard's home is a townhouse whose "pale facade had [shown] the rich and foolish self-importance of a parvenu." It is moreover "flanked by a large conservatory."[24]

Daudet's *Numa Roumestan* includes a rich catalogue of such metaphors in addition to a rich fictional cast of characters who represent these various themes of platitude, imitation, hollowness, exhibition, and performance. The action of the novel, which takes place around 1875–1876, focuses on Numa, a right-wing opportunistic member of Parliament, and his mistress, Alice Bachellery. Like Zola's Sauvaire and his Rougon family, Numa is a man from the south of France, or from the sunbelt. He likes to strut about in public on podiums and platforms "in full view"; he is "all show, in his voice and his gestures, like an opera tenor," with "an ever-ready storehouse of ideas and stock phrases." As a representative of the people, he passes his time attending sessions of

---

[23] Of course, the metaphor of the glass house is the same one used by Zola in his critical and theoretical writings when speaking of the type of naturalist writing he was trying to promote. In contrast to Zola's character Sauvaire, Taine's character, Thomas Graindorge sums himself up by describing his "habit of containing himself and his distaste for any type of display."

[24] At the time he was writing *La Curée,* Zola was planning a play entitled *Les Parvenus,* of which he left only a sketch of a few pages. Novels of the nineteenth century were simply fascinated by the parvenu along with other exhibitionist characters like the actress, the traveling salesman, the joker, and the "representative" of the people. See for example Féval's *Les Parvenus* (1853) as well as numerous plays by A. Rolland (1860) and H. Rivière (1870).

the chamber of deputies[25] where he "stages theatrical coups." His mistress Alice is "one of those divas that the boulevard consumes at the rate of a half-dozen each season, her paper reputation inflated by gas and puffery, which brings to mind those little rose-colored balloons that live only one day in the sun and the dust of the public gardens."[j] Numa's protegé, Valmajour, is a *taborist*, a pretentious, pestering poseur who plays at being the artist and whose career Numa and his mistress try to launch publically via a campaign of gigantic posters plastered all over Paris. These posters which reproduce the silhouette of the *taborist* are:

> enormous, printed in loud colors that come out under the gray and rainy sky. At every corner, on every vacant space of a bare wall, and on planks of temporary fences. They showed a gigantic troubadour, surrounded by a border of tableaux vivants in dabs of yellow, green and blue, with the ochre tabor placed across the figure . . . [It was] a coarse, explosive advertisement, that stupefied even Parisian gawkers.[k]

In the concert hall where he appears, "the walls were covered with posters and advertisements of every color setting forth the virtues of pith helmets, shirts made to measure for 4 francs 50, announcements for candy shops alternating with the portrait of the tabor-player."[26] In this

[25] There is always a bit of the ham actor and a bit of the sales representative in the representative of the people. See Daumier's series "Les Représentants représentés." The word *representative* and all the word plays that could be made with it were very much in use after 1848. See *Les Murailles révolutionnaires* (of 1848) by Charles Boutin (Paris: Picard, 1851): "Everyone wanted to yell: 'Et ego in Arcadia! And I too am a representative!' Contained at first, the representative craze spread to everyone." The three-act light comedy by Dumanoir, Clairville, and Labiche, *L'Exposition des produits de la République* (1849) includes, among others, caricatures of an English tourist visiting an exposition, a revolutionary street urchin, Father Suffrage, a lorette, and a woman parliamentary candidate named Jeanne Bédouin. Here is an excerpt:

| | |
|---|---|
| JEANNE BÉDOUIN: | They push me away, they tear up my posters! |
| GLOBCHESTER: | Ah! Madame is on display? |
| JEANNE BÉDOUIN (SINGING): | I want to represent! Give me your vote. . . . I want to represent! |

Daudet's Numa Roumestan is even more vacuous than Eugène Rougon's brother—one of Napoleon III's ministers—in Zola's *Son Excellence Eugène Rougon* (1876). A scene at the end of Zola's novel describes a session of the Chamber—another photographic term—where Eugène is presented as an actor on stage inspiring ovations from the audience, throwing out empty words, and making full use of "the fiction of parliamentarianism" and his theater in order to satisfy his hunger for power (vol. 2, 369). In Daudet's work, Numa is a former theater columnist.

[26] Alphonse Daudet, *Numa Roumestan*, trans. anon. (Boston: Little Brown, 1889), 292.

[j] Ibid., 144.

[k] Ibid., 282.

passage, one finds a systematic compilation of the themes of fakery and emptiness, of everything that is semantically opposed to solidity, plenitude, and stable volume. The thematic cluster that Daudet rehearses here—involving posters, puffery, inflation, off-stage prompting, empty phrases, ephemeral balloons, imitations, voids (such as the hollow of the drum), the theater, gawkers, and flatness (the silhouette and the dab) pointedly deflates the Romantic thematics of the monumental. Everything is interconnected around this network of characters who form a system of correlated metaphors and similes; for example, the parvenu, the sales representative, and the representative of the people are on display with actresses, just as the draper's assistant is exhibited with the seamstress, or with the woman who crafts Parisian luxury items.[27] The character of the actress—a woman whose exposure is so often associated with the problem of sexual reproduction (whether or not to have children—usually the problem of how not to have them, which is Nana's permanent obsession), or the problem of reproduction and resemblance (most notably in Maupassant)—is but another example of reflection on erasure of differences and artificiality. The dandy— who had so fascinated Stendhal, Barbey d'Aurevilly and Baudelaire— can be read as the self-controlled and refined heightening of the parvenu and the actress. Both on display and reserved, the dandy is a being created out of appearances and fashion, yet his irony is the opposite of the silly joke and his pose is the obverse of exposure: "As a mixture of irony and reserve, ostentation and desire, the dandy engages in both self-defense and self-display but he never mingles with the crowd."[28]

The stupefied gawker was often at a loss for words as he stood wide-eyed before the wonders of the boulevard or the exposition. By contrast, performing artists of appearance such as the sales representative, the

---

[27] One example, found in an excerpt from Céard's previously mentioned novel *Une Belle Journée*—a post-Flaubertian catalogue of platitude—clearly shows the permanent presence of the multiple themes of exposition (i.e., representation, display, theater, society as theater, clothing, and advertisement). The following is a description of a ball:

> Wine merchants' shop assistants stiff in their black suits . . . stroll with the ceremonial propriety of extras who represent mute guests on a second-rate stage, . . . the svelt dressmaker displaying the good taste of her appearance like a living advertisement for her shop, . . . a well-known accountant [walking with] his mistress. . . . Mothers . . . criticized him for "making a spectacle of himself" in this way (162 ff.).

[28] R. Kempf, *Dandies, Baudelaire et Cie.* (Paris: Seuil, 1977), 38. Germain Nouveau in the five sonnets in his *Bouts de notes*, itemizes a list of his own repulsions: *laughter*, the dandy and the actor (a Gilles "with dangling clothing"), and the wordly *salon* (with their "poufs").

actor, the artist, the society lady, and the parvenu are usually extremely talkative, perpetually exposing their opinions and principles, continually promoting their theories or ideas. Homais, for example, passes his time "exhibiting his general opinions and personal allegiances";[29] M. Duhamain, the architect in *Une Belle Journée,* "who had read Balzac," bandies about his unique theory concerning "a husband's duties";[30] in *Education sentimentale,* Sénécal, Pelerin, and Deslauriers spend their time "presenting [their] theories";[31] in *L'Argent* Zola describes the political theorist Sigismond whose "need to proselytize would, at the least provocation, launch him into a presentation of his system."[32] The literary text constructs something resembling a glass house around such a character; the type of exposition found in nineteenth-century novels that usually take place in salons describes the individual not through "roundabout conversation" (in the words of Barbey d'Aurevilly) nor through the lively dialogues that make Stendhal's salons the idyllic sites of a shared communion between characters, rather through compact, juxtaposed slices of frozen and stereotyped speech that form an exposition gallery of the received ideas and opinions of social discourse.

In a world of display and platitude where all distinctive traits, are, like privacy and intimacy, increasingly threatened and reduced in scope, the most distinguishing and personal aspect of characters—their proper names—also tend to obey this general law of hucksterism and exhibition. We have observed elsewhere how sensitive the nineteenth-century literary text had become to intrusive tourist graffiti on walls and monuments. Flaubert writes that "the names of imbeciles are everywhere" on Egyptian monuments. Similarly, writers had become increasingly aware of the store sign: "*Lettres d'or qui soudain bougent / En torsades sur la façade: . . . Lettres jusqu'au ciel, lettres en or qui bougent*"[33,l] as well as by the proper nouns of advertising posters. But in the fictional worlds these characters inhabit names tend to be inscribed, detaching themselves from the person they belong to, then turning into an abbreviation, signboard, or signpost following a sort of *widespread epigraphy* recurring most often in the exposition of the works themselves. Thérèse

[29] Gustave Flaubert, *Madame Bovary* (Paris: Gallimard, 1972), 169.
[30] Céard, *Une Belle Journée,* 11–12.
[31] Flaubert, *Sentimental Education,* 124.
[32] Zola, *Les Rougon-Macquart,* vol. 5, 43.
[33] E. Verhaeren, "Le Bazar," *Les Villes tentaculaires.*
[l] "Gold lettering that moves suddenly / In fringes of the facade: . . . Letters up to the sky, golden letters that move."

Raquin's name appears on the storefront of the shop selling notions just as Homais's takes up the "width of his store" at the beginning of part two of *Madame Bovary*; the first thing that the traveler sees in the opening passage of *Le Rouge et le noir* is the name of Sorel writ large on the roof of the sawmill. Many texts open in this way, with an inscribed name, as in *Les Travailleurs de la mer*, or a name mumbled out, as in "Charbovary" at the beginning of *Madame Bovary*, or a name majestically unfurled, as in *Le Ventre de Paris* or "Vauquer" in the opening of *Le Père Goriot*, or a name printed on a poster, as in *Nana*. The familiar signature of Nadar—itself a pseudonym—covered the entire facade of the building on boulevard des Capucines which housed his studio. The way Arnoux's name is displayed, both as a written and spoken sign, in the expository scene of *Education sentimentale* seems to have taken Nadar as its inspiration:

> The unknown person responded with one breath: "Jacques Arnoux, the proprietor of *L'Art Industriel*, Boulevard Montmartre." *L'Art industriel* was a hybrid establishment, including a fine-arts journal and a picture gallery. Frédéric had seen the title there, on many occasions, in the display of the local bookshop in his hometown, on the immense advertisements where the name of Jacques Arnoux unrolled majestically.[34]

In the first chapter of *Bouvard et Pécuchet* both characters expose the names they have inscribed inside their hats. In this way, a character's name comes to appear as an external and independent entity, and thus allows for all kinds of manipulation. In *La Curée*, Saccard chooses a pseudonym to obliterate the name Rougon, and succeeds in real-estate speculation with the help of assumed names and limited companies (*sociétés anonymes*) that nevertheless have grand-sounding names. Such

---

[34] The theme of the posted name, that is put on display recurs in chapter 3:

> Just beyond the rue Montmartre a traffic jam made [Frédéric] look round and on the opposite side of the street he saw a marble plaque which read: JACQUES ARNOUX. . . . Behind the tall, clear glass windows was a skillfully arranged display of statuettes, drawings, engravings, catalogues, and copies of *L'Art industriel*. The subscription price was also printed on the door, the center of which was adorned with the editor's monogram.

Furthermore, Jacques Arnoux spends a good deal of time exposing his theories and quoting himself. Balzac's illustrious character Gaudissart was also a living handbill. See also the signs for Baudu's and Mouret's store that Denise sees in the first pages of *Au bonheur des dames*—a name which is an indirect ethopeia of Gervaise's character, Bonheur, at the beginning of *L'Assommoir*—the names, the signs and the hieroglyphs offered to the eye of "conscientious flâneurs" by the facade of Chevrel-Guillaume's firm at the beginning of Balzac's *La Maison du chat qui pelote*, as well as the traveling animal trainer's sign at the beginning of Eugène Sue's *Le Juif errant*.

manipulation can however result in curious cases of dispossession or alienation.[35] But, remarkably, this epigraphic exhibition of names tends to become part of the textual frame itself, most notably in opening passages of the novels. The sign posted at the entrance marks the entry into a text, providing an inaugural threshold whose concluding epigraphic homology, the epitaph,[36] completes the system of framing. If *Madame Bovary* opens with the mumbled name of Charles Bovary, it closes with a list of Homais's publications and a monumental epitaphic parody of a great Romantic lapidary inscription:

> He had fine ideas for Emma's tomb. First he proposed a broken column surmounted by drapery, next, a pyramid, the temple of Vesta, a sort of rotunda . . . or else a large pile of ruins. As to the inscription, Homais could think of nothing finer than *"Sta viator,"* and he got no further. . . . At last he hit upon *amabilem conjugem clacas!* which was adopted.[m]

The overall experiences of the character, like the sequence of events in reading a novel, tends to reduce itself to a succession of inscriptions— names, abbreviations, symbols or signatures on architectural objects or supports.[37]

Faced with these diverse characters on display, two seemingly symmetrical variations emerge: on the one hand the *dandy,* the litotic character of self-display, reserved and in control, who prefers the ironic double entendre to serious discussion, a character who poses rather than exposes. On the other hand, there is the dandy's inflated counterpart, the joker or prankster (*blagueur*) who, unlike the dandy, has a great deal to say. Both of these characters, in the degree to which they

[35] Curiously enough the encounter with one's own name in the streets can lead to despoilment unless one is able to reclaim it, in the form of a narrative, in order to restore its meaning. See Laforgue in *Mélanges posthumes,* 31: *"The surprise of coming upon one's own name* on a shop sign and constructing antediluvian novels around it."

[36] At the end of Balzac's *Ferragus* a profusion of epitaphs in Père Lachaise can be compared to the description of the posters and inscriptions found in the novel's inaugural passage ("vile words" and graffiti on the walls and statues as well as on posters): "You can read jests carved in black letters, epigrams at the expense of the curious, pompous biographies, and ingeniously worded farewells. . . . You see trade signs in every direction. . . . Here is Paris over again—streets, trade signs, industries, houses, and all complete, but it is a Paris seen through the wrong end of a perspective glass, a microscopic city, a Paris diminished to a shadow of its former self" (Honoré de Balzac, *The Thirteen and Other Stories,* trans. Ellen Marriage [Philadephia: Gebbie 1900], 181).

[37] Such an itinerary is emphasized by the epigrammic modifications of a name on display, in the treatment of the name César Birotteau at the beginning of Balzac's novel: "No more retail for me . . . I shall burn the sign *The Queen of Roses,* and the words 'César Birotteau (LATE RAGON), retail Perfumer' shall be removed from the storefront. I shall simply put up *Perfumery* in big gold letters instead."

[m] Flaubert, *Madame Bovary,* 252.

are literally figures of speech, would come to fascinate the nineteenth-century writer. "Pose, pose, and make jokes (*blaguer*) everywhere," Flaubert wrote to Louise Colet in 1854. The French word *blague* appeared at the beginning of the century, originally meaning a bag or tobacco pouch. Metaphorically, then, it refers to an empty or boastful speech and implies glibness, mockery, or mendacity.[38] In the first chapter of Daudet's *Tartarin de Tarascon* we find a tobacco pouch (*blague*) left upon the hero's table. Whereas the dandy is a figure with "values" and ethics, "it's all the same" to a blagueur. In a return to the theme of platitude, his words tend to level everything into undifferentiation—according to French grammar, the verb *blaguer* can in fact take an object or remain intransitive, an absolute act. The blague differs from the laughter of, say, Hugo's *L'Homme qui rit*, just as it is distinct from irony, which is never coarse or untrue, and indeed presupposes a whole shared system of values. The blague could serve as a model for subversive writing: Flaubert, for example, dreamt of writing novels from the perspective of the "higher joke" (*blague supérieure*), in which the reader would never quite know "if the joke was on him." It can also act as a contemptuous foil for society and its mores in such characters as the glib pseudo-artist or salesman, or, more importantly, for the realist or naturalist writer whose basic qualification in this type of writing is, according to Erich Auerbach, that of the serious anthropologist. This form of speech, which is nothing more than pure enunciative "facade," is embodied, as we have seen, by fictional characters who inhabit devalued habitats. Thus in *La Curée* Maxim not only goes to the Opéra "to humbug Wagner" but he also "smooths out problems" (*essuyer les plâtres*) as the first occupant of his father's newly constructed buildings. For Zola, Maxime embodies the young Parisian deadbeat (*crevé*). Such metaphors and labels collect around a logic that associates the envelope of the blague—the tobacco pouch—together with the flattened character and the parvenu's house of whitewashed facades. The assumed name of Saccard contains within it the word *sac* (bag), an empty envelope. On the one hand there is the metaphorical field of the flat and the

---

[38] For a study of the lexical field of the joke in the nineteenth century see Jean René Klein: *Le Vocabulaire des moeurs de la vie parisienne sous le Second Empire* (Louvain, Brussels: Bibliothèque de l'Université, 1976), 373ff. See also Lorédan Larchey's article on this term in the *Dictionnaire historique d'argot*, 16th ed. (Paris: Dentu, 1888), 44ff. On the character of the joker see among others *La Physiologie du blagueur* (Paris: Garnier, 1841) and *Le Testament d'un blagueur* (1869) by Jules Vallès. Hugo gives a whimsical etymology of this term in *L'Homme qui rit* (vol. 3, 3), and *Littré* gives its origins as being from the Gallic meaning "to blow." Balzac calls it a "barracks term."

fake (face, facade, effacement) and on the other, the envelope that envelops only a void: a bladder, or cavity, the blagueur, and crevé, who are either spaced out, bombastic or swelled up.[39] The hot air of the blowhard directly opposes stones that mark off differentiated spaces, thus constituting a space that is architectural (architecture is the art of enveloping bodies). This metaphorical field is essentially negative, staging scenery that is antithetical to "true" architecture, which, after all, produces something monumental, intelligible, and stable, which possesses value and meaning.

The Goncourts often refer to the character of the blagueur. Médéric Gautruche (the name sounds almost like the French word for windbag—*baudruche*) is a blagueur from the streets, a sign painter (all his characteristics hold together) in *Germinie Lacerteux*:

> The street had given him his confidence, his language and his wit. . . . All that sinks from the upper portions of a great town to the lower—filtrations, fragments, crumbs of ideas, and knowledge, all that is borne by the subtle atmosphere and laden kernel of a capital—the rubbing up against printed matter, the scraps of newspaper serials swallowed between two half-pints, dramatic morsels heard on the boulevards had imparted to him that fortunate intelligence without education which grasps everything. He possessed an inexhaustible, imperturbable glibness (*platine*) . . . The picturesque naturalness of open-air farce . . . And only to look at him, people would laugh as at a comic actor.[40]

Cultural disparity here intensifies the jumbled bric-a-brac of expositions. The blagueur is the modern, one-dimensional ham actor without any of the secret dimensions or "backstage wings" of the Romantic actor: Gwynplaine, the hero of *L'Homme qui rit*, for example, is "comic on the outside but tragic on the inside." Instead he resembles a character from the Goncourts' *Manette Salomon*, the painter Anatole with the nickname "la Blague," who imitates or apes everything. The Goncourts continued the extended architectural metaphor, writing that he embodied "the vulgar, merry-making, great modern form of univer-

---

[39] In his *Physiologie de l'amour moderne* (Paris: Plon, 1890), 60, Paul Bourget, in reference to a deadbeat (*crevé*) would speak of a vacuous character. The *crevé* [from the verb *crever* meaning "to burst" or "to go flat"—trans.], which is an appropriate term when speaking of "envelopes" and "the mounting of exhibitions" of an individual, is also a fashion term [meaning "slash" or "slit"—trans.].

[40] Edmond and Jules de Goncourt *Germinie Lacerteux*, 191–192. The word *blague* is applied to this character. We note that the slang word *platine* that is emphasized in the text is formed from the adjective flat (*plat*) and means *wit* and *glibness*.

sal doubt and national Pyrrhonism: the nineteenth-century joke—that great demolition expert."[41]

One English variation of the verb *blaguer* is "to humbug." "Le Humbug" was also the title of an 1863 Verne short story set in the United States, the country of advertisement and worship of the almighty dollar. An extraordinary number of themes converge in this text: hollowness, expositions, hype, bluff, transparency, posters, and spectacular fakery. The story recounts a succession of swindles set up by the illustrious huckster Augustus Hopkins.[42] He declares that he wants to get his own universal exposition in Albany off the ground, "one of the colossal undertakings which up until now had been monopolized by the state."[43] In order to do this, he razes the historic ruins of an old English fort. His project creates a rush to buy into his imaginary stock thereby allowing him to gain fictional currency all over the region. Moreover, in the basement of the foundations of the future Exhibition Park, he claims to have discovered the fossil of a prehistoric man that he uses to promote his exposition. Of course, the skeleton is, like the exposition itself, nothing but "hype, bluff, and humbug."[44] The exhibition is promoted by word of mouth, yet the skeleton is the result of an even more systematic use of promotional salesmanship: "Augustus Hopkins, who had been so reserved about launching the Exposition, used all his ardor, inventiveness, and imagination to *place* his miraculous skeleton in the minds of his compatriots."[45] The hucksterism of the pseudoskeleton was accomplished by

> enormous multicolored posters. . . . Hopkins exhausted every known form in the poster line. He used the most stunning colors. He plastered the walls, the embankments of the quays, the tree trunks of the walkways. . . . The advertisement spread out in monstrous letters. . . . Men walked the streets, clothed in shirts and jackets that illustrated the skeleton. At night, enormous transparent slides projected it in black in outline against the light.[46]

[41] *Manette Salomon* (Paris: Union Générale d'Editions, 1979), 42. The character Anatole is accompanied by a monkey named Vermillon who "rubbed off" on his master who in turn "apes the ape" (147–148). His art which is described as a "type of superficial rendering, that only scratches the surface of its subject," is yet another example of an aesthetics of platitude.

[42] Jules Verne, *Hier et demain* (Paris: Livre de poche, 1967), 182.

[43] Ibid., 171ff.

[44] Ibid., 177.

[45] Ibid. Note the play on *pose* and *expose*.

[46] Ibid., 177–178. Verne in *La Journée d'un journaliste américain en 2889* (1889) would take up this theme of celestial publicity or advertisements projected onto the clouds, already mentioned in connection to Villiers de l'Isle-Adam. This sort of overdeveloped hype (*puff*) is consistent with the etymologies and the metaphors of wind, vacuousness, and levity of publicity and commercials displayed against the blown up emptiness of natural and mobile clouds.

The charlatan went on to invent other enormous swindles at the exposition, simply overwhelmed by "the difficulty in choosing what subjects to show, promote, and to exhibit."[47]

Even clothing, "man's second home," as Hugo terms it, the "semiophoric" envelope accessible to any number of "vestignomonic" readings such as those found in Balzac's works, becomes illegible. New habitats and new inhabitants require new garments. It is as if masculine and feminine attire embody the two distinct and basic criteria for this new industrial world: repetition, represented by men's clothing, and excessive, ephemeral decoration, as symbolized by women's fashions. Masculine attire somehow becomes the inverse, individual counterpart of the collective and universal glass house; the bourgeois—the one-dimensional being par excellence—dons his black frock coat as though he were in uniform.[48] The question of "the modern man's second skin" (*pelure*)—to use Baudelaire's coinage in an article on the Salon of 1846, *De l'héroïsme de la vie moderne*—remained a topic throughout the middle of the century. There is Emma's description of Charles Bovary: "His back was irritating to behold, and she saw all his platitude *spelled out* right there, on his very coat."[n] Wanting to give his wife a gift, Charles of course thought of a "daguerreotype of himself in his black suit." According to Ruskin, this item of clothing was "untreatable" in figurative art—be it painting or sculpture. For Quatremère de Quincy, who deals with this issue in his *De l'imitation,* the modern suit of clothes is "anti-imitative," meaning that it was either far too repetitive or far too fleeting as it followed all the changes in fashion.[49] J. P. Boncour, in *Art et démocratie* from 1912, criticizes the "growing tendency that pushes us to clutter our city squares and to transform our gardens and our parks into necropolises where dismal frock coats carved in marble perpetuate memories that are in no way historical." The serious journal *La Construction moderne,* in its 17 December 1887 issue wondered about Broca's and Lebon's new statues in the streets of Paris:

> In this time of statuemania, the task of the sculptor is becoming more and more difficult. How can a sculptor create an original work when he has to portray the same frock coat over and over again? . . . A bust is enough to immortalize famous men; we can thus avoid the tedium of bronze or marble devoted to reproducing our miserable modern dress. . . . Today, the unifor-

[47] Ibid., 185.
[48] Richepin, *Le Pavé,* 204. On nineteenth-century clothing, see J. Perrot, *Les dessus et les dessous de la bourgeoisie* (Paris: Arthème Fayard, 1981).
[49] Ruskin, *Seven Lamps*; Quatremère de Quincy, *De l'Imitation,* 424.
[n] Flaubert, *Madame Bovary,* 44.

mity in both poses and costume of every figure requires a pedestal that can get one's attention and can be itself decorative.[50]

Modern statuary figures not only as an aesthetic problem but as a problem of the status of memory and its supporting monuments in the modern city.

In his *Du principe de l'art et de sa destination sociale* Proudhon makes fun of the statue of Napoleon in the place Vendôme. Atop the Vendôme column—itself the focus of a novel by Lucien Descaves called *La Colonne*—the statue does not portray Napoleon in his legendary grey frock coat, but in a costume from classical antiquity. It was the only "possible" frock coat under the circumstances. But like any other object of exposition that is a product of industry, the statue finishes up as a paper "coat," as the poster and sign for a department store on the rue de Rivoli called "A la Redingote grise" (At the gray frock coat), reduced and emptied of its prestigious occupant. It recurs in many naturalist descriptions of the streets of Paris as an image punctuating the vacuousness of the century. Zola, in *Son Excellence Eugène Rougon,* has its tower over the baptism of Napoleon III's son like a gigantic symbol of farcical repetition of the uncle's empire by his nephew.[51]

As men's clothing came to represent repetition, social signs and distinctions would therefore take refuge in the female body and women's fashions. But in this case, it would limit itself to pure ostentation, observing increasingly shorter cycles of fashion and the ever-quickening pace of the tyrannical dictates of style. Women become novelties or, as Zola writes in *La Curée,* "the signpost of [male] speculation."[52] On the boulevard as in the drawing room she is an object on exhibition, a representation of her husband's status: "A salon is an exposition," writes Taine's

[50] Page 114. We can compare this to a letter from December 1862 from Flaubert to Sainte-Beuve. Here Flaubert, speaking of the conflictual relationships between description and narrative, uses a similar architectural metaphor in a discussion about his difficulty with his novel's "paper" characters; Flaubert wonders about his Salammbô, and whether the "pedestal" (i.e., description) is not "too big for the statue" (i.e., the character).

[51] This is an actual poster and sign created by the poster artist Rouchon, a pioneer of the colorful poster on large surfaces. This poster seems to have struck writers such as Céard, Edmond de Goncourt, Laforgue, and Germain Nouveau since they all mention it in their works. It can also be found in all the newspapers of the period in their advertisement sections. Zola ends chapter four of his novel *Son Excellence Eugène Rougon*: "The only distinguishable thing in the midst of the muddled gray of the facades was the giant frock coat, the monumental advertisement, hung by some hook on the horizon, the bourgeois cast-offs of a Titan whose wrath would have consumed the limbs" (*Les Rougon-Macquart*, vol. 2, 109).

[52] The mistresses whom Saccard displays are "the golden signposts of his speculations" (ibid., vol. 1, 429).

character Thomas Graindorge, "you are a commodity, and the only way to invest a product with importance is to expose it."[53] It is significant that the great novel of Parisian demolition and speculation, Zola's *La Curée,* is at the same time a novel about the heroine Renée's successive dresses, bills, and accumulated debts at the great design houses of the city. Just as Renée is the assumed name or signature of the real-estate speculations of Saccard, she also functions as the signpost for the couturier Worms (based on the historical figure Worth) for whom she becomes the female equivalent of the sandwich man—since "she wore a Worms." Renée is nothing more than Worms's insignia, monogram, invoice, and label. The final sentence in the book serves as Renée's epitaph: "The next winter, when Renée died of acute meningitis, her father paid off her debts. Worms's bill came to 257,000 francs." The dead woman reduced to an invoice is symbolic of the loss of the female body—a real, visual, and erotic loss that takes on the additional forms of obscene overexposure, such as the naked Nana in her on-stage crystal cage, or in the stifling constriction of an excess of envelopes or deceptive trimmings. Proust writes of Odette's body as "something admirably built," it was impossible to "make out its continuity" and so complicated was the play of superimposed layers of clothing that it gave the impression that her body possessed an "imaginary stomach"; "disappearing in the balloon of her double skirts," Odette had the air of "being composed of different sections badly put together," in no way attached to a "living creature, who, according to the architecture of these fripperies either drew them towards or away from her own, found herself either strait-laced to suffocation or else completely buried."[54] One should also notice in this passage, aside from the reference to architecture (a dress is "constructed" the same way as a cathedral, as we have seen elsewhere in Proust), the reference to the balloon.

The metaphor of the balloon has an obvious and logical place in this field of corporal envelopes. The balloon was the fetishized machine of the nineteenth century: it figures prominently in the universal expositions, the 1871 siege of Paris, Nadar's photography, "the Douanier"

[53] Taine, *Thomas Graindorge,* 57. Taine's hero ironically proposes the foundation of a "universal matrimonial agency" (ibid. 169) (we find once again the adjective so often applied to expositions) that would feature photographs of potential candidates. Henry James in the preface to *Awkward Age* tells how "the grain of subject-matter" of his book, "the access to salons," and the first "exposition" of the young girl had been furnished by the city of London itself. Of the society woman J. Péladan says that "her destiny is permanent exposition" (*L'Initiation sentimentale* [Paris: Edinger, 1887], 200).

[54] Proust, *Remembrance,* vol. 1, 197.

Rousseau's paintings, various works of Verne, and Maupassant's *Le Voyage du Horla*. In its negative aspects, the balloon is an absolute anti-architecture. Something both empty and filled with air, it is semantically and etymologically linked to themes of hype, blague, and the young deadbeat. Numa Roumestan's mistress has a "paper reputation, inflated by gas and puffery," that brings to mind "a rose balloon." Advertising balloons, publicity tools for Octave Mouret's store, often appear as a kind of leitmotif in *Au bonheur des dames*: "Red balloons, with delicate rubber skin, bearing the name of his store in big letters, were held from the end of a string, flew through the air, and carried a lively advertisement through the streets!"[55] Moreover, the balloon metaphor, as in Flaubert's description of Charles Bovary's hat, which was "a sort of bag," and "ovoid and stiffened by whalebone," can serve to incarnate an unstable, fake, and hollow universe. Laforgue in his *Grande complainte de la ville de Paris*, a mimetic poem-collage of the walls and hubbub of the Parisian streets, notes in a variation on this encounter of spectator with spectacle—whether "things seen," or things made up—that forms a conjunction between two vacuums; the "dog who barks at a balloon overhead." "A ballon sky," was a note Villiers de l'Isle-Adam made to himself when writing a sketch of his *Nouveau conte cruel*, "L'Amour du naturel" (1888), part of an anthology that was also an ironic judgment of the general loss of the state of nature in the modern world. Balzac, in *Gaudissart II*, said of the sales clerk (a draper's assistant): "outside his store . . . he is like a deflated balloon." Poe wrote a short story about a canard and a balloon called "The Unparalleled Adventure of One Hans Pfall" in which "a *balloon* manufactured entirely of *newspapers*" resembles "a huge *fool's* cap," a redundant object that triply alludes to "hollowness." Poe's character, Hans Pfall, whose very name sounds like *puff*, is himself a "former mender of *bellows*."[56,0]

The one-dimensional bourgeois, the balloon-like woman, the draper's assistant, the blagueur, the promoter of hype, and the woman who buys on credit comprise a list of forms lacking substance or volume, emblems of superficiality, or of non- or antimonumentality. Clothing the human

[55] Zola, *Les Rougon-Macquart*, vol. 3, 612–613, 620, 643.

[56] On the theme of the balloon, see the special issue of *La Revue des sciences humaines* 200, 1985. The term and its synonyms, serves also to designate a certain type of light poetry (*Ballons* by Gouffé, *La Bulle de savon* by P. de Koch). In 1862 Manet drew a balloon as a frontispiece to one of his collections of engravings, a balloon which could well be an allusion to Poe, or a parody of Verne's serious *Cinq semaines en ballon* that was published the same year.

[0] Edgar Allan Poe, *Collected Writings*, vol. 1, *Imaginary Voyages* (Cambridge: Harvard University Press, 1978), 388–399.

form sparks a perpetual debate; Mallarmé in *La Dernière Mode,* echoes it in opposing clothing that hugs the figure with the various poufs, puffs, and crinolines that "devour the buttocks."[57] This opposition doubles as a stylistic problem: how does one write about nothing, notably the ephemeral architecture of the female body and fashion, whose essence is change? In a sense, as editor of *La Dernière Mode,* it seems inevitable that Mallarmé should linger on the subject of women's clothing. The same is true of such related paper or fabric objects as fans and handkerchiefs which can be folded or unfolded and decorated with embroidery or inscription. "His mind clouded by fabrics,"[58] and fascinated by fashion magazines, a literary genre with neither past nor future, devoted only to the present, and already out-of-date before even published, Mallarmé muses:

> A dress, studied and composed according to fashion dictates that hold only for a single winter, does not become obsolete or stale as quickly as does a newspaper column, even one published every fortnight; to have the same life span as the illusion of tulle . . . is the dream harbored by every sentence that seeks to pen the latest news, instead of tales or sonnets.[59]

As a dialectic of the empty and the full, the stable and the ephemeral, of memory and amnesia, of the signifying sign and the designating signpost, any discussion of envelopes is interchangeable, whether it involves clothing, habitat, or language.

A strange osmosis seems to occur between the type of fabric worn by characters and wallpaper decorating the bourgeois interior. It is an osmosis documented, more or less sarcastically, by painters such as Gustav Klimt and the Nabis, and authors such as Maupassant. His story, *Une Vie,* recounts how a character named Jeanne is wrapped up in tapestries depicting fables from La Fontaine, and Ovid's *Pyramis and Thisbe.* The increasing use of decorative prints would pass from exterior to interior, transforming the bourgeois salon into a variation on the

---

[57] This is Flaubert's phrase (from a letter to Louise Colet 29 January 1854). The Robert dictionary defines *pouf* (or *pouff*) as: "Fabric gathered in a way that causes the skirt or the dress to puff out in the back." Mallarmé often speaks of the *pouf* in *La Dernière Mode* and opposes its use to the tight-fitting suit, which, by eliminating such accessories, lets the "woman, herself, show through, visible and finely delineated, with the total grace of her outline or the main lines of her person" (20 December 1874). Labiche in *La Poudre aux yeux*—here we are still in the world of bladders—speaks of a feminine *mongonfliére.* It is also interesting in the act of carving stone, the term *pouf* has a technical meaning that designates a stone which is of bad quality that crumbles when it is worked on.

[58] *La Dernière Mode* first issue (6 September 1874).

[59] "Chronique de Paris," signed by Ix. [Mallarmé] no. 5 (1 November 1874).

decorative frame of an official Salon or a streetcorner wall plastered
with posters: "Vieilles verdures, vieux galons / O croquignoles végé-
tales! / Fleurs fantasques des vieux salons," wrote Rimbaud in "Ce
qu'on dit au poète à propos de fleurs."ᴾ In his work *Cosmopolis,* Paul
Bourget speaks of "the interior-decorator mentality that distinguishes
modern novelists." Mallarmé, in *La Dernière Mode,* reminds his readers of the delicate issue of choosing flowers for women's outfits, "take
into account the color or shadings of the wall paper, in other words, the
background setting against which one leans in every salon." The characters of nineteenth-century fiction are often literally wall flowers. In
contrast to such outdoor types as the man in the street in the solid-color
frock coat, the sandwich man, or the strolling woman-as-label, we encounter the petit bourgeois man sealed up in the paper universe of his
parlor, surrounded by the bric-a-brac of his collected baubles, having
removed his frock coat to put on such semiophoric garments as shabbily
embroidered slippers, dressing gowns, and ascots. Verlaine's well-
known portrait of Monsieur Prudhomme in *Poèmes Saturniens* culminates in the final line: "And the flowering spring shone on his slippers"
(Et le printemps en fleurs brillait sur ses pantoufles). In Edmond de
Goncourt's *La Fille Elisa,* "the son of the house," shows off "tapestry
slippers with an embroidered nine of hearts."⁶⁰ In *Une Belle Journée,*
Céard describes the semiophoric interior of the architect Duhamain—
for which Homais's pharmacy undoubtedly served as a model—as having a "lithophanic lampshade [that showed] the figure of a hunter out of
comic opera blocking the way across a bridge while trying to kiss a milk
maid." The interior also features flowered wallpaper, family portraits,
and slippers belonging to the man of the house—"tapestry slippers
depicting Alsace on the right foot and Lorraine on the left, crying in

---

⁶⁰ Edmond de Goncourt, *La Fille Elisa,* 5th ed. (Paris: Charpentier, 1877), 42. See also
Baudelaire's poem "Les Petites vieilles," describing old women with "their tiny handbags
embroidered with flowers or puzzling patterns," "clutching [them] against their ribs."
Regarding the literary history of the house slipper see the pair of embroidered slippers that
are the heroines of a short story for children by E. Deschamp called "Pantoufles! . . .
Pantoufles!" which is included in a collection entitled *Nouvelles choisies de divers auteurs,*
ed. S. de la Madelaine (Paris: Bibliothèque des Demoiselles, René, 1841), Hugo's house in
Paris has on display a pattern that represented the author, that had been meant for a pair
of slippers. Slippers, Greek skull caps, embroideries, and fabrics are of course related
metaphorically and metonymically with the objects and practices of the writer—who is a
stay-at-home as well as being related to writing.
ᴾ Old greenery, old galloons / O vegetable cracker! / Fantastic flowers of old salons."

their national costumes, and the corsage decorated with a tricolored *cocarde,* while in a border of green vines, woolen letters across a band read: "She is waiting."[61] There is the further example of Judge Popinot's home in Balzac's *L'Interdiction,* with its "papers in flower vases," "piles of open books," "legal briefs arranged in rows," "bouquets of artificial flowers," "frames in which Popinot's initials were surrounded by hearts and everlasting flowers," "commemorative plaques" and "tokens of gratitude" given to the judge by those indebted to him, "embroidered pincushions," "needlepoint landscapes," and "crosses made of folded paper with flourishes that were evidence of inordinate amounts of handiwork." In her first appearance in the exposition of *Education sentimentale,* Madame Arnoux is shown working on her embroidery. This universe of the interior no longer affords the possibility of lapidary inscription on monumental stone, nor the rhetorical and symbolic grandeur of the "flowers of evil." Instead, flowers there are only to be displayed, printed, woven into carpets, or put on display, most particularly in the course of demolitions to make way for the new city, as well as in the destruction caused by popular revolution, both of which reveal the floral wall-paper and baubles of private homes—a scene that recurs with great frequency in novels by mid century. Thus in the famous scene of the 1848 revolution in *Education sentimentale:* "The houses were riddled with bullets, and their frames were showing beneath the chipped plaster. . . . Doors opened onto empty space. One could see the interior of rooms with their wallpaper in shreds; sometimes the most fragile things were spared. Frédéric noticed a clock, a parrot's perch, some engravings." In this passage that combines the exposure of anonymous private lives, the autopsy of ruins, and the juxtaposition of random objects, we encounter an ironic rewriting of the Romantic writer's visit to the great monument. One readily observes in this quotation the doors opening "onto empty space," the reference to plaster, and the eminently repetitive or mimetic character of these exposed objects. The engraving reiterates the described scene and the clock restates the time, while the

---

[61] Céard, *Une Belle Journée,* 198–199. Wallpaper is the object of many misgivings for a meticulous hygienist discourse. For example the liberal regulations of the ideal city of Verne's *Cinq cents Millions de la Bégum* pursue it ruthlessly: "Two dangerous elements of disease which are veritable nests of miasma and laboratories of poison . . . are strictly forbidden: rugs and wallpaper. . . . Comforters and quilts, powerful allies of epidemic diseases are also quite naturally prohibited" (chap. 10). The imperceptible is here the antithesis of the scientific panoptic.

parrot—the ever-so-Flaubertian animal that would reappear in *Un Coeur Simple* as a stuffed relic—can only exhibit language by repeating or "aping" it.[62] What remains on display among the ruins of the monumental, even in the pathetic detritus of this passage, is the problem of Mimesis.

---

[62] See Phillipe Bonnefis: "Exposition d'un perroquet," in *Mesures de l'ombre* (Lille: Presses Universitaires de Lille, 1987). For Léon Daudet: "The nineteenth century could be called ... the century of the parrot" because it repeats and drones empty words like *progress, hygiene, rights of man, Le Stupide XIXème Siècle* (Paris: Nouvelle Librairie Nationale, 1922), 17.

CHAPTER V

# Lyric and Exposition

*De la vaporisation et de la centralisation du Moi tout est là.*

[The vaporization and centralization of Self, this is what it
all comes down to]

> —Baudelaire, *Mon coeur mis à nu*

More than any other type of text, the lyric meticulously tests the status
of the architectural object. During the nineteenth century, it seemed
especially well-equipped to accept the ambivalence of the widespread
(over)exposure of the real and the resulting tensions between plenitude,
transparency, and platitude. Beyond certain stylistic oppositions, such
as verse/prose, literary/nonliterary, narrative/non-narrative, and elegiac/
lyrical, the question of the subject seems to be the unifying force of the
lyric field; the diverse texts that constitute this field all deal with a
subject's own construction or rehearsal through writing and the ensuing
problem of the subject's sites and their location. It may be noted in
passing that the genre of autobiography shares in these very same problems and that it is sometimes difficult to say which one of these two
genres is the subgenre of the other.

Curiously enough, the traditional key words most often found in
poems and their titles to designate essentially lyric stances are themselves products of metaphors—sometimes taken quite literally—with
strong underlying spatial associations: *Elevation* is a movement up-
ward; *humility,* a downward motion; *composure,* a centripetal ingath-
ering; and *effusion,* a centrifugal flow. These terms immediately imply
sites or zones of expressiveness, and define a volume, that can expand or
contract, thus giving the subject room to maneuver in its exploration of
the self. Interestingly, Paul Valéry saw the poem as "a way of maneuver-
ing myself by myself." In order to orient itself, this subject, exposed to

all the risks associated with a quest for the self, attempts a *mise en demeure* in a space ideally embodied in a precise architecture that serves to transform the subject into an inhabitant of a world where he would (or would not) feel "located," as Laforgue writes in his "Complainte de Lord Pierrot." The complicity between poem and architecture is perhaps signaled by the word *stanza,* which derives from the Italian term for *dwelling, residence,* or *resting place.*

The realist and naturalist text is quick to underscore the neutrality of the referent, since anything, even nothing can figure in the literary work as long as the work can in turn methodically redistribute this referent within its storehouse in the form of classified documents and by the use of transparent language. However, the lyric's reflection on the real seems more selective. For someone like Valéry, there exist certain privileged objects at the heart of the "mollusc we all live in" (*L'Homme et la coquille,* 1937). These are not objects that the text is somehow obligated to *cite* or that have been given a *citation* or summons to appear in the court of *representation* simply because they are themselves *representative* of a certain time or place—such as the gaslights, boulevards, theaters, advertisements, and newspapers that occur in accounts of the Second Empire. Rather, they are objects that *incite* or *solicit* representation by virtue of some sort of structural and intrinsic property. According to Valéry, those objects "commit [the poet] to a feat of attention and wonder," for they stand out against the "ordinary disorder of perceptible things" and "elicit the gaze and lead it to a kind of organized vertigo." These objects of the concrete world "expose their full power to seduce the senses." This holds true for those objects like the crystal and the shell which seem to waver between the natural and the manmade, while "exhibiting" and "exposing" their structure. They therefore seem to be the product of architectural design and seem defined by some sort of a priori spatial rhythm. This brings to mind the *zoèmes* evoked in Claude Lévi-Strauss's *Mythologiques,* vol. 4, defined as certain animals that fascinate mythical thought because of their basic ambivalence and ambiguity. Using Lévi-Strauss's notion as a model, it would be possible to come up with the concept of the technemes to define those architectural objects such as doors, windows, stained-glass windows, partitions, and passageways which invite structural thinking while functioning as the concretization of its questions.

The issue of the subject's difference and identity leads immediately to questions about its most characteristic aspect as an individualized body linked to an individualized language—that is, its voice. Its most minimal form of expression may correspond to the lyric "O." This pure exclamation, this nonsemantic punctuation of the origin of speech, this fundamental phonemic signature or biophoneme is enough to position the subject not simply as a subject but as a localized subject, situated at the very source and center of the concentric waves generated by its act of speech. As Rimbaud writes in his poem "Jeunesse IV" in *Illuminations*: "Toutes les possibilités harmoniques et architecturales s'émouvront autour de ton siège."[1,a] This founding act is not without its ambiguities. Since the modern lyric is a written text, how can this form of deferred utterance objectivize a location that can only be effectuated by a voice speaking in the present or as a presence? To quote Valéry once again, the lyric could be defined as "the development of an exclamation." Of course, the term *development* can be taken in either the photographic sense (a print exposed to developer) or the expositional sense (a display, or unfolding, or disclosure of the virtualities of the subject). Thus this self in search of a site is first and foremost engaged in a nostalgic quest for that natural and immediate locus constituted by the natural oral act of speaking. Speaking locates the self vis-à-vis the other by means of interlocution, just as it locates the self vis-à-vis time and space by means of language's shifters and deictics: *here, there, today, you, tomorrow, now, this, that*. Such are the fundamental themes and the lexicon of the lyric.

Baudelaire's prose poem "Anywhere out of the world"—whose architectural referents make it comparable to "Le Cygne" and "Rêve Parisien"—is a veritable catalogue of lyric obsessions concerning the subject's location. All the elements of the complex thematics of the lyric

---

[1] The /ô/ is both a "small word," according to Apollinaire in "Acousmate"; a circular letter, a sound and a vowel according to Rimbaud in "Voyelles"—"O suprême clairon plein des strideurs étranges." (O, supreme trumpet full of strange screeches)—a sign of lyric apostrophe, a signal that indicates that a text belongs to the lyric genre, and an index that registers the presence of a speaker. Blaise Cendras in "Opoétic," a poem in which all the O's are capitalized, makes fun of poets "*qui parlent la bouche en rond*" ("who speak with 'O'-shaped mouths"). There is also the fin-de-siècle poem by André Remacle entitled "Sièges et trônes" in *La Passante*:

> Avoir lieu—Siège ou Trône—être un point vibrant, ETRE,
> Centre de vue et d'ouïe, actif et un ancêtre,
> Enfant perpétué, chanter l'enivrement,
> D'ETRE, d'avoir lieu—Trône ou siège—absolument!

> [Take place—seat or throne—to be a vibrating point TO BE,
> center of sight and hearing, active and whole, ancestor,
> Perpetuated child, to sing of drunkenness
> OF BEING, of taking place—Throne or seat—absolutely!]

[a] "All possibilities of harmony and architecture will rise up around your seat" (Rimbaud, *Complete Work*, 221).

can be found here: the topical and the utopic; presence and ubiquity; identity and ambiguity. Moreover, we encounter once again the theme of "relocation" (*déménagement*). A theme that cuts across not only the journalistic discourse of a contemporary of Haussmann's like Victor Fournel, but that also traverses fantastic literature's discourse on madness (for a literal incarnation of the French expression used in reference to a madman—*il déménage* [nobody is home]—see Maupassant's short story "Qui Sait?"). In Baudelaire's prose poem the narrator engages in a dialogue with his soul:

> *Il me semble que je serais bien là où je ne suis pas, et cette question de déménagement en est une que je discute sans cesse avec mon âme.*[b]

The soul suggests Lisbon:

> *ville . . . au bord de l'eau; on dit qu'elle est bâtie en marbre, et que le peuple y a une telle haine du végétal, qu'il arrache tous les arbres. Voilà un paysage selon ton goût; un paysage fait avec la lumière et le minéral, et le liquide pour les réfléchir!*[c]

The various elements that are itemized here derive from the logic at work whenever architecture provides the referent: It associates immobile and stable stone (in this case marble, its most hyperbolic form) with agents of cyclicity, of recursivity, and mobility—vegetation on the one hand, the stars and the seasons, on the other. Furthermore it associates the fixed rhythm of the building with the flowing rhythm of the sea. The mirror, obligatory *techneme* and identifying leitmotif of the lyric per se, materializes in this poem in themes which are themselves at the heart of lyric self-reflexivity: doubles; reflections; echoes; dialogues with the self; and inversion. *Exposition* only comes about within these relations between the unique and the multiple, between the periodic and the permanent, between the describable, nameable, and reassuring architecture of discrete volumes and forms and the ineffable effusion of nature. In his poem "Le Cimetière Marin," Valéry writes of "l'âme exposé aux torches du solstice."[d] This could stand as the lyric figure par excellence.

Of course, references to architecture in the lyric have very different functions and motives. Despite this diversity, however, Baudelaire's

---

[b] "It seems that I would always be content where I am not, and I constantly discuss that question of relocation with my soul" (Baudelaire, *Paris Prowler*, 119).

[c] "That city is next to the water; they say that it is built of marble, and that its inhabitants hate vegetation so much that they rip out all the trees. Now there's a landscape to your liking: a landscape made of light and minerals, and of the liquid to reflect them" (ibid.).

[d] "The soul exposed to the torches of the solstice."

phrase from "Mon coeur mis à nu"—which serves as this chapter's epigraph—condenses them in two principal points. On the one hand there is the centripetal role of a fixed, central point, on the other hand the centrifugal vaporization brought about by a multiplicity of points. These two tendencies constitute the limits of the lyric subject which in regard to space seems to constantly vacillate between two inclinations— agoraphobia or agoraphilia. As Wilhelm Worringer writes in *Abstraction and Empathy*, references to architecture may therefore well serve to ward off "the spatial anxiety experienced when the mind is confronted by the motley confusion and arbitrariness of the phenomenal world."

Many lyric texts of the second half of the nineteenth century offer an "I" engaged in an eternal quest for identity. Subjects such as the one in Nerval's "El desdichado" who begins by asking: "*Suis-je Amour ou Phoebus, Lusignan ou Biron?*"ᵉ search for themselves in such sites as "a tomb," "a destroyed tower," and a "grotto," or in particular time periods that must be conjured up or rediscovered. Such subjects often present themselves by resorting to the rhetorical play of the figure (which according to Pascal, "bespeaks both absence and presence") and, significantly enough, often have recourse to architectural metaphors where the "I" likens itself to an edifice. The lyric speaker's identification with an edifice, a monument, a tomb, or a room is first and foremost a direct consequence of having to use a semantically "empty" pronoun ("I") as if it were a proper noun. The use of a shifter (or "egocentric particulars" as Bertrand Russell might say), which in its written form is free-floating and interchangeable, therefore requires the anchor of a metaphorical discourse. As a result, we get statements that run: I (my mind, my soul, my heart) . . . is . . . (a castle, a palace, a ruin, a monument).[2] A term devoid of significance (the pronoun "I") is thereby stabilized and filled with meaning, thus permitting a portrait of the "I" to emerge. Moreover this metaphor also provides a means of uttering the gramatically correct but existentially improbable and impossible phrase—"I am dead"—as well as a means of denying death by assimilating it to architectural structures which resist time and survive

---

[2] Some well-known examples from Baudelaire: "*Je suis un cimetière abhorré de la lune / . . . une pyramide, un immense caveau*" ("Spleen," I am a graveyard that the Moon abhors / . . . a pyramid, a vast grave); "*Notre âme, piteux monument*" ("L'Irréparable," That pitiful monument, our soul); "*Mon âme est un tombeau, que, mauvais cénobite, / Depuis l'éternité je parcours et j'habite*" ("Le Mauvais Moine," My soul is a tomb in which for centuries I have moved to and fro and lived, an unworthy monk); "*Mon esprit est pareil à la tour qui succombe*" ("Chant d'automne," My mind is like a tower, crashing).

ᵉ "Am I Amor or Phoebus, Lusignan or Biron?"

their inhabitants. Since every building is a monument that solicits activities similar to those of the reader—who both restores meaning to written texts (themselves like semantic ruins) and revives concrete situations
of (re)utterance—it is therefore fitting that the lyric "I" identify itself as
a building in the hopes of being resurrected by a reader–visitor. In this
sense, every lyric text is something of a stela, epitaph, or tomb.

Not only is architecture the preferred metaphor for the lyric subject,
but it can also be the preferred object of its descriptive voice or contemplative gaze. Architecture can be evoked for a variety of reasons: as a
medium of vision (looking through a window), as an object of vision
(buildings that one contemplates), or as a metaphor for things seen
(while in America, Chateaubriand describes the clouds as "old towers"
and speaks of a papaya tree as a "carved silver style crowned by a
corinthian urn"). In all these cases, the allusion to architecture allows
the lyric viewer to believe that he is regulating, controlling, and mastering the amorphousness of space and time, and that he is the point of
origin of a world that has been reticulated by thresholds, templa, windows, and perspectives. In this sense the lyric text does not differ from
the reticulations at work in the realist or naturalist novels already discussed. But, whereas the reticulations of the realist or naturalist text—
to the left, to the right, far away, behind, to the north, on top of, in front
of—primarily serve to construct the legibility and visibility of the storehouse work and to fabricate a space that airs out and arranges the
objects of the real, the lyric by contrast attempts to locate a subject in
relation to the real. Thus the need to establish a residence for the contem-
plator here outweighs the desire to reduce the real to an exposition
space as well ordered as the Champ de Mars or the Palace of Industry.
Just as a painting places its subject at a point that corresponds to the
vantage point of the painter's eye, at the center of the intersection of
lines of perspective, so the lyric endeavors to define a subject point that
can be deduced from the different intersections, lines of sight, figures,
and foci evoked by references to architectural objects and sites.[3] It is as

---

[3] Crosses, windows (croisées), crossroads, intersections, and aisles (rayons) that we
have already encountered in discussions on the organization of the storehouse text are
also part of the most obsessive terms and themes of the lyric. Some examples: "I flee and
cling to all the windows" ("Je fuis et je m'accroche à toutes les croisées"; Mallarmé, "Les
Fenêtres"); "Entre les fenêtres qui se croisent on n'écoute pas" (Reverdy, "Le voile du
temps" Between criss-crossing windows one does not listen"); and Baudelaire's "intersections" of "many relationships" of an "enormous city." Of course the word "line" (ligne)
is associated with these other terms (the lines of perspective that define a center at a
vanishing point, and the lines of the text itself):

if the lyric subject, when confronted with the choice of either being dispersed into nature by effusion and "vaporization," or being confined to his room and almost anaesthetized by sleep, dreams, or disease,[4] could only recover or recognize himself in and through the systematic configuration of a given site—in other words, through architecture.

The lyric is clearly fascinated by the reassuring propensity of any construction to stabilize time and space by providing a center, measure, and articulation. And yet there are also certain more disturbing aspects to the edifice, such as its propensity to organize ambiguity—an ambiguity embodied in its technemes (windows, stained glass, walls, mirrors, doors, shutters, partitions, and balconies), a class of prefabricated objects which constitutes the discriminating, filtering, selectioning, pivoting, or reflecting parts of the building. Such ambiguity is directly attributable to the properties shared by these objects: a wall both separates and connects; a balcony is both indoors and outdoors; a vestibule is both private and public; and, as Walter Benjamin has shown, an arcade (a "house turned inside out" to use Jacques Réda's expression)[5] is both an interior and an exterior; a door or a window (which can involve either dormers or leafs) can be either opened or closed.[6] The lyric is

---

*Dans la ville où le dessin nous emprisonne, l'arc de cercle du porche, les carrés des fenêtres, les losanges des toits.*
*Des lignes, rien que des lignes, pour la commodité des bâtisses humaines.*
*Dans ma tête des lignes, rien que des lignes; si je pouvais y mettre un peu d'ordre seulement.*

(Reverdy, "Traits et Figures" in *Poèmes en Prose, Plupart du temps*)

[In the town where pattern imprisons us, the arch of the porch circle, the squares of windows, the diamonds of the roofs.
Lines, nothing but lines, for the convenience of human buildings.
In my head lines, nothing but lines; if only I could make some order of them.]

On certain spatial obsessions of the lyric text, see Michel Collot, *L'Horizon fabuleux*, vol. 1, XIXème Siècle (Paris: José Corti, 1988).

[4] See Aloysius Bertrand's descriptions of rooms or Verlaine's, where the Self dissolves: "*Une sorte à présent d'idyllique engourdi / Qui surveille le ciel par la fenêtre*" (Verlaine, *Sagesse* I, 3, A sort at present of idyllic numbness that observes the sky from out the window). See also Verlaine's *Sagesse* III, 3, or Laforgue's descriptions of rooms in *Complainte d'un autre dimanche: "Seras-tu donc toujours un qui garde la chambre?"* (Will you always be someone who stays in your room?).

[5] Jacques Réda, *Châteaux des courants d'air* (Paris: Gallimard, 1986), 93.

[6] On the "system" bridge–door see Georg Simmel's brief but stimulating essay "Pont et porte" (1909). The Folio Junior anthology, *Fenêtres en poésie* (Paris: Folio, 1981) proves the frequency of the theme of the window in poetry. See also the titles of an author like Pierre Reverdy—*Lucarnes ovales* (oval skylight), or René Char—*Fenêtres dormantes et portes sur le toit*.

equally intrigued by architecture's propensity to organize reversibility: one can enter a place and then leave it, go from the inside to the outside, and vice versa; one can go up or down the same staircase, take a street in one direction and then in the other, allowing one to say: "I am here, and you are outside, but soon you will be here, and I will be outside."[7] At issue in these references to architecture, that art of envelopes, is the status of the "I" as a body or as a "skin ego" (to use Didier Anzieu's expression) at once opened and closed, ingesting and evacuating—as is the status of the "I" that marches towards the irreversibility of death, the "I" that exercises its natural, fundamental, and reversible functions of orality.[8]

Nostalgic for orality in all its various possibilities, the lyric text tends to define itself by its own impossibilities. First of all, the lyric text is destined to be forever deferred by writing and therefore it can only offer absence where orality imposes presence. Second, because of the split inherent to writing—a split between the present of writing and the past of the act, between the self who is composing and the self who is reading the product—it can never attain a full union between the spoken and the speaker. Finally, condemned to the linearity of the written word, it cannot achieve the reversibility of dialogue. Its recourse to the metaphor of architecture merely reinforces all this in a two-fold fashion: first by referring to architecture, which in a sense embodies the very objects of the lyric subject's angst and nostalgia (identity, presence, unity, and irreversibility of death); and second, by the fact that this reference to architecture itself takes the form of metaphor. A metaphor is after all a rhetorical operation that organizes ambiguity, blurs semantic partitions, and functions as both transport and transfer of meaning on the basis of shared analogic identity. Although it may be purely coincidental that the words door (*porte*) and *trope*, and window (*vitrage*) and *vertigo* are virtual anagrams of each other, it nevertheless underscores the role of these technemes in inducing ambiguity. For examples see the use of the

---

[7] In the dedication of his prose poems to Arsène Houssaye, Baudelaire writes of his own book: "everything in it is both tail and head alternatively and reciprocally." We have already mentioned Kevin Lynch's work (*The Image of the City*) where the problem of the reversibility of perspectives and pathways of the inhabitants and users of a city is discussed strictly from the point of view of the architect and urban planner: how to organize sequentially and univocally the development of motives of a street which can be taken in any which way?

[8] Emile Benveniste, dealing with subjectivity in language in *Problèmes de linguistique générale* (Paris: Gallimard, 1966), 260, encounters the problem of reversibility in analyzing the polarity of the "I" and the "you" in utterance, which are "complementary but only according to an opposition such as interior/exterior, and at the same time . . . are reversible."

word *vitrage* in Mallarmé's poem "Sainte," or the "regulated vertigo" of which Valéry speaks in *L'Homme et la coquille,* or the title of Reverdy's "Figure de porte."

Technemes, deictics, and shifters—each one a metaphor for the other—are all part and parcel of the lyric's lexicon. Thus Baudelaire's prose poem "Paysage"—the inaugural poem in the section "Tableaux parisiens" of *Les Fleurs du mal*—sets up a carefully articulated site around a garret where a narrator, sitting at his window, looks out upon the city's windows and listens to the noises below. In certain respects, this poem could be an ironic paraphrase of Victor Hugo's preface to *Voix intérieures* and that author's theory of the poet as echo chamber. The entire poem "hinges" on the moment in the middle of the text when the "I" closes the "doors and shutters" (*portières et volets*) (line 15) thereby splitting the text into something like the two "volets" of a diptych; later Francis Ponge would use this same object as a metaphor in his text "Le Volet suivie de sa scholie." The first half of the poem is devoted to the outside world with its moon and the lamp at the neighbor's window, while the second part turns inward to focus on the "sun" within the narrator's heart. Just as in so many of the opening expositions of naturalist novels, this poem mimes the operations of the heliographic art of photography: it prepares a "chamber"; opens it up to the lit objects of the outside world; and then closes it up again in order to "print" (*tirer*; line 25) an image. It thereby enacts a series of dialectical relationships: between camera lucida and camera obscura, between hidden images and ones revealed through development, between movable and immovable, between interior and exterior, and between container and contained. Frequently found within the rooms and interiors of lyric texts, lamps act as variations on exterior cyclical agents such as the sun, stars, moon, and plant life. Not only can they be the sign of a certain intimacy—the coziness of home—but they can also signal the inversion of privacy. At night, an interior lamp can transform the normal diurnal observatory of the spectator gazing from his window upon a real world lighted by the sun into a spectacle to be observed from the outside by an unseen spectator in the shadows. Lit from within, exposed, and displayed to the gaze of any outside voyeur, the intimacy of the home is transformed into "publicity." Moreover, for those who approach it at night, the transparent window changes into a reflecting mirror. Similarly, darkness transforms the stained-glass window, normally a beautiful narrative object visible only from the inside, into a spectacle visible to those on the outside gazing upon this window which is lit from within.[9] In the lyric, these "pivotal" moments or moments of inversion dealing with a quest for identity are often of a narrative nature and occur in descriptions of just such a place that is meticulously articulated by these "technemes/tropes." See for example the pivotal moment in Mallarmé's poem "Les Fenêtres": "*Je fuis et je m'accroche à toutes les croisées / D'où l'on tourne l'épaule à la vie, et béni / Dans leur verre . . . Je me mire et me vois ange! . . . Que la vitre soit l'art, soit la mysticité.*"[f] According to Valéry, in *Tel quel*, the window is a *topos* of the lyric stance: "Cette barre de fenêtre, ce plan poli d'une vitre, où le front s'appuie, accessoires de l'être, décor, système entre lesquels les pensées et les impression se meuvent."[g] Mallarmé's "monstrance window" in *Sainte* can be understood as a place where a subject who is otherwise unplaceable, dispersed, and sealed-off can perform ostentive or ostentatious acts. This is a theme that would be shared both by lyric poems and fantastic tales. Here a room described by Villiers de l'Isle-Adam, in his short story entitled "Véra" in *Contes cruels*:

> Through the window he looked at the darkness spreading across the heavens; and Night seemed *personal* in his eyes. He saw her as a queen walking sadly in exile, [with] the diamond clip of her mourning tunic. Venus, alone shone above the trees, lost in the depths of the sky. . . . He looked all around him. The objects in the room were now lit by the hitherto indistinct glow of a night light that was tinting the darkness blue and to which the night sky gave the appearance of another star. It was the incense-scented flame of an iconostasis, a relic belonging to Véra's family. The triptych made of precious old wood, was hanging by its Russian esparto between the mirror and the painting. A quivering gleam of light from the gold inside fell on the necklace among the jewels on the mantelpiece.

This text, which could clearly stand alongside a number of symbolist interiors, is also interchangeable with a good many realist or naturalist interiors because of the underlying logic of its system of technemes as well as its function within the work. Clearly, the articulation of this

[9] Let us note that after 1840 there was a return in both public and private as well as in religious edifices of the stained-glass window which had all but disappeared since the beginning of the seventeenth century. We have seen that colored glass was a leitmotif in Baudelaire, Zola, and Champfleury in their discussions of the problem of representation. For this theme see the collection by Laurent Tailhade, *Vitraux* (Paris: Lemerre, 1894).

[f]     I flee and I cling to all the windows
        From which one *turns* ones back on life, and blesses
        In their glass (. . .) I look at myself and I see an angel.

[g] "This window barrier, this polished plane of windowpane, against which the forehead is pressed, [are] accessories to being, the scenery and system between which thoughts and impressions move."

passage is set up by a system of technemes: outside, inside, window, mantelpiece, mirror, painting, displayed relic, and the gleam of the jewels. Moreover, like a realist or naturalist description, this text produces the illusion of a person's presence—Villiers does after all emphasize the word *personal*. Of course through the use of analogy and symmetry this person is vaporized, since the narrator equates Véra and Venus, and the necklace is compared to a star. This person also wavers between the status of an inhabitant (yet what kind of inhabitant could there be for such a habitat?) and an exile (which is how the night in this passage is described).[10] Thus the locale of this tale becomes the potentially disquieting instrument of "dislocation." As André Gide notes in his prelude to *Le Voyage d'Urien* (1892), the poet is one who "wets his brow against dew on the window-pane." And, of course, Mallarmé creates an entire *art poétique,* in *Le Démon de l'analogie,* around the encounter of a passerby and objects in a display window.

In this context, Baudelaire's prose poem "La Soupe et les nuages" is also of interest. Just as in his poems "Paysage" and "Le Balcon," the dining room's opened window acts as a boundary between worlds that are simultaneously at odds and linked. Baudelaire writes of "les mouvantes architectures que Dieu fait avec les vapeurs, les merveilleuses constructions de l'impalpable."[h] Thus, Baudelaire presents the motif of vaporization side by side with more prosaic elements such as soup, digs in the ribs, and vulgar language ("*Sacré bougre de marchand de nuage*")[i] not to mention the beloved's "hoarse," "hysterical" voice

---

[10] For the combination within the same poem of a mirror, a window, a wall, a mobile source of light, an image (painting or stained-glass), we could cite many texts by Mallarmé, Verlaine, or Apollinaire. But certain fin-de-siècle symbolist or decadent novels would also frequently express their fascination for such combinations by constructing ambiguous chambers where subjects attempt to recompose and localize different aspects of their personalities. One example is found in *Tout bas* by Francis Poictevin:

> When the houses have entered darkness and only some windows keep a light, it seems that a soul dwells behind these windowpanes, a soul crammed behind that illusion of glass. Certain tall windows opened and luminous, more isolated, pour out philtre, which is not of this earth. Towards the hour of shadows the head of anyone looking at themselves in a mirror seems to be sinisterly awash in mercury. And the brightness of their eyes is alarming as if a survivor within a cadaver. The constellations, like within a window frame, far away, entangles indefinitely in our thoughts. . . . Last night, under the overcast sky in the window, a masked brow under which orbits carved themselves out, that livid alienated reflection of myself threw back at me an enactment of my death. ([Paris: Lemerre, 1893], 105–107)

[h] "the moving architectures that God fashions from vapors, the marvelous constructions of the impalpable."—Baudelaire, *Paris Prowler.*
[i] "God-damn cloud peddler"—ibid.

"husky from brandy." The text also erects a *templa*—both *contemplate* and *contemplation* are terms found within the poem—making a correlation between the intake of food and the escape into the outer world, between the palpable and the impalpable, as well as between liquid and vapor. Here again the lyric subject seems to hesitate between the reassuring and stabilizing assimilation made possible by architectured sites that on the one hand organize identities and differences, and on the other hand enable a total abandonment to the ambiguity, reversibility, and confusion embodied in these sites.

The lyric also often draws on certain myths that associate stone and voice. Baudelaire's "Spleen" ("*J'ai plus de souvenir que si j'avais mille ans*"), for example, begins with the itemization of the various monumental envelopes and incarnations with which the narrator identifies. He compares himself successively to a chest of drawers, a pyramid, a boudoir, a tomb, a communal grave, a graveyard, and a granite sphinx. All these places either contain writing in the form of verses, love letters, receipts, or accounts, or they are sites of unanswered speech, as is the case of the sphinx and its enigmas. After making a reference to the moon, which seemingly "abhors" the poet, the text ends by resurrecting the sphinx-like granite statue which allows him to rediscover the lyric activity par excellence: song. Contrary to the myth of Memnon, where Aurora's first ray of daylight empowers her son's statue to live and sing again, this rewriting relates the life and song of a statue to the *setting* sun. And yet the two texts share the same theme of a monument exposed to the sun which exchanges song for the gift of light. Clearly, this poem about reflection, itself a reflection of another text, both locates and "dislocates" a voice—since quotation and rewriting are ways of echoing the voice of other texts when it cites the myth of Memnon. It is worth noting that the myth of Memnon itself seems to be the rewriting of yet another myth involving an exposed child—the Oedipus myth. In the case of Oedipus, one day his parents decide to abandon their son, while in the myth of Memnon, Aurora rediscovers her son each day. In the one myth a son kills his father, in the other a mother brings her son back to life. This myth of Memnon not only recurs in lyric discourse, but in the discourse on living architecture (Ruskin makes Memnon the symbol of an architecture of truth), as well as in the entire Romantic discourse on ruins. It is also taken up again by other myths whose eponymous heroes are associated with the quest for the self, or with the sun, song, or carved stone: Daedalus, Orpheus, Babel, or Amphion—

"*dont la lyre enfante le temple* [*et*] *attaque le désordre des coches*"ⁱ to quote Valéry.[11] Thus stone and voice are part of the same system. Apollinaire's "La Chanson du mal aimé" begins with London's "wave of bricks" and ends in a Paris saturated with cries and chants as well as with a reference to the myth of the siren. In *Calligrammes,* the poem "Il pleut" speaks of "*l'univers de villes auriculaires.*"ᵏ Baudelaire's "Rêve parisien," a delirious product of architectural fantasy, speaks of "unbelievable stones" ("*pierres inouïes*") and the "*Babel d'escaliers*" ("Babel of staircases").

It would be interesting to study the lapidary motif of the *jewel* as a variant on the cluster of themes. In naturalist and realist texts the jewel often occurs in depictions of Parisian manners, such as in Maupassant's story "La Parure" (The jewels) or Zola's *La Curée* (The quarry) where it recurs as a leitmotif in relation to the woman-as-sign who displays her husband's wealth. Authors also draw on this theme when discussing the loss of meaning that has afflicted the world of precious stones; in *La Curée* for example, jewels play a role in Saccard's real-estate speculations. As we have seen, jewels also act as an extended metaphor for imitation and plate—the so-called *articles de Paris.* The lyric text by contrast reinvests this little lapidary object with particularly rich symbolic value. For value, in his poem "Les Bijoux," Baudelaire praises "[*le*] *monde rayonnant de métal et de pierre*"ˡ and the narrator states: "[*j'aime*] *à la fureur* / *Les choses où le son se mêle à la lumière.*"ᵐ The "Ouverture Ancienne" of Mallarmé's "Herodiade" presents yet another variation on the Memnon myth with its references to Aurora, space, and

---

[11] Verlaine ends the epilogue of *Poèmes Saturniens* with a long reference to "the serene masterpiece, . . . new Memnon" awakened by the "Posterity-Dawn." Chateaubriand mentions Memnon during his trip in Egypt; Poe evokes the myth in his poem "The Coliseum" (1833); Laforgue in his "Complainte des grands pins: dans une villa abandonnée" writes: "*Chantons comme Memnon, le soleil a filtré* / . . . *Memnons ventriloquons!*" (Let us sing like Memnon, the sun has filtered through / . . . Memnons, let's ventriloquate!). Hegel in his *Aesthetics* makes Memnon a symbol of architecture. *Le Magasin pittoresque* devoted a long article in 1857 (81ff.) to this Egyptian statue, famous since antiquity. To travel towards the Orient for Nerval and for Romantic travelers, for the Flaubert and Du Camp hieroglyphic mission, or for Rimbaud in *Une Saison d'enfer*—"*Je retournais à l'Orient et à la sagesse première et éternelle . . . l'Orient, la patrie primitive*" (I returned to the Orient and the first and eternal wisdom . . . the Orient, the primitive country)—is to go towards Dawn (*Aurore*) and towards monuments to be resurrected. We can find the elements of the myth in a text like "Aube" from Rimbaud's *Illuminations,* where he presents a child, a goddess, an awakening, dawn, architecture, a living precious stone, and song.

ⁱ "whose lyre sires the temple" . . . "and attacks the disorder of gashes and cuts."
ᵏ "a universe of auricular cities."
ˡ "the glittering world of metal and stone."
ᵐ "I furiously love / Those things in which sound and light are combined."

its mention of a monument, in the form of *"une tour cinéraire et sacrificatrice / Lourde tombe."*[n] Scintillating stones replace or reinforce the cycle of stars as well as the echo of the reverberating voice. The domestic jewel is also water, since we speak of a diamond's water and fire—Rimbaud's "Barbare" associates "carbonization," water, fire, as well as the "female voice." Of course, the building has traditionally and logically positioned and exposed itself in relation to all these mobile actors. Thus the allusions to jewels in these various poems reveal the hope of miniaturizing and controlling the world by way of these tiny stones that are worn so close to the body, and which are themselves scale models of those vaster, enveloping stones in which those very same bodies dwell. In the very first issue of *La Dernière Mode*, Mallarmé makes explicit the relation between jewelry and the edifice: "I would advise any woman who is hesitant about commissioning the design of a desired jewel to ask the architect who is building her townhouse to draw up the plans." It therefore becomes possible to use classical architectural metaphors of jewelry in order to speak of the poet's text and work. Examples can be found in Verlaine's "Art poétique" (1874) where he defines rhyme as a *"Bijou d'un sou / Qui sonne creux et faux sous la lime"*[o] or Mallarmé's well-known text *Crise de vers* in which the poet *"cède l'initiative aux mots, [qui] s'allument de reflets réciproques comme une virtuelle traînée de feux sur des pierreries, remplaçant la respiration perceptible en l'ancien souffle lyrique."*[p]

The intertextual nature of the lyric as well as its predilection for myths associating stone and voice are not theoretically incompatible with a certain autobiographical stance; both attempt to make present an originating and original voice, even if the reverberations of the voice of the Other tend to dislocate the voice of the text. The theme of reverberation fascinates the lyric text: Ovid's Echo is inseparable from the theme of stone and from the character Narcissus; the lyric *ego* is often presented, whether euphorically or anxiously, as an *echo*, an "accousmata"—*"une voix quiète d'absence"*[q] as Apollinaire writes in his poem "Acousmate"—or as an entity that lives within an "echo

---

[n] "a cinerary and sacrificing tower / Heavy tomb."

[o] "A two-bit jewel / that is hollow and does not ring true when under the file."

[p] "Yields to the initiative of words, [which] flare up with reciprocal reflections, like a virtual streak of fire along a string of precious stones with the ancient lyric breath being replaced by perceivable respiration."

[q] "a calm voice of absence."

chamber."[12] In his preface to *Voix intérieures* (1837), Hugo, as we
know, develops a theory of the triple echo—the echo of an inner voice,
the song of the outside world, and the rumblings of political events—
"Isn't man totally understood through this triple aspect of life: the
home, which is our very heart, the fields where nature speaks to us, the
streets where that confusion of carts that we call political events,
storms as parties crack their whips." These voices or echoes, although
heard in unison in a written text, which by virtue of certain textual
constraints, is deferred and submits to the regimentation of absence,
can pose certain problems. To return to Baudelaire's quote, the echo is
certainly the vaporization of the voice. Whether produced in a natural
site or inside a cavernous edifice, the voice is multiplied, disseminated,
reflected, and dislocated; the echo adds multiplicity to immateriality
while maintaining its presence. Therefore this phenomenon serves as a
particularly apt autodescriptive metaphor that allows the text to speak
of the poem's textual and intertextual operations. As a stylistic operation, quotation is a transfer or a reduction of the space and distance
between texts just as a trope within a single text erases the distances
and space between disconnected semantic fields. The echo of another
voice is therefore a reference to an inheritance, and to an ancestry—
ancestor worship always involves the erection of tombs, and the story
of Memnon is of course a touching story of a mother–son relationship.[13] The echo of citation is also one of the preferred means of *ironic*
utterance, as is evident in Baudelaire's "Paysage" which is saturated
with references to the literary genres of the idyll and the eclogue.

[12] Some examples of lyric reverberation: "*Dans nos coeurs maudits / Chambres d'é-
ternel deuil où vibrent de vieux râles / Répondent les échoes de vos De Profundis*" (In our
condemned hearts—those chambers of eternal mourning—in which death rattles and vi-
brates from gone times, the echoes of your De Profundis respond; Baudelaire, "Obsession"); "*C'est étonnant comme les pas de femmes / Résonnent au cerveau des pauvres
malheureux*" (It is amazing how the footsteps of women / Reverberate in the brain of poor
wretches; Verlaine, *Sagesse* III, 3); "*O, pour moi seul, à moi seul, en moi-même / Auprès
d'un coeur, aux source du poème, / Entre le vide et l'événement pur, / J'attends l'écho de ma
grandeur interne, / Amère, sombre et sonore citerne, / Sonnant dans l'âme un creux toujours
futur*" (Valéry, "Le Cimetière marin," For me alone, to me, within myself, / Close to the
heart and at the poem's spring, / Between abeyance and the pure event, / I await the echo of
my secret depths, / A salt, sombre, sonorous well resounding, / An always future hollow in
the soul). In Baudelaire's "Les Phares" art itself becomes "*Un écho redit par mille laby-
rinthes*" [an echo repeated by a thousand labyrinths].

[13] On the link of the theme of the echo and intertextuality in the lyric text see John
Hollander, *The Figure of Echo: A Mode of Allusion in Milton and After* (Berkeley, Los
Angeles, London: University of California Press, 1981). And let us not forget that *l'écho
de Paris*, the gossip column, which is a genre, style, and discourse, is almost an obligatory
presence in the Parisian press of the nineteenth century.

Within such an ironic stance where the location of the source and the identity—two obsessions at the heart of all lyric—of utterance in an identifiable "site" is already problematic because of its dispersed voice. Reverberated by intertextuality, on the one hand, and by its "vaporization" and "effusion" on the other, scattered by the anagrammatic game of the poem, seeking a "composure" in sites which are always precarious or ambivalent, the lyric voice is often therefore literally unplaceable. In his "Complaintes de Lord Pierrot"—a text which is full of quotations and irony—Laforgue writes that the lyric "I" feels: "*Malheureux comme les pierres . . . de moins en moins localisé.*"ʳ

A final word on this vaporization of the self: Baudelaire's "Spleen" ( "*J'ai plus de souvenirs . . .*") ends by evoking a desert, specifically, "[*un*] *Sahara brumeux*" (line 21), "*entouré d'une vague épouvante*" (line 20), "*ignoré du monde*"ˢ (line 22). It is as if a tabula rasa were necessary in order to resurrect the lyric voice. This final destination contrasts sharply with the poem's list of specific architectural sites (the chest of drawers, the boudoir, the pyramid, and the tomb) at the outset of the poem. This hazy, vague desert, this pure, neutral space is triply indistinct: Not only does it fail to offer any physical "distinction," but it is also emotionally unavailable and inaccessible to any lucid gaze; is a- or anti-architectural, and radically undifferentiated. Here we confront an aesthetic of disorientation (*dépaysement*) reminiscent of the aesthetic of the *sublime*. This confrontation not only exceeds the thresholds of representation, but also will not suffer distinction and is indescribable. In fact, when the lyric subject "does not fall back on his skills as an architect when dealing with poetry," (as Mallarmé wrote of Edgar Allen Poe) and when it does not itemize lists of sites, of *templa*, light or black boxes that carefully fit together or compartmentalize, it will instead often tend to select types of negative and undifferentiated antisites: Baudelaire's abyss; Mallarmé's Azur; Hugo's oceans and shadows; Coppée's wastelands and amorphous suburbs;[14] Paul Verlaine's snow that effaces topographical distinctions, as well as the plain of "interminable boredom" into which his name dissolves by way of an anagram; not to mention an assortment of voids,

---

[14] The suburb (*banlieue*) is the place of banishment of the subject to a demonumentalized habitat, an unlivable intermediary zone between nature—where one can open up one's heart—and the city—where one is concentrated within rooms. Jean Richepin writes in *Le Pavé*, 2d ed. (Paris: Dreyfous, 1886) that one can visit the suburbs if one is "one of the crazed modernists who find a strange charm in trees with no leaves, and buildings with no architecture, horizons with no line, and skies with no purple shades, who are fond of the lifelessness of shriveled and mute nature in an indolence of an old valetudinarian."

ʳ "As unfortunate as stone . . . less and less localized."

ˢ "a hazy Sahara"; "shrouded in a vague horror"; "unknown to the world."

deserts, mists, and clouds. Verlaine's mist and Baudelaire's vaporization bring to mind once again the themes of hype, the balloon, and levity seen in a great many novels. In this case, though, they act not as an absolute form of anti-architecture but rather as a form of temptation or a way of surpassing those values of stability, permanence, and solidity that are embodied by architecture.[15]

Vaporization acts as a foil to the inhabitant of an architectured site, for it opposes its amorphous and undifferentiated mobility to a universe of stability and differentiation. This opposition, which informs many narratives involving the subject's quest for itself, underscores the fundamental vacillation of the lyric stance between *vaporization* and *centralization*. Thus, in what may be a reference to the lines of a text in Baudelaire's poem "La Beauté," the fear of a "movement which disturbs lines"[t] and upsets beauty like "a dream in stone" (*"une rêve de pierre"*), or, of the ocean which "disturbs all lines [and] disintegrates all symmetry" in Hugo's *L'Homme qui rit,* confronts the systematic exploration of the dialectics of effacement versus construction that unleashes destructive forces. As Rimbaud's "Nocturne vulgaire" puts it:

> *un souffle ouvre les brèches opéradiques dans les cloisons, brouille le pivotement des toits rongés, disperse les limites des foyers, éclipse les croisées.*[16,u]

---

[15] The steam engine is the emblematic machine of the period. The last line of Apollinaire's "Un fantôme de nuées" from *Calligrammes* which could be seen as an epigram for the nineteenth century is: *"Siècle, ô siècle de nuages"* (Century, o, century of clouds). A window which acts both as "frame" and stabilizes clouds, such as in Baudelaire's "Paysage" where the narrator speaks of "the rivers of coal" or the scenery of "La Soupe et les nuages," could constitute a fundamental figure of the lyric text of the nineteenth century. All these texts rewrite the clichés associated with the poet who "has his head in the clouds" or, when he is not "building castles in Spain," is building "castles in the sky." The poet who is an acrobat that makes "tropes" and as Apollinaire writes in "Un Fantôme de nuées," "*[fait] des tours en plein air*" does "spins in mid-air."

[16] Note the terms windows (*croisée*) and hearth (*foyer*) in this passage from Rimbaud which are focal points and reference points. There is also the reference to theater, the presence of technemes and the allusion to the operations of which they are metaphors: the "pivot" and the "partitions" that separate. The trope, in this case *la porte* ("the door"), as we have seen is what "confuses" the topos or distinction. Rimbaud likes to exacerbate to the point of illegibility the discrete side of his paper architecture: "*L'opéra-comique se divise sur notre scène à l'arète d'intersection de dix cloisons dressées de la galerie aux feux.*" ("Scènes," The opéra-comique is divided on our stage at the line of intersection of ten partitions placed between the gallery and the footlights [Rimbaud, *L'Illuminations*]).

[t] "mouvement qui déplace les lignes."

[u] "A gust of wind makes operadic cracks in the partitions, confuses the pivoting of the worm-eaten roofs, blows away the walls of the hearths, blots out the windows" Rimbaud, *Complete Work,* 235.

Certainly, the "illegible" poetry of someone like Reverdy at the beginning of the twentieth century, in such texts as "Fronton," "Figure de porte," "Couloir," and "Porte entr'ouverte" in his collection *Pierres blanches* (1930), reflects an obsession with meticulously constructed architectural scenery that takes the dislocated lyric subject and the semantic disinvestment of its voice and pushes them to the limit. Of course, works of this type closely resemble mystical texts which attempt to constitute a subject that is empty, de-architectured, destabilized, nomadic, and thus open to the structure and plenitude offered by transcendence. Those empty rhythms, which, according to Verlaine's laconic testament, Rimbaud had hoped to compose, may have been the ultimate and most radical reduction of the poetic text to its purest form of architecture.

# Index

| | |
|---:|:---|
| Designer: | U.C. Press Staff |
| Compositor: | Huron Valley Graphics |
| Text: | 10/13 Sabon |
| Display: | Sabon |
| Printer: | BookCrafters |
| Binder: | BookCrafters |